1994

RURAL COMMUNITIES IN ADVANCED INDUSTRIAL SOCIETY

Development and Developers

Ted K. Bradshaw and
Edward J. Blakely

PRAEGER SPECIAL STUDIES • PRAEGER SCIENTIFIC

Library of Congress Cataloging in Publication Data

Bradshaw, Ted K
  Rural communities in advanced industrial society.

  Bibliography: p.
  1. United States--Rural conditions. 2. Sociology,
Rural--United States. 3. Rural development--United
States. 4. Community development--United States.
I. Blakely, Edward J., joint author. II. Title.
HN59.B72   301.35'0973   78-19736
ISBN 0-03-041626-4

PRAEGER PUBLISHERS
PRAEGER SPECIAL STUDIES
383 Madison Avenue, New York, N.Y. 10017, U.S.A.

Published in the United States of America in 1979
by Praeger Publishers,
A Division of Holt, Rinehart and Winston, CBS, Inc.

1234567890 038 098765432

PREFACE

This book is the result of a rare and happy collaboration of two scholars who had been examining similar issues from different perspectives which, as it turned out, could be integrated effectively with each other. The project started with a series of discussions in which we progressively discovered that our interests were complementary and that a study of rural California would be a way to join our long run research aims. While one of us (Bradshaw) was interested in the development of advanced or post-industrial societies and their impact on public policy, the other (Blakely) was concerned with the changing nature of rural areas and the consequences of these changes for rural policy makers and community developers. What we shared from the start was a curiosity and excitement about California as a special setting in which advanced industrialism, rural policy, and community development practice lead to new solutions for old problems as well as to another generation of issues needing the attention of policy makers.

We decided that by focusing on the rapid and diverse set of changes affecting rural California we could produce a study that would be useful to scholars and policy makers who had been finding a growing gap between the social and economic conditions described in the literature about rural society and the conditions they actually observed. California, where these developments are seen particularly clearly, provided an opportunity to explore changes which we believe have relevance in many other rural states and regions as well. The formulation, development, and revision of each chapter was shared by the two authors. Bradshaw had the primary responsibility for the parts dealing with advanced industrialism and rural economic and social institutions, while Blakely had primary responsibility for the integration and the analysis of community development.

As we began work, we realized that the task we set for ourselves was enormous. We wanted to provide a new perspective on rural America that embraced the widest possible theoretical and empirical orientation rooted in emerging macrosociological theories of advanced industrialism, and we wanted to do this with the practical needs of the community developer in mind. We were entering an arena where we would find little help from the literature. As Howard Newby has argued in a forthcoming review of trends in rural sociology, the concepts used to study rural phenomena are insufficient, and rural sociology must adopt "a more holistic approach which addresses itself explicitly to the question of rural change under conditions which predominate in advanced industrial societies" (Newby, 1978: 38). Similarly in a review of community development James Christenson (1978) notes an absence of a coherent theoretical perspective for the field. Nonetheless, we thought that recent work on change in modern society and its implications for policy offered models that could be applied to the study of rural communities.

Although we were not modest in the task we chose for ourselves, we are modest in our assessment of how far we have gone. This book is an initial undertaking which inaugurates a series of studies which will be conducted in the coming years. We are publishing our general perspective now, not as a final statement but as a working report to generate debate, discussion, and collaborative work. There are three areas where collaborative efforts would be particularly useful: First, case studies need to be carried out in rural areas outside California that are being affected by many of the same developments we have identified but are different in other important ways. In addition, better quantitative analysis is needed, and data should be collected and analyzed that more accurately reflect trends since the 1970 census. Finally, greater input and more insights of an interdisciplinary nature need to be added from diverse fields such as economics, political science, geography, health, social welfare, and others to supplement our contributions from sociology and community development. While we have tried to integrate material from all these fields, deficiencies remain.

An important dilemma we faced had to do with the balance between the achievements of a state such as California and the problems and crises which such development entails. In our discussions of changes in the major social institutions in rural California we portrayed a number of successful developments which brought rural areas into a new kind of social relationship with the rest of the society and provided new opportunities for rural residents, old and new. However, we also stated that, along with positive development, new problems were created with which rural policy makers and community developers must cope. We make no final judgments about these changes. We are neither convinced that advanced industrialism is the best solution, nor the worst outcome for rural areas. We take exception with those who think that the developments seen in California are the cure for rural problems elsewhere, just as we disagree with those who think there is nothing of value in the California experience. A balance is needed; but, above all, other areas should learn from California's mistakes just as California should move to correct its new problems.

The role of the community developer further illustrates this tension between achievement and the creation of new problems. Our analysis shows that the community developer has a more sophisticated and complicated part to play in California, requiring new skills and professional training. This may be seen both as a social organizational success or as a shortcoming. The growing importance of development specialists is clearly an organizational and professional success in dealing with complicated problems; but their widespread employment is also an indicator of a shortcoming in that social problems remain so intractible that they demand extraordinary response.

This project has been made possible through financial assistance from the University of California Agricultural Experiment Station. The Institute of Governmental Studies at the University of California, Berkeley, not only provided necessary materials and services for our research but also furnished the rich, stimulating, and supportive environment that scholars always seek but never seem to find. The Institute's Library gave valuable service at every stage of the research. Gala Rinaldi provided help with the field work and was particularly skillful in tracking down information on the variety of community development projects reported on in the book. Betty Lou Bradshaw reviewed and edited the entire manuscript; her critical sense challenged us to improve many instances of loose thinking, and her eye for style helped us to say the rest more clearly.

We also received much valuable assistance from a number of persons who have given us data and information during the last two years. Bill Myers of the California Employment and Training Advisory Office has been a continuing source of information and ideas on critical issues at times when we needed them most. Glen Hawkes, Ralph Palmer, Tom Parsons, and Tom Haller have also assisted us in particularly important ways during the study. Many other persons who furnished information and assistance can not be listed here, but we thank them collectively—they created and are carrying out those projects which have made the study of California so interesting to us.

Among our Institute colleagues help and encouragement came from John Cummins who initiated the meetings leading to our collaborations and from Todd LaPorte who was critical in helping us to understand the importance of systematic and analytical studies of California. Other colleagues who have discussed aspects of the study with us include Dean MacCannell, Alvin Sokolow, John Kushman, Phil Martin, Orville Thompson, Claire Christensen, Emmett Fiske, and Joan Randall. Finally, Gertrude Allen, Catherine Winter, Pat Rameriz, Pat Thomason, and Francis Wilcox deserve special recognition for their efficient and competent assistance in typing various drafts of this work.

CONTENTS

LIST OF TABLES, FIGURES, AND MAPS

1

The Rural Society
and Advanced Industrialism

INTRODUCTION

The changing character of social relations in response to industrial development has long preoccupied social scientists. Currently, a great deal of interest and attention is being devoted to new or emerging stages in the process of social and economic development termed "post-industrialism," "advanced industrialism," the "new industrial state," or the "technetronic era" (Bell, 1973; Touraine, 1971; Bradshaw, 1976; Galbraith, 1967; Brzezinski, 1970). These research efforts have put forward the notion that America and other leading industrialized nations are at or embarking on a new stage of development with profound implications for the entire social fabric and economic structure. Although these theories are dominantly urban in orientation, recent data suggest that rural areas are experiencing similar developments that foretell vast changes in the possibilities and the problems of rural economic and social development. Rural advanced industrialism, it will be argued, is not, as it may seem, a contradiction in terms but a new frontier in the development of rural areas.

Rural sociologists as well as community developers and other human resource professionals have begun to sense that these changes in society have implications for their work, a theme elaborated by W. Keith Warner in his 1974 presidential address to the Rural Sociological Society titled "Rural Society in a Post-Industrial Age." He argued that "the challenge of a post-industrial age for persons interested in knowledge about rural society is not the loss of significant work to be done, but the overwhelming scope and complexity of the task before us. We have still to figure out the meaning and implications of what we think we know, as well as to verify it. There is not too little to do, but too much" (Warner, 1974: 316). Similarly, Charles Anderson has noted that "a social science designed for the concerns of post-industrial society might view the problem of development differently from the social science of a high industry society"

(Anderson, 1971: 30). These differences include using techniques from the social indicators movement, the emergence of ecology as a policy science, and changes in the value system, all of which may introduce a note of uncertainty into development theory. Finally, Olaf Larson and Everett Rogers (1964: 59) suggest that many aspects of rural society are facing confusing vigorous social change and that these changes need to be articulated and taken into account both in theory, policy formulation, and professional practice. This book merges these themes and elaborates a conceptual framework that is useful to academics and practitioners interested in the problems of rural community development today.

Interpreting the New Rurality

Recently scholars are ending their long neglect of rural America. While libraries are still filled with much more recent analysis of the rural parts of underdeveloped countries than of this country, a number of new studies provide a new awareness of the American rurality. Frank Clemente, in the preface of an issue of the *Annals* on the "New Rural America," notes that during the 1960s "to the extent rural areas were examined, they were often done so as the residual of urban studies." However, he continues, "in recent years there has been an increasing recognition among researchers and popular commentators that rural America is alive and generally doing well" (Clemente, 1977: vii). Furthermore, a powerful new history of rural America by John Shover cuts past the mythology and glamor of past studies and shows that rural Americans have become a distinct but vastly influential minority in American life as their function in producing food has become essential to the worldwide battle against hunger (Shover, 1976). Politically, too, a new awareness of rural areas is emerging through organizations such as Rural America Inc., which is a large interest group applying pressure on government to be more attentive to the problems of nonmetropolitan regions.

In this book we join the new interest in rural areas and argue that post- or advanced industrialism is giving rise to new social conditions in rural America. Instead of the pastoral subsistence farm of the past, rural America is becoming primarily nonagricultural with only a small percentage of rural residents involved in farming. Instead of a long and persistent population decline, small rural communities are growing in population and new migrants are bringing economic and social resources with them. In many states the availability of educational resources in rural areas is giving residents opportunities for development of their human resources similar to those in the city, and educational institutions are becoming centers for local and regional development projects. Housing and health are improving greatly as governmental capacity increases; rural areas now provide increasing welfare services for the poor, who previously were forced to migrate to the city, and for the middle class, in the form of public facilities for the pursuit of desired life styles. In parallel with the development of many advanced industrial characteristics, rural society is faced by problems which had previously passed it by. Crime is on the rise, racial tensions are increasing, pollution and crowding are marring areas which used to be primitive and isolated, and growth control is advocated, especially by newcomers who do not want to share their new communities' benefits. In short, this is the making of a new rural age.

Some time ago Frederic Jackson Turner noted that the frontier had played a critical part in the development of this country. On the frontier individualism prevailed, and opportunity was open to any man who wanted a new start, free from most of the restrictions of congested society. To Turner (1962) the closing of the frontier marked the end of this type of opportunity. In one way Turner was right, but in another, more critical sense he was wrong. Today some rural regions are opening another frontier, a frontier of the advanced industrial society where experimentation, individuality, and the new start not only characterize the people but, what is novel, *their communities*. In this frontier the community developer functions somewhat like the shopkeeper, pastor, and police in making some things happen and other things not.

Themes of Rural Advanced Industrialism

This book develops three basic themes which are woven together in the chapters which follow. The first is that advanced industrialism is changing and has changed the structure of rural society so as to mandate a new understanding of rurality in developed countries. Although many rural areas remain isolated and poverty stricken, a new rurality is emerging that promises growth, new opportunities, integration with the rest of society, and new problems. In a sense, advanced industrialism adds another layer of social structure to rural communities, solving some but not all of the preexisting problems and adding new problems of its own. Our goal is to examine the character of advanced industrialism in rural areas in order that we might understand not only what is occurring in rural regions but what is possible.

Post- or advanced industrial societies differ from traditional and industrial societies with more sophisticated scientific technology, new emphasis on knowledge resources, the expansion of public organization and welfare services, and increased quantity of interdependence. We shall show, first, that the use of new sophisticated technologies has altered rural economic opportunities and occupation patterns, and that the accompanying growth of the service sector has itself been developed through new social technologies of the professions and marketing, etc. Second, it will be shown that the creation and diffusion of knowledge through education have worked to enhance human resources in rural areas so that growth which is desirable to the local population can take place. Finally, increasing social interdependence within rural regions and between rural and urban areas has led to new planning and government intervention activities, often taking the form of "welfare state" services in health, housing, and leisure. The theoretical development of these changes will be undertaken in the third section of this chapter, and they will be elaborated in detail in chapters 2–4.

The second theme, noted in detail by demographers but paid little attention by community developers, is the so called "reverse migration" of population from urban to rural areas. After many decades of population decline, nonmetropolitan communities are increasing in population (Beale, 1975; Beale and Fuguitt, 1976; Sorenson, 1976). Young people are not leaving small towns so rapidly; new retired and middle-class persons are moving to the country to find opportunities in nonfarm, advanced industrial employment. Businesses seeking new locations, fewer restrictions, and a healthy atmosphere are attracted to rural areas. Government has become increasingly important in providing jobs and the infrastructure for new growth. Finally, many persons experiencing the urban problems of crime, drugs, pollution, noise, and frustration have hope that these problems may be avoided in rural areas. Thus, in many ways, the growth of rural population is in part a response to the changing social conditions of the largely advanced industrial society. Our analysis of population growth in rural areas is aimed at understanding the structural conditions that seem to underlie the changes from declining to developing regions. The details of this argument are elaborated in the fourth Section of this chapter.

Finally, our third theme is that there has been a considerable change in the nature of community development activities in rural regions and in the professional roles played by community developers. Community development aims to facilitate the éstablishment of needed services and opportunities in rural areas in order to improve the quality of community life (Warren, 1975; Sanders, 1970; Lauderdale and Peterson, 1971). This aim has not changed but the methods have. It is no longer adequate for community developers to work on the level of assisting individuals who come to them with personal problems. Nor is it adequate for the community developer to be a group organizer who establishes groups to work for needed improvements. The community developer in the advanced industrial society does many tasks long part of his profession but must also add the new roles of resource coordinator and network facilitator. The community developer no longer restricts his work to the level of the community but coordinates resources and people over a whole region. Our tracing of the changing role of the community developer aims to show how new roles are created during social change and how effective community development requires that community developers adopt strategies appropriate to a dynamic advanced industrial society instead of a lagging region. The changing role of the community developer is the subject of chapter 6.

These three themes combine to make a whole with analysis at several levels. At the most general level, it is an explication of a theory and the way the theory helps to explain the character of rural areas that no longer fit the predominant descriptions offered. At the more specific level, it is a study of a region experiencing change, including population growth. Finally, it is a study of professional community developers and their changing involvement in the processes of community. At this level, the analysis focuses most specifically on the individual practitioner who is involved in day-to-day decisions about how the community is changing and how it might change more closely in line with the desires of the population.

Objectives of the Study

The elaboration of these themes has a number of important consequences. First, the concept of a rural advanced industrial society is needed in order to provide an accurate description of nonmetropolitan life in America. We agree with Rural America, Inc. that rural parts of the nation are diverse in their problems and prospects (Rural America, 1975). Nonetheless, rural regions are still too frequently portrayed only in terms of their poverty and lagging economies (Hansen, 1970). Yet, in some rural regions, changes are occurring that foretell a vastly different future, especially with recent population increases. Thus, we will describe a set of conditions emerging in rural areas that is different from those described in either sociological studies or in the popular literature.

These themes are also important for their value in elaborating social theory. Concepts of post-industrialism or advanced industrialism (Bell, 1973; Brezezinski, 1970; Bradshaw, 1976) have come almost entirely from the urban experience, even implying that the post-industrial world would be one of well-functioning large cities. The extension of the theory into rural regions may correct some of the distortions in the urban theory and, more importantly, may provide the setting in which to test some implications of the notion of advanced industrialism. The processes may start in the cities, but they soon have substantial effect on rural areas. If the impact of advanced industrialism on rural regions is not consistent with the developing body of knowledge, a new assessment of the concepts may be needed. Thus, the elaboration of the theory in a very different setting from that in which it was developed will further theoretical thinking (for example, see Stinchcombe, 1968: 18-22).

A careful analysis of rural advanced industrialism is also relevant because the social changes have vast policy implications. Rural areas are facing new challenges as well as opportunities. The most important problems facing the nation during the 1970s and 1980s have a particularly strong implication for rural areas. Energy provides one example where coal boom towns, nuclear waste disposal and even renewable energy sources, such as solar collectors, wind generation, and biomass, will make considerable demands on land in rural regions. Water policy and the exploitation of forests and minerals also provide evidence of strong impacts on rural regions. Policies relating to the solution of urban problems themselves are strongly tied to ideas about rural areas, particularly because many urban problems stem from rural-urban migrants. Policies regarding highways and parks strongly affect rural tourism industries.

Our emphasis on community developers is central because they are almost always facilitators to public agencies that are mandated to carry out federal and state policies. Because of this, a better understanding of the rural community development profession is needed so that the quality of developers' performance and the potential of their contribution may be increased. Thus, it matters how rural areas are understood in view of the important policy decisions that will affect these areas in the next decades.

APPROACH—RURAL CALIFORNIA'S ADVANCED INDUSTRIALISM

Our approach to the analysis of advanced industrial rural society is to concentrate on a nonmetropolitan region which—more than other regions of its type—is already experiencing the impact of advanced industrialism. Although we will develop our argument for rural society in general, we feel that California is the best place to look for empirical data on rural areas that are socially and economically affected by the changes of advanced industrialism. California may be thought of as a prototypical advanced industrial society (LaPorte and Abrams, 1975) which may be studied for its leadership in social trends and policy innovation. We recognize that California's rural areas are unique, shaped by the state's particular history and resources, but there are also many similarities with other rural areas; thus a close look at California may be instructive for understanding rural areas in the United States and other developed countries, as well as for community development professionals, wherever they face the challenge of aiding rural communities in a complex society.

California: A Prototypical Advanced Industrial Society

More than any other state, California has developed in a way that combines the most important aspects of economic and social development characteristic of an advanced industrial society (Bradshaw, 1976). As Todd LaPorte and C. J. Abrams (1975) suggest, California was one of the earliest states to develop as a post-industrial society, having over half its labor force in service-type employment more than 30 years before the nation as a whole reached this mark. It is the state best known for the development of sophisticated technology; for example, the largest telescopes, the development of the aircraft industry, atomic physics, which included the research that led to the atomic bomb, the computer industry in Santa Clara County, and agricultural developments, which included the tomato-picking machine and the hard tomatoes specially developed for it. The California educational system has set a pattern which has been followed by scores of other states and many foreign countries. The state legislature and other public bodies have gained notice for their innovative policies in such areas as energy, recreation, law, welfare, and services to the disabled and aged. California life styles set patterns that are copied (or ridiculed) virtually everywhere but which stimulated the movie and television industries and, increasingly, for the publishing industry as well (Bradshaw and Blakely, 1979). These are characteristics we will have occasion to refer to again because they are the characteristics that make California a unique natural experiment in which many of the changes, thought to be most important in tracing the changing social order, are to be found.

We are not the first to use California as a case study of patterns that fore-tell the future. Writers have been using California in this way for decades. For example, Michael Davie wrote of California in his book *In the Future Now* (1972); Ross McDonald described it as "one of those leading new places" (Mc-Williams, 1977); Peter Schrag (1975) described California as "just like the rest of America, only more so." California is portrayed as being the epitome of the American dream by several generations of writers between 1800 and 1915, according to a literary analysis by Kevin Starr (1973). At the same time it has also been described as a nightmare, and a dream unfulfilled.

California has a complex history shaped by the longest and most rapid population growth of any region in the industrial world, not excluding Japan and Israel (Davis and Styles, 1971: vi). What Neil Morgan called the *Westward Tilt* (1961) has been so rapid that more things in the state are new than else-where. In Carey McWilliams (1949: 25) brilliant *California: The Great Exception*, he stressed the impact of such immense change:

> If asked to name the most important respect in which California dif-fers from the other forty-seven states, I would say that the differ-ence consists in the fact that California has not grown or evolved so much as it has been hurtled forward, rocket-fashion, by a series of chain-reaction explosions. . . . Elsewhere the tempo of development was slow at first, and gradually accelerated as energy accumulated. But in California the lights went on all at once, in a blaze, and they have never been dimmed.

Although California is the most urban state in the nation, with more than 90 percent of its population living in counties classified in 1970 as Standard Metropolitan Statistical Areas (SMSA), it has a vast rural area. Because many of its counties are huge, the 90 percent urban datum is somewhat misleading. Many residents live in metropolitan (SMSA) counties, yet are more remote from a sizeable city than are rural people in small counties in other parts of the country. Just over 46 percent of the state's land area is in metropolitan counties, and this includes large areas of desert, forest, and prime agricultural land. The five metro-politan counties having the largest land area (San Bernardino, Riverside, Fresno, Monterey and Kern) have significant urban populations, yet their total land area is so large that, taken together, it exceeds the size of any one of the 18 smallest states. Within these large land areas lies a significant part of rural California.

A slightly different indicator of "rural," as defined by the Census, includes "farms, open countryside, and places of less than 2,500 persons both within and outside of SMSAs" and provides a different perspective on the relevance of California's rural areas. California's rural population measured in this way ranks tenth among all states with nearly two million persons. It is instructive to examine the 1970 rural population of these ten largest rural states because it alters our perception of the rural population of the nation and reinforces our claim that California is an important case for the study of rural areas (see Table 1.1).

TABLE 1.1

Rural Population in the Ten Largest States, 1970

Pennsylvania	3,363,499
North Carolina	2,796,891
New York	2,633,254
Ohio	2,636,320
Michigan	2,321,310
Texas	2,275,784
Illinois	1,884,155
Indiana	1,821,609
Georgia	1,821,501
California	1,817,089
Total Top 10 States	23,361,412

Source: U.S. Bureau of the Census, *Statistical Abstract*, 1976.

The top ten states constitute 43 percent of the rural population in the United States, and what is interesting is that included among these are the major industrial, sophisticated, affluent, and progressive states, based on urban images of development. In short, large parts of the U.S. rural population are in states not having the dominant agricultural base of Kansas, for example, or the poverty of Mississippi, or the isolation of Idaho. California's rural experience, thus, has close relevance to many other rural areas.

Our focus on California is not an attempt to promote or justify the state's activities. We do not believe that trends are destiny, or that trends seen in California are necessarily going to be replicated in the rest of the nation. Thus, the trends we are examining serve the primary function of teaching us how to think about the options for an emerging rurality. Furthermore, we do not make the judgment that California's rural regions are developing in the best way; we simply argue that California is an unplanned social experiment that must be evaluated and understood because it may point to emerging processes other regions might be facing and to experiences from which other regions might benefit. To analyze California in the manner described is difficult without a methodology that provides both quantitative and qualitative dimensions. We believe we have selected and developed such a method in this work.

Social Anticipation: A Research Strategy

While we ground our analysis in presently existing rural developments, our attempt is to make statements about future developments in rural life, to call attention to trends which are just emerging, and to help shape activities by community developers that will affect the future of nonmetropolitan areas.

These future-looking activities require a methodology that is considerably different from forecast or prediction techniques used in other research.

There are three broad categories of future-study methodologies. The first uses time-series projections into the future. The second uses models and simulations, while the third looks at qualitative and holistic estimates of the future. Time-series and future projections are in many ways the simplest of the three methodologies and the most commonly used. These techniques, more or less, extrapolate historical patterns into the future. This may be done through simple linear extensions or more complex methods of using moving averages, exponential smoothing, substitution and growth curves, envelope curves, and simple and multiple regression. Another use of trend data involves the identification of relationships which have historically predicted results, such as "precursor" events, leading to the construction of models. In some of the more complex of these, relationships are identified with confidence levels given for deviations from the patterns.

The second main type of futures technique involves the use of models and simulations. Instead of a concentration on trends, more complex relationships are patterned mathematically. This involves identifying interactions among events, alternative patterns of relations, secondary and indirect effects, and relationships which are manipulated by computer to extend into the future.

The final group of techniques are holistic and employ qualitative and intuitive processes. Many of these techniques lack precision but take advantage of this flexibility to cover a wider range of possible futures than the other methods. Group processes like Delphi forecasting collect expert opinions and then develop consensus among the experts about the future. Other techniques such as scenario building take a few central events and try to elaborate associated events into a plausible whole. Others, such as values forecasting, try to project future societal scenarios from changes in social values, presumed to be more indicative than behaviors (Miller, 1977).

In many ways each of these methodologies is limited because it does not include features of the others. Trend extrapolation is too simplistic in that it does not look at interrelationships. Holistic analyses do not look carefully enough at the way present trends and empirical evidence condition the options for holistic futures, many of which are versions of lay science fiction. Models and simulations, like trend extrapolation, are severely limited by the quality and quantity of input data and the quality of the relationships presumed by the models. In the latter case a slight error in the model can have implications which become magnified over time. As society becomes more complex, mathematical models to describe important relationships become almost impossible to deduce as Brunner and Brewer (1971) show in an attempted restructuring of a set of hypothetical data patterned in really quite simple ways. As the complexity of the relationships increases, the error approaches completeness. In general, the major limitation of most forecasting techniques is the lack of an adequate theory about the relationships which are under study. If the theory had adequate explanatory power, more accurate projections could be made about future events.

In an attempt to overcome these limitations in currently existing forecasting techniques, we have used a methodology we term *social anticipation research*. Its characteristics are that it identifies "cutting edge" developments in key places in society, integrates them into a theoretical framework to verify that they are meaningful, and compares them with similar phenomena in other places and times.

Social anticipation is grounded first in social theory. It involves theoretical consideration of macrosocial structural variables which, in combination, may affect the options available for the future. The theory is holistic in that it attempts to include a wide range of both social structural and individual level variables as they are related to one another. It is historical in that it starts with observed patterns in the past, examines their relationships, and considers the probability that these relationships might change. The theory of advanced industrialism is such a theory in that it identifies emerging relationships between major sectors of the social structure in advanced industrial society, and contrasts them with relationships prevalent in industrial society.

In addition, social anticipation is grounded in empirical evidence. The future does not impinge on the whole world at exactly the same time, although some limited events, like the oil embargo, do have worldwide impacts that emerge quickly. The best way to understand the future is to discover those places, events, and situations where emerging events might theoretically be considered "cutting edge," or illustrations of the future working itself out. Thus some states and counties develop in ways that are replicated by other areas later, and in this way they are case studies of future developments. The distinction of cutting edge developments from ones which are just different or bizarre is difficult and involves a qualitative trend analysis. Our technique for making this choice is to identify areas with past experiences of developing new patterns that were later adopted by others as partial evidence that *other* patterns of the community will be anticipatory as well. Our choice of California as a prototypical advanced industrial society is based on the evidence that in the past California—as a sociotechnical system—has served as a model that other parts of the country have followed in innovations and important patterns of social development.

In doing research which suggests what the future will be like reliance is made on using ideal types, in the sense that Weber (1968) used them. The ideal type is an abstraction for which the data only approximate the model, and exceptions are frequent and notable. However, the theory that is embodied in the ideal type helps us to systematize the pattern of observed events and to make order of them. Over time it is suspected that the empirical evidence will come to resemble the model more closely.

Obviously, new cutting edge developments of the future are found existing side by side with older developments of the previous order. In fact this is implied in the theory of advanced industrialism. New social orders rarely replace existing orders but gradually the new takes on a larger and larger importance. Today in California there are pockets of largely subsistence, preindustrial culture, especially in the Indian reservations and in some of the more primitive farming areas. Yet side by side, new technologies are found that supplement the traditional. Although we often talk more about the new than the old, the importance of the old remains significant because it constitutes a large, though declining, part of observed current behavior and is part of the social reality new development must take into account.

In essence, then, the shape of the future can be assessed *via* empirical observations and illustrations carefully linked to social theory. This research methodology reaches into the future by examining emerging change rather than attempting either to intuit futures, as in future forecasting, or to quantify them, as in predictive research. The method offers flexibility since the landscape of future society is not orderly, but will be composed of irregular events which not only shape the perception of what is possible but serve as landmarks for the evolution of something new.

THE ADVANCED INDUSTRIAL SOCIETY

A number of recent social commentators have called attention to the emergence of a new stage in development of American society which is distinct from the industrialization of the last hundred years. Daniel Bell (1973) marked the end of the industrial era and the emergence of the "post-industrial society" when service employment came to include over half of all employed workers. Brzezinski (1970) described the emerging "technetronic age" characterized by increasing reliance on science and technology. Other social scientists have noted new leisure societies, welfare states, and over-developed societies. MacCannell (1976) points out that a new tourist society has emerged.

We have chosen to view these changes as the development of an *advanced industrial society*, thus acknowledging the continuity between the industrialization process and the present, yet stressing the changing social patterns brought about by the use of high technology and new industrial forms. Furthermore, our emphasis is derived from existing social theory in that it calls attention to changes in the processes of development which have been at the root of sociology since Marx, Weber, Durkheim, Toennies, and other early analysts of industrialization. The advanced industrial society in this sense does not represent a sharp break with earlier patterns of industrialization but is the next iteration in the socioeconomic development of Western civilization. It is in effect a continuation of scientific western society beset with both new problems and new potentials.

Post Industrial Theories

The most important post-industrial analysis is by Daniel Bell who argues (1973: 14) that American society has become a post-industrial society that may be subsumed under five dimensions or components:

1. Economic sector: the change from a goods-producing to a service economy;
2. Occupational distribution: the pre-eminence of the professional and technical class;
3. Axial principle: the centrality of theoretical knowledge as the source of innovation and of policy formulation for the society;
4. Future orientation: the control of technology and technological assessment;
5. Decision making: the creation of a new intellectual technology.

For Bell, these changes in the social structure, particularly the declining importance of the industrial component of society and the rise of the intellectual elite, have implications for the political system and the culture, creating a new set of social relations, just as the industrial revolution created a new social order with the decline of agricultural society.

Brzezinski prefers to call the emerging society a "technetronic" one, a "society that is shaped culturally, psychologically, socially, and economically by the impact of technology and electronics—particularly in the area of computers and communications. The industrial process is no longer the principal determinant of social change, altering the mores, the social structure, and the values of society" (1970: 9). He continues to show that scientific and technical knowledge affects not just the industrial process, but the world political structure as well.

Touraine (1971: 61), a French radical sociologist, argues that the post-industrial society is a "programmed society," in that class relations are transformed from ones of owner/employer vs. worker to ones between decision makers and consumers.

> The principal opposition between these two great classes or groups of classes does not result from the fact that one possesses wealth or property and the other does not. It comes about because the dominant classes dispense knowledge and control *information*. . . . This is the reason—in our eyes justified—why the idea of alienation is so widespread. We are leaving a society of exploitation and entering a society of alienation.

Thus, unlike other analysts of the post-industrial society, Touraine deals with the emerging problems of the highly technocratic social system.

Rural Postindustrialism

In all these analyses a perspective on the significance of rural areas is missing. None mentions it. None suggests that the changes discussed will have implications for the rurality. None develops examples from rural areas nor evaluates the interdependence of rural areas with urban settings where the changes generally take hold first.

Furthermore, the general adoption of the term "*post*-industrial" to represent the development of a new stage of society is highly misleading because there is little evidence of an actual decline in manufacturing industry. During the last 75 years the proportion of employment in manufacturing has changed little, fluctuating around the 30 percent range in the United States. In contrast, the agricultural sector has steadily declined and the service sector has increased. Thus, the growth of the service sector has been at the expense of agriculture, *not industry*. Therefore, it is our preference, in the light of these developments, to use the term "advanced industrial society," which reflects the increasing importance of new and advanced technology in creating social changes of vast proportions, and to reserve the term "post-industrial" for possible future developments (Table 1.2).

If the concept of advanced or post-industrialism is to be generally applied in the description of processes in the emerging society, then it should be applicable to the rural parts of the society as well. Put another way, the theory of the advanced industrial society has drawn largely on urban developments, but if the same processes have similar implications for the rural areas, the theory is significantly strengthened. Unlike the industrial revolution which left rural areas to decline, advanced industrialism promises to revive and strengthen them. In fact, it can be argued that the rural areas of more advanced regions of the nation, such as California, provide an environment in which many of the most important developments of advanced industrialism are being worked out with exceptional freedom from restraint.

Some are Left Behind

The theory of an advanced industrial society does not imply that changes of the same sort affect all parts of the society at the same rate and in the same way. Some parts of the society remain unaffected by changes and remain tied to social patterns characteristic of traditional or industrial societies. For example: some depressed mining towns, marginal agricultural communities, poverty stricken urban areas, and traditional assembly or garment industries are found in California alongside new aerospace and electronics plants, with virtually no influence upon one another. In other cases, the advanced industrial society creates profound changes when a new college, industry or communication link brings the community to the forefront of the twentieth century. The point is that traditional, or less advanced, communities are not eliminated in the ad-

TABLE 1.2

Characteristics of Industrial Society, Advanced Industrial Society, and Rural Areas of Advanced Industrial Society

Characteristic	Industrial Society	Advanced Industrial	Rural Advanced Industrial
Technology	High energy-consuming machinery substituted for human labor	Knowledge-intensive technologies substituted for bulky machinery	Knowledge-intensive agriculture in a highly integrated food industry; movement of electronics and other high technology plants to the rural area
Services	Services introduced to the marketplace; growth of transportation, utilities, communication and trade	Professionalized and extensive network providing specialized services	Specialized agricultural service, expanded tourism, and wider distribution of professional and welfare services.
Knowledge	Development of literacy and mass primary schooling	Nearly universal higher education and extensive, institutionalized research network	Better distribution of educational opportunities, research taking place on farms, new educational structures outside of schools, new atmosphere of need and interest in education
Relationships	Traditional relations replaced by rationalism and secular concerns	High degree of interdependence and complexity which demands planning and coordination	Rural towns integrated into regional networks; media create increasing awareness of outside developments; emergence of regional governmental systems

Source: Compiled by the authors.

vanced industrial society. If these older systems continue, they are the subject of public scrutiny or intervention, as in Appalachia, or they become representatives of the romantic past and, as such, become touristic monuments. In short, the essential feature of the advanced industrial society is that something important has been added, not that the other parts have been eliminated.

Four Characteristics of Advanced Industrialism

The advanced industrial society is defined in terms of four basic characteristics. Such a society, current literature suggests, is found

1) to make disproportionate use of the most advanced physical science and social science technologies and to use these technologies in a manner that multiplies productivity and create both physical and human waste.
2) The concentration of labor activities shifts into service employment, and particularly to professional occupations. Along with this alteration in the character of employment is the development of a welfare state which makes available, through governmental intervention, the services of income and program support to both individuals and political systems at the local level.
3) The advanced industrial society is a heavy user of knowledge, and devotes considerable effort to the generation and transmission of both basic and applied research.
4) The most important consequence of these developments is the increase in interdependence in the economic and social structure. Individuals and groups are tied to each other in many more complex ways than before.

Table 1.2 summarizes these characteristics, contrasting them with the old industrial society, and illustrating their impact on rural areas.

High Technology

Advanced industrial societies have an intensive concentration of industries that make use of technology, developed through the application of science and research, to manufacture products not even available 50 years ago, or to manufacture goods which involve new processes and materials. The technology is not simply concentrated in a few sophisticated industries, though it is most easily seen there, but is diffused throughout the entire economic and social system, including agriculture, public institutions, and community social structures.

The use of sophisticated technologies means that an increasing proportion of the value of a product is a consequence of investment in scientific and engineering knowledge. In contrast, the value of a product in industrial society comes mostly from physical labor, mechanical energy, or raw materials. In high technology production processes the knowledge behind them becomes increasingly complex. Nathan Rosenberg points out that as industrial society becomes more advanced, "we may be moving up the scale of increasing complexity in the knowledge base underlying economic activity—from the mechanical to the electrical and electronic, chemical, biological, etc." (1972: 167-8). Indeed, Freeman Dyson has described the "next industrial revolution based on a new technology [which] must grow out of an understanding and mastery of the basic processes of biology, just as our existing technology grew out of a mastery of the processes of chemistry and physics" (1977: 2). Some of these biological processes will surely be used to solve problems of adequate water, energy, and raw materials and, in so doing, will have important impacts on rural land use.

In rural areas the impact of new technology comes both from the expansion of the newest industries, made possible by advanced technology such as electronics and aircraft, and from the use of the most sophisticated technology available for more traditional industries: for example, agriculture, wood processing, sport and recreation equipment, communications, and retailing. Agriculture becomes an integrated, complex food industry with processing linked to growing and harvesting through specially designed machinery and special hybrid seeds. Experts take over large parts of the agriculture process, including the control of pests, application of chemical fertilizers, and determination of irrigation patterns and rate of water delivery. In California, during the drought of 1975-77 these technical information systems were so effective that production in the state's fields declined only minimally, although water use was cut 60 percent.

The challenge new technology poses for understanding rural areas lies in the fact that technology is more than a set of devices and physical structures, or is more than a set of theoretical principles that describe the dynamics of the devices so that we can predict and control their behavior. As LaPorte (1974: 13-14) points out, citizens, government officials, and employees all experience technology as a *social experience*:

> Beyond the external physical changes wrought by the technological advance, changes occur in people's ability and capacity to do things— to change the shape of social life itself. These are the changes, generally widespread, that stimulate both the enthusiasm and uneasiness about technical development. And they are the changes which require the active cooperation of many people to accomplish. Thus, it is essential to understand that "technology" is also a system of human beings cooperating in quite complex ways, ways combining to create a new or improved capacity which others may use to alter their life's experiences.

The sophisticated technology found in the advanced industrial society creates massive social change because it is a social system that reaches into both rural and urban areas.

Technology creates new professions because it seems to require increased specialization for its implementation in social organization. In agriculture we have already mentioned the various specialists that have evolved, ranging from

agronomist to nutritionist to community development specialist. Others, including radio and electronics operators, quality control persons, and the like, are
all part of the control staff required for the implementation of new technological systems.

Technology creates new expectations as well. In areas where there are
many new technologies there is a general expectation that the development of a
new technology will continue to be available to solve many other problems. A
parallel expectation is that the new technology will have increasingly painful
second- and third-order consequences in terms of waste products, job displacement, and regulatory complications. In short, there is the expectation, increasingly felt by unions, homeowners near construction sites, and city councils,
that things do not always work as well as they are supposed to work for all
parties involved. This does not mean that all criticisms of technology are valid.
As Victor Ferkiss (1969) has shown, there are many compensating balances to
the problems created by technological change.

Service Sector

The second changing arena in the advanced industrial society is the growing service sector. The distinction between service and manufacturing sectors of
society was developed by Colin Clark (1960), and has become the basis for much
of the census classification of industry. The classification characterizes industries,
first, as primary if they take things from nature—that is, raw materials, including
agricultural products and mining. The second industrial category includes the
processing of these materials through manufacturing processes. The product of
manufacturing is goods of a wide variety. The third category covers the production of services rather than goods—and is the "tertiary" or service sector. The
advanced industrial society is shaped to a large degree by a growing service sector which has increased in the United States from 37 percent of the labor force
in 1910 to 64 percent in 1970. This expansion includes a growing proportion of
employment in industries such as communications, transportation, insurance,
sales, education, and government. The relative growth of the three sectors for
the United States and California is shown in Figure 1.1. There has been a considerable growth in service employment in California and in the nation, though
California started with a higher proportion and now has the highest level of
service employment of any industrial state (California, Governor, 1976: 17).
This large proportion of service employment has a number of consequences for
the social development of rural areas.

The large service sector has created an expanding class of white collar
workers with skills for processing information, not materials. If one examines
the proportion of persons employed in white collar occupations, one notes that
California exceeded 50 percent white collar employment before 1940, while the
nation as a whole did not reach this mark until the 1960 census (see Table 1.3).
With virtually all economic growth occurring in this sector, minority ethnic and

FIGURE 1.1

Percent Employment by Industrial Sector in California and the United States, 1910–70

Percentage

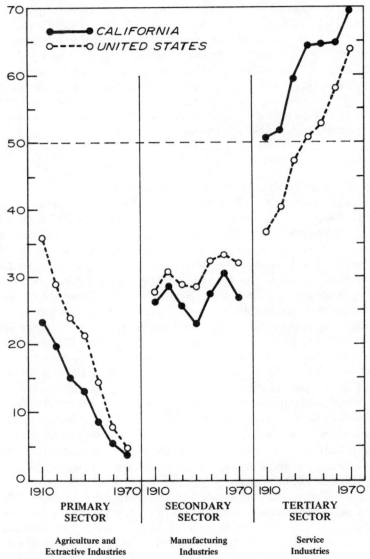

Source: Todd R. LaPorte with Ted K. Bradshaw, "Advanced Industrial California: Employment Patterns," *California Data Brief*, 1, no. 4 (July, 1977): 2.

TABLE 1.3

Percent Employed in White Collar and Service Occupations: California and the United States, 1930–70

	1930	1940	1950	1960	1970
California	48.8	53.1	56.0	57.7	67.0
United States	37.5	43.1	47.0	52.5	61.0

Source: Todd R. LaPorte with Ted K. Bradshaw, "Advanced Industrial California: Employment Patterns," *California Data Brief,* 1, no. 4 (July, 1977): 1.

TABLE 1.4

Percent Employed in Professional Industries: California and the United States, 1910–70

	1910	1920	1930	1940	1950	1960	1970
California	6.4	7.7	9.4	8.8	9.7	12.7	20.1
United States	4.5	5.2	6.7	7.5	8.5	11.7	18.5

Source: Todd R. LaPorte with Ted K. Bradshaw, "Advanced Industrial California: Employment Patterns," *California Data Brief,* 1, no. 4 (July, 1977): 3.

racial groups having different values and literary training are increasingly relegated to a persistent underclass.

A second change is reflected in the composition of the service sector. Along with its growth have been important internal changes from personal service to professional employment and from independent employment to large scale operations that are capital-intensive and highly bureaucratized. For example, service employment includes working for the telephone company, but many telephone workers deal with machines not people; they are in one of the most capital-intensive of all industries. At the same time personal services such as rendered by shoeshine boys have virtually disappeared. Professional industries incorporating these changes have grown significantly, from only a few percent of the labor force in 1910 to over 20 percent in California today (shown in Table 1.4).

In the service sector professionalization signals another important trend—the employment of sophisticated social technologies to manage and coordinate large social systems. Social technologies imply the use of innovations such as computer simulations, cost-benefit analysis, econometrics, information theory, multivariate analysis, attitude surveys, and opinion sampling to solve social and managerial problems. These technologies have been available for use only since 1945; most have been developed since 1960. Although data are not available for all these, it is clear that the service sector is influenced by the new sets of social technologies for improved organizational management in ways similar to many industries that were affected by innovations in the handling of raw materials to produce consumer goods.

Unfortunately, however, social technologies are not as subject to prediction and accuracy as are physical ones. The service sector is subject to massive breakdowns of social technology when, for example, national economic and financial efforts do not produce expected upswings in the national economy; when new philosophies of education produce a whole generation that has difficulty reading; and when Planned Program Budgeting increases paperwork but does not effect more rational government efforts.

As will be shown in Chapter 2, California's rural areas are being shaped by a growing service sector. Not only are professional services generally available in many small towns and communities, but many services industries are growing in rural areas to serve the needs of urban residents. Tourism, for example provides a major source of growth for many rural communities. But while tourism has brought many second homes, shopping centers, and civic facilities to rural regions, it has also caused congestion and rising home values, taxes, and crime.

Finally, the growth of the service sector has been due in part to changes in the role of government and its increasing size. Many of the important developments we describe were introduced through government programs of many kinds. Employment by the public sector in the 1970s was used in an attempt to cure high unemployment rates, in particular through the Comprehensive Employment and Training Act (CETA) and other programs. During the last decade government has been the fastest growing sector of the economy.

However, in June 1978, California voters passed Proposition 13, the Jarvis-Ganns Initiative, which was the first of many tax limitation proposals in a so called national "antitax revolt," the extent or implications of which are not known as we write. We think that the political change resulting from tax limitation will have implications for the development of the service sector and for community development in general, but the directions of overall social change we will chart will, most likely, not be reversed so much as slowed down.

Knowledge and Information

The third characteristic of an advanced industrial society is the intense rate at which knowledge is generated and transmitted. This knowledge is needed by industry to support and continue the high technology which is essential to the economy; but it is also needed in the service sector, in government and social programs, and by groups which are interested in changing the opportunities in the society. An advanced industrial society is therefore a knowledge-based society.

This has caused significant structural changes in the character of the educational system which transmits knowledge from its source to persons who need it. Whereas knowledge used to be a commodity for the power elite and could be provided for the most part by schools aimed at the young, the advanced industrial society has such changing and continuing needs that the concept of lifelong learning takes on increasing importance. Furthermore, during the life cycle, education comes to mean more than simply preparing for and acquiring skills; it means the provision of tools for coping with an increasingly complex world and finding enjoyment in it. Thus, the educational system has become involved in the personal lives of many adults over a long period of time.

Equally important, the educational system has increased in scale so that very high proportions of high school graduates receive further training in post-secondary educational institutions prior to taking employment in a career. In rural as in urban areas there are now facilities for the improvement of human resources of youth before they enter the labor market, and there are increasingly specialized programs to meet varied expectations. While general education in the liberal arts tradition is not the most rapidly growing section of higher education, increasing attention is being given to it by administrators who believe that it is the only way to adequately prepare youth for the many changes they are likely to encounter during their lives.

The school in rural areas of an advanced industrial society becomes a resource for the community. Schools are not neutral resources but advocate planned change for social improvement. Of all institutions in rural areas, schools—especially at a postsecondary level—are least likely to be isolated and hampered by traditional philosophies. They provide the capacity out of which changes can come. Indeed, many individuals who are going to be doing community development actually work in schools because of their centrality to developments in the advanced industrial society.

If the needs of the society are for education, the needs of education for new banks of knowledge are equally great. In many rural areas a significant amount of research is conducted by universities, corporations, and private groups. The need for this research effort increases the pressures for linkages between rural areas and central cities for information. Indeed, the research that takes place in rural communities becomes a channel for cosmopolitan influences.

Interdependence

Finally, an advanced industrial society is characterized by increasingly dense networks of exchange and transfer of resources, information, and goods of all sorts. Increasing interdependence means that more goods and services of varying kinds are exchanged among units in the society at a more rapid pace, with greater potential disruption when the flow is broken. The innovation of industrial society was to bring rationality and secularism to social relations, while the innovation of the advanced industrial society is to magnify and institutionalize the networks of exchange among individuals, businesses, governmental agencies, communities, and other societies. This involves new patterns of bureaucracy and innovations in every sphere.

As technological development increases, a larger variety of specialties are needed by each firm or organization; to gain access to these skills, each group must deal with a greater number of other groups. For example, a traditional toaster factory has low interdependencies, needs a relatively small number of supplies such as metal, heating elements, plastics, tools and cardboard boxes. The company markets the toaster through a network of distributors and warehouses that deal with similar items. But an advanced industrial firm manufacturing computers or aircraft needs many more kinds of materials and tools, each with fewer substitutes. In turn, these materials and components are more complex, have more parts, and originate from more suppliers. The output of the advanced industrial plant is then distributed through a more complicated network, whose installation services and special adaptations increase the number of interdependent links.

The government becomes increasingly involved as more regulations are needed to govern relations among firms. Also, there is more interdependence among the various components of government itself, for example, more links among governmental agencies and between state and local levels. For example, Jones, Magleby, and Scott report that local government is increasingly linked to state programs and funding (1975: 47). Furthermore, local governments must deal with regional governments, such as area-wide planning agencies and independent water districts (Fujimoto and Symonds, 1971). Such interdependence becomes a major source of both strength and confusion for advanced industrial societies.

Probably the most important difference for rural areas in the advanced industrial society is the increasing interdependence in which local communities are embedded. The rural community is no longer isolated from developments in the whole society but is rapidly affected by them. Interdependence means that what happens in Washington has ever larger impacts on social programs, and it means that processes of getting things done require coordination and planning among many organizations, not simply among a few individuals.

For example, the Federal government spends an enormous amount of money in California, much of which finds its way into rural areas. Military spending for salaries is concentrated in bases situated in relatively rural areas. Thus, Beal, Travis, Edwards, and March Air Force bases, and the Vandenberg missile complex are in rural locations. Furthermore, Army bases including Fort Ord are in rural or semi-rural locations. The impact of federal money in the State Water Project and much of the Interstate Highway Program found its way into rural communities. Finally, the communities in California are able to compete favorably for federal funds and have received a disproportionate share. California's peculiar position as the nation's most urban state, combined with one of the largest land areas of any state, attracts considerable federal resources.

All of these issues will be sketched in more detail in the following chapters; they provide an organizing theory for the study of new rural society and of the professional roles of community developers who attempt to improve the human resources in rural areas.

Advanced industrialism, thus, means that there are changes in the structure of the technological base in the society that affect people and their institutions. One of the important ways this has affected rural areas is that population trends, which were depleting rural areas of their population bases, have been reversed; now people are finding their way back into rural areas and are bringing with them the interests and opportunities they enjoyed in urban areas. Furthermore, in the high technology society where service and knowledge-intensive economic patterns are found, rural areas can be enjoyed today for their high quality of life and yet remain connected to the city. Thus, the new rural frontier is a context within which hopes for both social and economic development arise. With this in mind, we now turn to a consideration of the patterns of population migration which are giving increasing evidence that rural areas are not only becoming newly viable, but indeed are thriving. Yet, as we shall see, the new growth is giving rise to frustrations and problems which accompany these changes.

NONMETROPOLITAN POPULATION GROWTH

One of the most interesting consequences in the growth of the advanced industrial society may be the potential for altered patterns of urban population distributions. While the growth of central cities has been a part of the process of industrialization, evidence suggests that the advanced industrial society, and other developments, may lead to a reversal of this pattern and to the growth of rural areas instead. In this section we will review data about the "reverse migration" nationally and present data on the changing character of rural population distributions in California. The growth of rural areas suggests that they are at the frontier of social and economic change while the cities may be left with many of the problems of the past.

Calvin Beale first noted the rapid turnabout of population migration in the United States in 1973. Between 1970 and 1973, Beale showed, nonmetropolitan counties gained 4.2 percent in population compared to only 2.9 percent for metro areas, reversing for the first time in many decades a trend of more rapid metropolitan population growth. During the 1950s a net of 5 million people left nonmetro areas. In the South during this same decade farm population dropped 40 percent. During the 1960s, however, the rate of out migration had slowed, and in the South some 250 nonmetro counties had out migrations of black population only and a net in migration of whites. Several large nonmetro areas started having relatively large rates of growth, but the pattern did not become general until the 1970s (Beale, 1975: 3-5). Confirming Beale in his analysis have been a number of other studies of this reversal of population movement. For example, Tucker noted that more recent evidence from 1975 confirms Beale's observations based on data for 1973. Tucker shows that during the 1965-70 period 352,000 persons migrated to metropolitan areas, but in the following five-year period these same metro areas lost 1,594,000 persons (1976: 437). Morrison estimated that the growth rate of rural counties with virtually no commuting to an adjacent SMSA declined at an average annual rate of -0.4 percent during the decade of the 1960s, while in the first three years of the 1970s the growth rate rose 0.9 percent annually. Thus Morrison concludes that "the more remote kinds of places—those that as a group used to be regarded as 'nowhere'—have today become 'somewhere' in the minds of many migrants" (1977: 214). Finally, DeJong and Sell show that over the longtime perspective this new rural growth represents a marked reversal of past patterns. The population within SMSAs, as defined by 1960 SMSA boundaries, increased 4.4 times between 1900 and 1970, while the population outside these boundaries increased only 1.4 times. In every decade the proportion of persons living in urban areas increased, while there was a corresponding decrease in the proportion living in rural areas. This trend apparently has been reversed. Although much nonmetropolitan growth is concentrated in areas close to SMSAs (an extension of suburbanization), DeJong and Sell show that growth is not confined to these areas but is widespread in rural counties (1977: 131-4).

While there is a great deal of consensus on the fact of a large migration to nonmetropolitan areas, there is less agreement on the reasons for this change. Zuiches suggests that communities which grow have large institutional activities located nearby—such as colleges or military bases. In fact, these factors alone accounted for a significant proportion of total in migration rates of a sample of nonmetropolitan counties using 1960 census data (Zuiches, 1970). Since the 1960 census there has been a significant increase in the number of colleges and, during the Vietnam war, an increase in activity on military bases. Similar analysis has been done by Beale and Fuguitt who showed that, whether or not a county was adjacent to an SMSA, the presence of a college between 1970 and 1974 led to rates of net migration some 20 to 30 percent above counties without such colleges. However, military bases no longer contribute to growth. Between 1950 and 1960, counties with 10 percent or more military personnel had an average growth rate of 4.53 compared to 0.23 in counties without this much military; in the 1960s they had a growth of 2.08 compared to 0.39 in counties with fewer military. However, this was reversed in the period of 1970–74; places with over 10 percent military lost population at an annual rate of -.30; at the same time other nonmetropolitan areas grew at a rate of 1.31. Beale and Fuguitt's data present several more surprises. There is a strong and consistently increasing importance of migration of older people into growing rural areas. Retirement counties—those with over 15 percent population over 60 years of age—grew at more than double the rate of counties with 10 to 14 percent older persons and at four times the rate of those with less than 10 percent. Further, predominantly black and predominantly agricultural counties continue to lose population to out migration, although the rate has slowed from earlier decades. Finally, Beale and Fuguitt show that those areas with the largest manufacturing employment were not necessarily the gainers in population. Those with medium amounts of manufacturing were the leading growth areas. The evidence points to expansion of employment opportunities in trade and other non-goods-producing sectors, rather than to manufacturing, as the leading impetus for growth (Beale and Fuguitt, 1976: 16).

Tucker has contributed to our understanding of migration patterns through an analysis of the age patterns of migrants. Although many reports of the growth of rural regions emphasize the "return to the countryside" of large numbers of urban youth and retired persons, the data show that this is more complicated. As expected, young adults aged 25–35 were more likely to move from a SMSA to a nonmetropolitan area during the 1970–75 period, as compared to 1964–70. On the other hand, Tucker points out that nonmetropolitan youth continued to move to the city at about the same rate as they did during the earlier period. However, Tucker's data also show low rates of migration of older persons to nonmetropolitan areas. The out migration rate for the over 65 group is lower than for any age cohort except the 45–64 year-old group. Among the oldest group 2.8 percent left rural communities for metropolitan areas while 4.0 percent moved the other way—from the cities to nonmetropolitan areas. Of course, because of the larger number of metropolitan residents, there is a net migration of persons over the age of 65 to rural areas, amounting to about 300,000 persons: an increase of 200,000 over the 1965–70 period (Tucker, 1976).

In addition to the special attractions due to institutions and retirement opportunities, rural communities are growing because of a number of other factors. Wrigley (1973: 58-9) summarizes the attractiveness of nonmetropolitan locations, mentioning six advantages. There are lower labor costs for industry, more available land at lower costs, less stringent pollution regulations, a more pleasant place to live, expanding opportunities for new types of industries, and market access through modern highways. Niles Hansen agrees that there are advantages in nonmetropolitan areas, but they may be different than supposed. Highway access, for example, is usually considered a very important factor, as in the list by Wrigley. However, Hansen shows that proximity to a good highway is strongly correlated with proximity to a standard metropolitan area, and that it is this proximity which accounts for the observed growth of many communities on new highways. Hansen concludes that "although there are isolated success stories, emphasis on the causal efficacy of highways with respect to development has diminished in favor of greater emphasis on their permissive role" (Hansen, 1973: 31). Furthermore, he shows that the nonmetropolitan counties which are growing most rapidly have had large increases in urban-type employments, including services and other non-goods-producing kinds of jobs (1973: 40).

Finally, a number of analyses have concentrated on the desire of people to live in rural settings instead of the city. These generally include "push" factors reflecting the problems of city life, such as pollution, crime, and the high cost of living, rather than the "pull" of job opportunities, better schools, and attractive housing. Fuguitt and Zuiches (1973) examined a number of surveys taken since 1948 and report that in eight out of nine surveys the large city is the community size least preferred, but in all surveys the small city or rural residence is most preferred. However, they also point out that most of the persons expressing these preferences actually desire those small city locations to be close to large cities rather than in remote regions. Finally, they show that the greatest potential interest in living in rural areas comes from young persons with high school diplomas, white collar occupations, and high incomes relative to present rural residents, who are older and less educated, have blue collar occupations, and earn low incomes. From these analyses we document a major attitudinal change from that which led to the earlier mass migration from rural areas to urban.

The growth of rural areas, then, is significant for a variety of reasons. However, for community development the surprising element is that the reversal of population appears to be the unanticipated consequence of a number of policy decisions which were completely outside the structure of past community development activities. Growth of rural areas has been desired by policy makers for several decades, climaxing with massive rural assistance programs, such as the Rural America Act of 1972; but the evidence does not suggest that such efforts were the cause of the growth of rural areas in the 1970s. Instead, it appears that present rural growth is an unanticipated result of a number of other policy decisions by both the state and Federal governments in such areas as energy policy, highway construction, park expansion, educational development, research, welfare policy, and intergovernmental relations.

Changing Population Growth Rates in California

From 1970 to 1976 California's nonmetropolitan counties grew at a rate three times the rate of the metropolitan regions—18 percent compared to 5 percent. In this period migration continued into the state as a whole, but the rate for metropolitan areas slowed to about one-fourth of the rate of the 1960s, while migration into nonmetropolitan counties doubled. Sokolow reports that only six of California's 52 counties had a net out migration during 1970–76, and four of them were the counties containing the state's oldest and most populous cities. By contrast, 15 small counties that recorded net migration losses in the 1960–70 period had net gains in the six years after 1970 (1977: 348). The interesting fact about much of this migration is that it is not simply an expansion of the suburbs out to the next tier of counties; it is an increased settlement of the "hinterland" as exists in California (Sokolow, 1978). Map 1.1 shows the recent population change in California.

Over the longer run, an important feature of California's development is that its rural areas have never experienced the dramatic out migration characteristic of much of the rest of the nation. From 1930 to 1976 there has been steady, although slow, growth in the 44 counties defined as rural in 1950. During this period California grew from a population of 5,678,210 to the largest state in the nation with 21,514,000 persons, representing nearly a 3.7 fold increase in people. Similarly, the rural areas grew from 1,125,000 persons to 4,410,300, an increase of 3.9 times. Thus, rural areas have grown at about the rate of the state as a whole during the last 35 years. However, much of the growth of rural areas has been centered in a few counties which have become classified as metropolitan areas since 1950. When these counties are excluded from the rural count, those counties now defined as nonmetropolitan grew from 559,540 persons to 1,559,400 during the period of 1930 to 1976, an increase of only 2.8 times. This relatively sluggish rural growth has turned around since 1970, in keeping with national patterns of rural growth. During the period from 1970 to 1976 these same rural counties had an overall growth rate of 14.3 percent in contrast to the overall state growth of only 7.5. The urban counties in northern California grew at a rate of 6.5 percent; the urban central valley counties had a growth rate of 10.3 percent, while the heavily populated southern California counties grew only by 6.3 percent.

Thus, the rural areas grew at a rate nearly double that of the state as a whole. We must caution that this does not reflect a large number of people; it does imply a new trend when coupled with similar trends in the rest of the nation. Our data suggest that the start of this trend was about 1970 or about the same time the national trend started.

MAP 1.1

Population Changes for California Counties, 1970–77

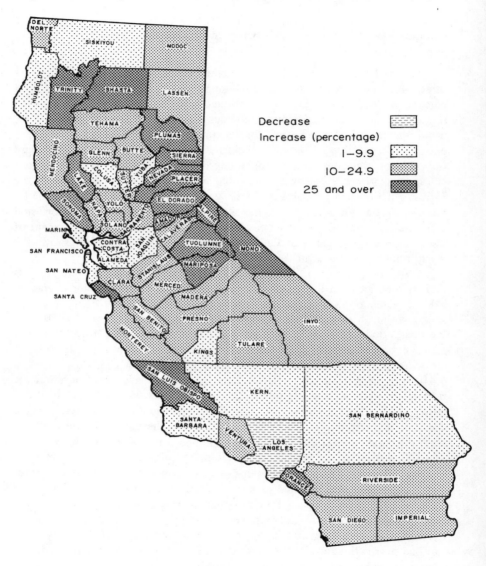

Source: Alvin D. Sokolow, "The Redistribution of California's Population: New Growth in Nonmetropolitan Areas," *California Data Brief*, 2, no. 1 (February, 1978).

RURAL COMMUNITY DEVELOPMENT— PUBLIC POLICY AND PROFESSION

Rural community development embodies both the process of affecting change in rural areas and the emerging professional specialists who are agents of change in collaboration with local policy makers. There are many definitions of community development (see Cary, 1970: 2; Sanders, 1970; Lauderdale and Peterson, 1971; Biddle and Biddle, 1965; Kramer and Specht, 1975: 6). We use the concept in a particular way to describe organized and intentional efforts undertaken on behalf of an entire community or region to create changes that improve the conditions of community life. Such efforts include improving economic opportunities and physical structures; stimulating more effective social resources, organization, information, and participation; bringing improved resources to disadvantaged parts of the community; and creating awareness of the potential for improving the community quality of life. The processes of bringing change to rural areas is not monopolized by the community development profession. Various scholars in disciplines ranging from anthropology to economics and sociology have labored to understand why, how, and when the processes of socioeconomic development can be stimulated in lagging rural areas. Our interest is not in the origin, history, or philosophy of community development but in the developmental processes that respond to a rapidly changing society such as rural California.

Development processes are related to the changing macrosociological conditions of society, especially as they are affected by changes of advanced industrialism and rapid population growth. These forces affect public policy in a broad sense, affecting the ways the policy institutions are configured and how they carry out their responsibilities with respect to rural or nonmetropolitan areas. Further, they influence the choices and opinions of rural policy makers in dealing effectively with the needs of rural areas, facing changes they can feel but do not understand.

Along with changing processes, we will describe the impact and implications of changing rural society on the profession of community developers. Community developers operate in both rural and urban settings, with many of the same goals and methods, but we shall restrict our analysis to rural development activities. Obviously, much of what is described is equally applicable to urban areas, although specific situations in rural areas are different. Our concern is discussing the practitioner is directly related to the basic goal of the community development profession—that it requires skilled professionals to stimulate and to manage changes desired by people in a community setting.

Community Development as a Policy Approach

Community developers perform a variety of activities that are central to the process of encouraging and facilitating change in rural communities. There are a number of approaches to community development which entail a variety of different community developer activities. In spite of this diversity, there is a general agreement that community development involves a number of specialists working with the citizens of a community to alter community organizational patterns (Lauderdale and Peterson 1971: 13). Community development in its most general sense is part of the overall public arena. Policy is the process of setting general goals and approaches to meeting those goals. Community development is a subset of policy in that it works within, and tries to influence policies set elsewhere, to achieve changes. Policy has other subsets, including political process by which communities select leaders and choose among policies and policy options, based on the power of competing interests. Another component of policy is the actual delivery of social services based on public administration. These efforts are contrasted with community development which is that part of the policy system responsible for interacting with citizens and their groups within policy guidelines and for helping establish organizational structures to reach community goals.

Although, as Figure 1.2 shows, community development is neither power politics nor service delivery, it is nontheless involved with both. It engages with groups in power politics in order to get policy set, and it often finds itself involved in service delivery because that is how things can get done. Similarly,

FIGURE 1.2

Public Policy and Community Development

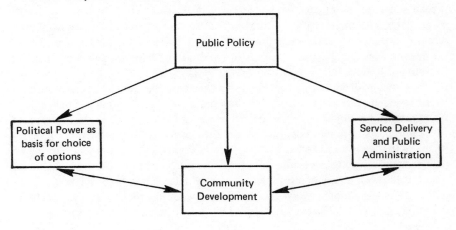

Source: Constructed by authors.

political processes and service delivery both use the community developer to gain assistance in reaching goals they seek. In its very conception, therefore, community development has a central integrative role and is a link or a process, rather than an end in itself (Sanders, 1970).

Activities of Community Developers

Community development activities include a diverse array of functions undertaken primarily for the benefit of a geographical unit (neighborhood, city, or region). These activities are usually initiated by a public entity and receive some form of government support. The most common of these activities is the *infusion of resources* into a community to alter the local economy. These efforts usually involve allocation of capital for building roads, installing sewers, creating industrial or commercial facilities, funding the construction of community centers, or similar projects. The emphasis here is on the identification of community needs for which some economic resource can be transferred into the local environment which will stimulate employment and bring about permanent improvements in local income and material quality of life. In addition, community development activities attempt to create solidarity, cohesion, and local leadership potential through the *stimulation of local group processes*. This latter activity is designed to contribute to political stability and to provide a socio-psychological environment in which political change, through debate and discussion, can proceed within a common or shared set of values.

Further, the community development process is essentially a *goal formulation* activity in which people from diverse backgrounds choose the direction their community should develop. According to John Huie (1975: 18), the goal-setting approach helps to build consensus about community objectives, clarify current problems, and analyze the potential means to overcome them. The community developer's role in goal-setting is to facilitate consensus development by designing mechanisms through which local citizens can mutually determine their needs and goals, as well as the means to attain their objectives. This can occur through the use of techniques ranging from small group meetings to political confrontations and demonstrations.

Finally, community development encompasses a set of activities related to the organization and delivery of a variety of human services supporting *socioeconomic change*. That is, the community developer is a "change agent," working in the schools, hospitals, housing programs, and agricultural regions, to integrate efforts to change these institutions in conformity with other goals within the domain of the planning structure in a manner that is catalytic to the development process itself.

These community development activities are vital to the analysis of the development of rural communities in the advanced industrial society. In each chapter we deal with the community developer's role and the way development activities are performed in new social and economic contexts.

Pressures on the Community
Development Profession

The community development process and the role of the community development practitioner are under increasing pressure for change in the advanced industrial society. As we will show throughout this study, the traditional activities and roles of the developer are being expanded and extended to include new public policy activities. The community developer is working with professionals from a variety of related social and human service fields who share the community developer's mission of improving the overall quality of community life. These changes in the profession create both new conflicts and new opportunities.

There are no precise estimates as to the number of professionals who are active community developers. Nor are there estimates of the number of professionals in related fields who use community development techniques and perform community development activities but are not identified as professional community developers. Presently, over 100 educational training programs prepare community developers in the United States, according to Lee Cary (1976). These training programs range from Ph.D. programs at some land grant universities to Bachelor's and Master's programs elsewhere. These programs, as described by Blakely (1974), place emphasis on the diagnosis of community problems, citizen involvement techniques, and various other human relations skills. Not only do the educational institutions offer degrees; they provide outreach activities as well and engage in community development practice through their faculty and staff.

Community Development and
Advanced Industrialism

In the following chapters we examine community development within the context of a changing society. We show how community economic development must take into account a variety of new economic issues and opportunities. In chapters 3-5, we give illustrations of how the community developer works within the context of social institutions in rural areas, particularly in educational institutions, government, and welfare agencies. Finally, in the concluding chapter 6, we combine our discussions of the problems and practices of community development into a discussion of how the development professional and the profession itself responds to the overall changes of the society.

In this book we offer a model for the understanding of new trends affecting the field of community development and a description of the new opportunities for community developers as change agents in rural settings. We do not offer a prescription for community developers, who are struggling with the new issues we describe, but we present a framework within which a better assessment of the problems and opportunities are possible.

2

Rural Economic Development in a High Technology Society

INTRODUCTION

Theories of economic development are ill-equipped to explain the new types of rural growth and changing economic patterns found in the rural areas of the advanced industrial society. Most of the current literature on economic development in rural areas is based on experiences of Appalachia or the rapidly declining farming areas of the South, Northeast, and Midwest (see Hansen, 1973, 1974; Marshall, 1974; and bibliography by Harvey, 1975). McGuire argues that rural economic development programs in the United States have traditionally been tied to specific, economically depressed regions through organizations such as the Tennessee Valley Authority (TVA) and the Appalachian Regional Commission (1971: 8). Research on the efforts of these agencies has been performed by land grant universities in the South and Midwest, and, for the most part, these research efforts have dominated thinking about the process of rural economic development. Similarly, rural community development strategies have emphasized industries with low-skill technologies from other areas with attractions such as tax incentives and industrial parks.

However, in rural areas of California and other states with characteristics of an advanced industrial society, economic development is taking place in new ways. Increasingly, research is turning up processes in the more advantaged and rapidly growing rural areas that may foretell patterns of rural development in the coming decades. For example, in some rural areas factories are not only being attracted from urban areas by prevailing low wages, nonunion labor forces, and tax credits, but factories in growth industries are choosing rural locations in order to take advantage of skilled labor forces and high quality of living. Furthermore, some rural areas are able to select the most attractive industries wishing to leave metropolitan areas. Perhaps most important, the bulk of new jobs are in service industries and the governmental sector, giving rise to new strategies and processes of rural industrial development. In advanced industrial rural areas, as in the economy as a whole, three new jobs are created in the service sector for every one in manufacturing. The expansion of marketing, communications, tourism, and social services to rural areas, therefore, may be a more important economic development for most rural communities than the attraction of a new factory. At the same time this leads to new problems and demands as many rural communities in California have discovered.

Wilbur Thompson (1975: 188) has noted that the South, with its recent attraction of industrial factories, "is going through the industrial and post-industrial age at the same time." For other parts of rural America the step will be directly from the agricultural age to the advanced industrial, with no intervening industrialization of the traditional sort; a fact that makes the experience of these small towns much different from the typical community of the last half century so carefully studied by sociologists and others (for example, Vidich and Bensman, 1958; Warner, 1953; Lynd and Lynd, 1929). As Conrad and Field argue, the new opportunities necessitate a new concern by community developers and others to protect smaller communities from overdevelopment or types of economic growth that would change the character of the locality and seriously impair resource quality (1976: 47).

In this chapter, changes in the economic structure of advanced industrial rural areas will be described, and economic development strategies appropriate to the new rural economy will be discussed. In particular, we will show how high technology and service sector growth are contributing to the economic revival of rural areas, and how these economic changes will require community developers to adopt new strategies suitable to the complexity of the new economic system. This chapter is not intended to be a review of the literature of economic development or to be an economic analysis of the processes of rural development. This has been done elsewhere. (See Kerr and Williamson, 1970; Hansen, 1970b; Tweeten and Brinkman, 1976.) Our analysis focuses on macrosocial conditions that are part of the evolution of a rural advanced industrial economy and aims only to point to trends which suggest the need for a new consideration of the emerging economic patterns shaping some rural areas.

The Problem of Rural Economic Development

The problem of economic development is indeed the most important problem facing the majority of rural areas. Hansen states that the most pervasive problem for rural workers is underemployment and low earnings (1970b: 32), due largely to the excess labor freed from farm employment. The President's National Advisory Commission on Rural Poverty (1967: 25) has emphasized the importance of economic development in rural areas:

The current situation in rural America is this: Employment in agriculture, forests, mines, and fisheries is declining faster than new jobs are being created in rural areas by construction, manufacturing, and service industries. At that, the rural unemploy[ed] get few such new jobs as are created. They often don't know the job exists, they lack the skills needed, and they can't finance a move to a new job. So they remain poor.

Indeed this grim economic situation forced the vast migration of rural persons to urban areas during the last half century.

Galbraith, for example, suggests that the problem of the poverty-ridden community is the lack of potential for growth: "There is stagnation in output and income, and this perpetuates itself year after year, and from generation to generation. One cannot extend the analysis of the advancing society to this stagnation" (1962: 14).

The result of these situations is that when rural industrialization does take place, it is often in industries that pay wages well below the average for all manufacturing industries and that are tied to the initial processing of natural materials (Tweeten and Brinkman, 1976: 226–230). Marshall points out that jobs in these industries often provide nonfarm employment for farmers with small operations or for wives of underemployed men. When high-wage firms are attracted, however, there have been few employment opportunities for local unemployed or underemployed persons, and more skilled workers are often attracted from outside the area (Marshall, 1974: 74). Some of the best examples of rural industrialization noted in the literature are communities that acquire a huge textile or steel mill (see, for example, Beck, Dotson, and Summers, 1973), but the number of these occurrences is small. When they do locate in a small rural community, the consequence is similar to the boom town impact of coal development and similar natural resource based changes (Gilmore, 1976). In contrast, small branch factories and the expansion of secondary processing of natural resources and farm products in rural areas are more common through all regions, though less centralized in their impact and less well studied.

Furthermore, changes in agriculture not only eliminated many of the traditional laborer jobs by which migratory families and lower skilled persons make their living, but these changes upgrade the skills required for the job, tend to make the job last longer, and, consequently, further restrict the opportunities for casual laborers. At the same time, the larger social organization of agricultural industries tends to remove many of the suppliers of farm machinery and chemicals from the local community and to concentrate them in larger regional communities. The changes brought about by new technologies in agriculture thus extend far beyond the local farm in terms of rural economic development problems.

Advanced Industrialism and Economic Development

An advanced industrial society is distinguished from its predecessors by a number of factors. The sophisticated technology used in the economies of advanced industrial societies is complex and scientific, but most important it requires knowledge that goes beyond common sense and is theoretical (Bell, 1973). Ordinary farmers cannot develop their own hybrid seed, breed Beefalo cattle or develop integrated pest management techniques; even engineers take years of testing and development to create a new electronics product; the primary economic contribution of professionals such as lawyers is their knowledge and training in a complex field of specialization. Furthermore, the knowledge of the advanced industrial society is concentrated in many products which process knowledge itself though symbols, rather than process raw materials through mechanical operations. The genius of the industrial society lay in its use of inanimate energy to perform mechanical operations in factories. The advanced industrial society utilizes much of its knowledge to minimize the use of energy and to free people from the confines of the factory organization. The advanced industrial society, in short, has proportionately more industries using technologies involving knowledge instead of raw materials, unskilled labor, and massive amounts of energy. These industries include electronics, aerospace, and instrumentation (Bradshaw, 1976).

Furthermore, the knowledge-intensive technologies of the advanced industrial society find application in every industry from the most resource-based like agriculture or mining, to the least like the professions. California's emergence as an advanced industrial society is evidenced by the high proportion of scientifically trained workers in its industries and by the mix of industries requiring the greatest amounts of specialized scientific knowledge. For example, as an advanced industrial society the economy of California is based on the design of computers rather than heavy industrial machinery, on the building of aircraft rather than automobiles, and the production of agricultural specialty crops rather than traditional grains.

Rural economies of the advanced industrial society reflect some of these developments, though to a lesser degree. Relative to other rural states, California's nonmetropolitan counties make great use of the most technologically sophisticated agricultural practices, favor industries having a high technology base, and emphasize extensive professional services. These characteristics are described in general terms in Table 2.1.

The economy of advanced industrial society is affected by a second trend of service sector growth which has significant consequences for both urban and rural areas. In traditional society few persons were needed to provide personal or public services—most individuals took care of themselves except for the affluent who employed numerous household workers. With greater affluence, social interdependence, and knowledge about the management of people in advanced industrial society, the service industries have responded to new opportunities. Personal services of the sort the affluent enjoyed have declined while the organized services of an increasingly knowledge-intensive sort have grown. Communications have used new technological developments such as the telephone and television, while trade, finance, real estate, and similar industries have provided

TABLE 2.1

Rural Economic Growth in the United States

Economic Characteristics	Traditional Society	Industrial Society	Advanced Industrial Society
Technology	Extractive, based on tradition	Energy intensive, factory production	Knowledge intensive, based on scientific knowledge
Manufacturing	Crafts	Heavy industry in factories	New products in electronics, aero-space and chemicals. New scientific processes for traditional industries
Agriculture	Traditional agrarian	Mechanized	Scientific
Service Sector	Personal services for affluent	Rise of trade and clerical industries, and early growth of professions (especially teaching, welfare, etc.)	Dominant source of employment. Growth in tourism, government, and professions.

Source: Compiled by the authors.

efficient transactions among people. The professions have grown with advances in their knowledge of fields such as medicine, law, engineering and education; public values have encouraged their use in the provision of welfare for the disadvantaged and widespread social security insurance programs for all.

Rural areas of traditional society have had few services. Widner (1974) suggests that such traditions have carried over into plans for the economic development of rural areas. For example, the lack of hardware stores and similar businesses in rural communities forces dollars from rural residents to be spent outside the area, further depleting the local economy. In the advanced industrial society many service industries are finding useful places in the economy, although many are more knowledge intensive than hardware stores. The community developer must construct regional economic strategies that will take advantage of new opportunities in the service industries through regional cooperation.

In this chapter we address the character of the changing rural economy in the advanced industrial society. The discussion is divided into three sections. The first two deal with the growing importance of knowledge-intensive technologies in the manufacturing and agricultural industries of a rural advanced industrial society. In the third we examine the growth of the service sector in rural areas. The changes in rural society brought about by the types of examples we examine in California pose significant challenges, as well as opportunities, for the economic development of rural areas and require the community developer to perform different roles.

KNOWLEDGE-INTENSIVE TECHNOLOGIES
IN RURAL SOCIETY

Although it has been generally assumed that the highest technologies would be located in central cities, the role of technological change in economic development has been recognized as important by economists and community developers alike. Wilbur Thompson's "filtering down" theory suggests that industries at the end of their growth period will leave the fertile central city and locate in the remote areas where low-skilled and cheap labor is available. As Hansen points out from a careful analysis of employment in six broad regions experiencing population growth, considerable decentralization of manufacturing plants into rural areas has been observed. However, an increasing number of innovative, high technology growth industries were also observed to be locating in some rural areas (1973: 162).

Central place and growth pole theory also emphasize metropolitan areas as the primary locational centers for growth. Morgan Thomas (1975) suggests that "propulsive" industries that are likely to bring growth to an area are in the early stage of a pattern of development. In general, industries that have innovative potential start with relatively high-cost and specialized development. During the second stage—the mass development phase—the industry moves into full production marked by cost reductions and gradual saturation of the market.

In the last stage—decline—the market is saturated and the process of production is routinized. This last stage is common for industries moving into the rural areas of much of the South today where the attraction of low-skill and inexpensive workers is substantial. However, an increasing number of these industries are moving to foreign countries. Apparel is one example of an industry with traditional growth of production in the South; but now, foreign countries account for much of the growth. Even so, advanced industrial growth in rural communities may still be consistent with the theory, as second-stage industries move into rural communities where skills and wages are higher, while declining industries go to foreign countries where greater economic savings are possible.

Rural areas offer many attractions for industries. Robert Wrigley has identified a number of traditional attractions of small cities for industrial expansion such as lower labor costs, greater availability of low-cost land, and less stringent regulations on pollution. He has also noted other aspects of rural areas attractive to knowledge-intensive industries such as greater livability, higher quality of life, improved market access through modern highways, and the availability of more skilled workers. Of the latter he writes (1973: 59):

> In recent years, "intellect-oriented" industries have become important—research and development activities, and some parts of the aerospace, electronics, and precision instrument industries. These industries, hiring a high proportion of scientists, engineers, and other professionals, particularly consider the desires and needs of their personnel. Although many firms of this type have located in the urban fringe of large cities, some are moving to small cities deep in rural territory, since they have found that the size of the city does not control the level of intellectual and recreational activity.

Rural advanced industrial regions are moving to attract this type of industry through regional planning bodies and economic development agencies, as in most of California's 40 rural counties.

The attractiveness of California's rural areas for high technology economic development may be seen in several examples in both traditional and new industries. In the far northwestern corner of California, traditional fishing and lumbering interests are being assisted by LANSAT satellites which provide information from space for the development of new forestry techniques and the location of fish at sea. The satellite data are also helping an Indian tribe assess its natural resources and develop a plan for their successful economic development (Northern California Signature, 1977). In Santa Cruz County, Monterey County, and parts of other rural counties, electronics plants have recently been started where the output is so miniaturized that a week's production may be transported in a pickup truck. In another area a strawberry cooperative has started using recently developed freeze-drying methods for preserving the fruits. In short, in several rural parts of California examples are found which suggest that considerable development springs from industries making use of sophisticated new technologies.

Knowledge-Intensive Employment in Rural California

In assessing the impact of high technology industries on the economic development of rural communities, we may first examine the prevalence of engineers and scientists who are the major professional groups responsible for implementing the technology. Data from the census are available to compare rural areas in California and the nation as a whole for 1960 and 1970, and although they are dated, the numbers do provide evidence that California's rural areas are employing more professionals who are the primary sources of knowledge-intensive technologies. Table 2.2 shows these data. In the rural parts of the state of California 1.8 percent of the employed male workers in 1970 were engineers, while in the nation's rural areas they accounted for only 1.4 percent of the work force. (For comparison, engineers accounted for 4.0 percent of the urban employed in California, significantly greater than the national proportion.) When scientist categories are included with engineers, the totals for rural California are 2.1 percent and the national rural totals are 1.6 percent. (Data not included in the table—available for 1970 only.) These proportions show some increase over the proportions just a decade earlier in 1960. At that time California's engineering workforce included some 1.6 percent in rural areas, while the national proportion was 0.9. While not all these engineers work in manufacturing industries

TABLE 2.2

Percentage of Rural Employment in Engineering Occupations: California and the United States, 1960 and 1970, Males

	1960	1970
California	1.6	1.8
United States, total	0.9	1.4

Source: U.S. Bureau of the Census, Census of Population, Detailed Characteristics, 1960 and 1970.

of high technology, the data suggest that significant technological changes should be on the increase by the time the 1980 census is published.

A more general measure is the proportion of the work force employed in all the professional occupations. These include some of the service occupations to be discussed later, but the general indication is that there is an increasing professionalization in rural California, which is leading the nation in this trend. Between 1950 and 1970 California rural nonfarm employment in professional occupations rose from 8.5 to 13.9 percent while professionals employed in rural farm areas rose from 3.6 to 8.7 percent. Comparable data for the nation were several percentage points lower. (See Table 2.3.) The rate of growth is substantial, especially in the rural farm areas: and if past trends are any indication, professional employment in California's rural nonfarm areas may be near 16 or 17 percent of total employment by 1980, with nearly 10 percent in the farming areas. We shall have more to say about these statistics later. The point not to be missed now is that professionals are the carriers of much of the society's knowledge-intensive technology, and the evidence shows that there are increasing numbers of them in rural California.

TABLE 2.3

Percentage of Employment in Professional Occupations: California and the United States, 1950-70

	Urban	Rural	
		Nonfarm	Farm
1970			
California	17.8	13.9	8.7
United States, total	16.1	11.5	6.9
1960			
California	14.1	11.1	4.9
United States, total	12.4	9.1	3.9
1950			
California	11.9	8.5	3.6
United States, total	10.3	7.8	2.4

Source: U.S. Bureau of the Census, *Census of Population*, Detailed Characteristics, 1950, 1960, and 1970.

Furthermore, as Bendix (1956: 216) points out, one of the unmistakable impacts of increasing industrial growth is the rise in the proportion of employees working in managerial positions. Census data also permit a comparison of the managerial function in rural areas. In 1970 California managerial employment totaled 9.3 percent in rural nonfarm areas, and 5.1 in rural farm locations. This is compared to national figures of 7.8 percent for rural nonfarm and 4.4 for rural farm areas.

Data such as those presented here are only indicators of larger social and economic trends in rural California. In contrast to the post-Sputnik era when there was a shortage of engineers and they desired to live in urban or suburban locations, today there are significant numbers of these well-trained persons who prefer living in rural areas. The rural community is becoming more closely linked with the advances of technology in the society, and employment opportunities are developing significantly for knowledge-intensive occupations in rural areas. Furthermore, for every engineer, scientist, or other professional working in a rural area, there are several other assistants and technicians who assist in the work. Thus, the work force closely associated with the technologies these persons practice is larger in rural areas than the small numbers indicated by table 2.3. Finally, while the difference between rural and urban areas is substantial, it is not as large as might have been expected and is decreasing in size over time.

High Technology Manufacturing and Jobs

The manufacturing industries that use professionals the most are electrical and electronic machines (which include computing and communications equipment), machinery (including office and computing machines), transportation (including aircraft), and instruments. In 1970 each of these industries had about 20 percent professional employment in California and were among the fastest-growing of the state's industries. Recent data on the changes in rural employment within these industries are difficult to obtain. The census does not publish adequate data by state, and alternative sources of data, collected as part of the unemployment insurance system, provide county data only for large SMSAs. Even then the data are not disclosed if there are only a few firms in a category (to protect confidential information).

Nonetheless, there are some data that show manufacturing plays an important part in the overall employment growth in rural California, although the bulk of new jobs are in the service sector. From 1965 to 1976 manufacturing added 26,748 new jobs in rural California, or 11.3 percent of the statewide total of nearly 237,429. Since rural areas in 1976 had about 7.0 percent of the state's total manufacturing employment, this represents a rapid growth in keeping with population increases in rural areas. However, the rural areas included a significant number of jobs in the highest technology sectors. As Table 2.4 shows, 5,000 new high technology manufacturing jobs were located in California's rural areas either in computing machinery, electrical machines and electronics, or instruments. About 19 percent of the new manufacturing jobs in rural areas have come from these industries (with nearly half the growth in urban employment coming from these sources). While these figures have possible inaccuracies, they do suggest that high technology industries are taking a significant place in rural economies.

In sum, the data show that where there are new manufacturing jobs, a significant, though not large, proportion goes toward the sectors of the economy that use the highest levels of technology. The pattern is increasing, and these sectors should show evidence of greater growth in the future. The total numbers are small in the high technology sector—perhaps 8,000 jobs out of a total rural

TABLE 2.4

Wage and Salary Employment in High Technology Industry,
1965 and 1976, Nonmetropolitan Counties

	1965	1976	New Jobs
High Technology Manufacturing	3,523	8,526	5,003
Computing	647	1,387	740
Electrical Machines	2,288	4,173	1,885
Instruments	588	2,966	2,378
Total Manufacturing	81,755	108,503	26,748

Note: Computed by subtracting metropolitan counties from total. Because of missing data, total high technology jobs in nonmetropolitan counties may be slightly lower than shown, but total new jobs may be higher. Missing data are for smallest metropolitan counties, especially in 1965.

Source: California Employment Development Department, *Employment and Payrolls*, 1965 and 1976.

California manufacturing employment of 33,000—yet it does constitute nearly one-quarter and is not the type of economic base that would be expected in rural areas.

Some work in high technology industries occurs in rural areas and is done by professionals who program computers and engage in research in a rural location, connected by phone to their urban offices. There is no estimate of the numbers of persons who work in these types of arrangements, but the examples are well known among industry persons. One reason electronics and other highly specialized industries are able to locate in rural areas is that the size of the industrial unit is relatively small. Unlike the type of plant required to assemble automobiles or airplanes, electronics and similar specialized instrumentation installations are typically small in scale. In part this is because a large number of applications can be made with the basic components. A microprocessor chip may be put to thousands of special uses and, often, separate companies develop the devices that allow such units to be applied to their particular process. Because land is cheaper in rural areas and the quality of life is high, this provides an opportune source of rural economic growth.

Knowledge-Intensive Processes
for Traditional Industry

The application of high technology to industry appears in new processes for traditional industries as well as for new industries. One of the best examples is in food processing. New techniques of processing fruits and vegetables for canning, and the development of processes such as freeze-drying have channeled the industry in a more knowledge-intensive direction. Furthermore, storage techniques for the preservation of fresh fruits, such as apples and pears, have provided longer seasons of availability for consumers.

In the lumber industry the number of materials produced has increased, the use of waste wood for new chip products has been developed, and mills have adopted sophisticated control and pollution abatement technologies. Furthermore, resources that were once wasted in some of the forest areas are being used as the basis for growing industries. For example, hardwood trees have long been considered a problem in the fir forests of northern California. Now, a recent migrant to Mendicino County, with the aid of foresters, is harvesting these trees and hopes to create a new furniture industry. Appealing to the "art" tastes of visiting tourists, these products are responding to new market opportunities in a rural tourist area. Persistent innovative pressures of this sort are common in rural communities in the advanced industrial society and offer recent migrants a new resource for economic development.

The traditional fishing industry has been able to take advantage of modern communications and radar devices to increase safety and to locate fish. This has opened up opportunities for expansion of radio repair facilities in rural areas and has helped to further increase the skills of this industry. Furthermore, persons working in high technology facilities provide a resource for further innovation. For example, one rural radio repairman, tired of fixing automatic pilot devices on the fishing boats, invented a transistorized device to do a better, more efficient job. He produced the product, employing local off-season farm workers who learned soldering techniques in Mexico to construct it. In many such small ways industry in rural areas is advancing through the use of more knowledge-intensive technologies and expertise.

Another industry finding a popular place in rural areas is specialty printing. Publishing houses for a variety of publications are locating in small communities in California. For the most part they publish materials for the specialty "art" interests and for the state's counterculture and diverse alternative groups (Bradshaw and Blakely, 1979). The small California presses are attracting a significant amount of national attention, printing everything from "do-it-yourself divorce" to fine hand-printed art and literature books

Finally, examples of changing energy-related technology promise to bring significant changes to rural areas. As the technology for new alternative energy sources such as biomass and solar are developed, the impact on rural areas will be dramatic. Already, experiments are being conducted on the use of manure and other farm wastes for the production of methane, and windmills and other wind-power devices are being proposed for placement in farming areas. A recent study suggested that by the year 2025 nearly all of California's energy could be produced by renewable resources, including solar, biomass, and other new energy technologies (Lawrence Berkeley Laboratory, 1978). However, the production of these energy resources will have severe consequences for land use, according to the study, because considerable land used for light agriculture will have to be converted to growing energy-producing crops. A secondary consequence of the change will be that some forms of energy will be relatively cheap in rural areas and will be an enticement for industry to locate near them. Chief among the concepts leading to this development will be cogeneration and the siting of plants near each other so that the waste heat from one process will be usable for another.

The social climate is good for the development of many of these new energy resources in California. The population has a consciousness about the need to find alternatives and the technology is available to implement new technologies (Lawrence Berkeley Laboratory, 1978: Chapter IV). Experiments have taken place near several university campuses in rural California, including a particularly well-known project in Davis, with the construction of all-solar homes. Firms in other small communities are constructing solar panels and insulation materials. Farmers are examining the use of hydroponics and other techniques in solar heated greenhouses. In sum, new energy-related developments will have a great impact on rural industry by bringing changing technology to rural life (Schwartz, 1977).

Conclusion

High technology industry and the use of new knowledge-intensive processes in traditional industries pose new problems and new opportunities for rural areas. On the one hand, local surveys in several California counties have shown that residents want new industrial development. In Plumas County, 80 percent of the respondents to a survey thought that some industrial growth was necessary for their county, while 73 percent favored small businesses over large. The emphasis was on encouraging new business and industry, instead of emphasizing either traditional timber-related industries or recreation (Davis, 1978). A similar survey in Siskiyou County had nearly identical results (Black, 1977). In both cases the respondents expressed the opinion that industrial growth was needed but that it should not lead to harmful effects for the county and its access to public facilities or natural resources. Response to a survey in Yuba City specifically favored particular kinds of knowledge-intensive industry and agricultural processing and urged an integrated planning effort to make sure that unwanted growth did not occur (Blakely, Schutz, and Zone, 1978).

The change in industry from resource-based to an increasingly knowledge-based technology means that there is a shift from physical to human resources in the essential ingredients that make an area attractive to industry. The community development task in the advanced industrial society is not one of concentrating primarily on the physical resources that a community can offer for industry to exploit, but to develop more human resources that can be applied to the emerging technologies.

ADVANCED INDUSTRIAL AGRICULTURE

The agricultural sector of the rural advanced industrial society has been more strongly affected by the impact of scientific knowledge-intensive technology than virtually any other. During the last century agriculture has been in the process of industrializing, moving from hand labor to the use of machinery powered by inanimate sources. This has resulted in rapid increases in productivity per farm worker leading to a decline in rural farm populations, and has been coupled with improvement in seed, irrigation, and chemicals to result in great increases in productivity per acre farmed. Our interest in agriculture is not in the long-run improvement in efficiency but in the technological innovations that link sophisticated scientific innovations in biology and chemicals with machinery and with new forms of social organization. The result may be called advanced industrial agriculture, and its impact on rural communities is as significant as other technological changes.

The implementation of technology is not an inevitable and uniform process of innovation and change. This is clearly seen in the development of farm technology in rural advanced instrumentalization. Technology itself involves three components, according to LaPorte (1974: 14). First, technology is the device used to do something—machines or mathematical procedures, for example; second, technology is constituted of the knowledge behind those devices: the theories and experiences about how and why they work as they should; and third, technology is constituted of social organization—the firms and professions necessary to implement the use of the devices. The technology of a factory or a farm machine requires a particular social organization of workers to make it effective. In farming, consequently, technological changes have had organizational impacts considerably greater than the simple displacement of labor that is so well known. Furthermore, because of increased organization interrelation in advanced industrialism, the technology is not developed and implemented simply. Its very creation is dependent on social conditions at a particular time.

Agriculture and Technology in California

California is the nation's most productive farm state with nearly $7.4 billion total sales in 1974 according to the Census of Agriculture (U.S. Bureau of the Census, 1974: 2). This position has come about through a combination of favorable soils, weather, and technology which has permitted the state to produce large proportions of the nation's supply of specialty crops (vegetables, fruits, nuts, and other nonstaples) as well as basic grains and animal products. The application of advanced scientific processes to the development of an integrated agricultural production has taken place in many product areas, such as the development of technology for the tomato picking machine and the harvest of lettuce.

Research and development activities in farm machinery have long been of major importance to the growth of agriculture in California. As early as 1880,

Bean suggests, one of the most significant aspects of wheat growing in the great Central Valley of California lay in its contributions to the development of agricultural machinery (1968: 272). Not only were new plows invented, that greatly simplified and speeded the cultivation of large fields by using multiple plowshares riding on wheels and pulled by teams of mules, but machines were developed that in one operation pulverized the soil and planted the seed, spreading earth over it. Later, in the Central Valley, use was made of the largest steam-powered "combined harvesters" in the world; tractors were first used there. Much of this development was aided by the research and development activities at the state land grant university which, in its early years, got most of its support from actively helping the farm community (Stadtman, 1970). Furthermore, the agricultural extension activities were strongly financed by state and federal money and to a greater extent than anywhere else in the nation.

Research in wine-making is an example of the application of scientific technology to the integrated agricultural process. For years, the Napa and Sonoma counties of California have been known for their naturally good wine-making conditions. Since the 1940s, however, the university has combined efforts with growers to develop scientific processes that have taken wine production from a specialty, best described as an "art," and made large portions of it into a science with careful chemical testing and processing at every stage to produce reliable (if not outstanding) wines. The grapes are cultivated in the fields with precise measurements of the chemical nutrients and water needed, and are harvested when their sugar content is exactly right. They are fermented with scientific precision and aged with the guide of chemical evaluation. The result of the greater understanding of the wine-making process has permitted grapes to be grown in rather ordinary soils and hot climates (for example, Central Valley areas including Fresno County) and made into good table wines. The process developed in California is being exported to Europe and other places where uneven quality is a major problem.

Technological Innovation in Agriculture

The technology involved in perfecting the tomato-picking machine for "canning" tomatoes is another example of the integration of a diverse set of research efforts to produce a major agricultural breakthrough. The tomato harvester required not only mechanical innovations but the breeding of a tomato variety that could stand up to the demands of the machine. As Rasmussen states (quoted in Schmitz and Seckler, 1970: 569-70):

> The invention of the mechanical tomato harvester contrasted decidedly with the development of the cotton picker. The tomato harvester resulted from a "system approach." A team made up of an engineering group and a horticultural group, with advice and assistance from agronomists and irrigation specialists, developed suitable

plants and an efficient harvester at the same time. The necessary changes in planting, cultivation, and irrigating were developed concurrently.

Despite the success of this example of mechanization, it was hardly the deliberate, long-planned effort suggested by the end-result. Early progress toward development of the machine came from the efforts of a single university researcher, often seen as a maverick, who worked on a machine thought ridiculous (Friedland and Barton, 1975: 22). Later, support from other researchers helped develop both the fruit and the machine so that by the time the government decided to end the Bracero program, which had brought considerable migrant labor into the fields from Mexico, the application of the machine could proceed. In 1963 only 66 machines existed, and together they harvested 1 percent of the tomato crop. By 1966 the number of machines reached 736 and harvested 66 percent. Two years later nearly 1500 machines were harvesting virtually the entire crop (23).

Social conditions strongly affect the rate and timing of implementation of a technological innovation. Friedland has made this most clear in his study of the development of a lettuce-picking machine. Such a machine, using gamma rays or X-rays to determine if the lettuce head is ready for picking, is a complicated project still awaiting completion. In contrast to the notion that agricultural technology comes unendingly from the research labs, Friedland has shown that its development and implementation are closely related to the uncertainties of labor. The introduction of a new machine is itself an uncertain process. At least in the early stages it is costly. The machines do not work as they are supposed to, and improvements come quickly, putting the early adopters at a disadvantage. In contrast, stable labor patterns provide continuity and, if all farms use the same labor, do not significantly affect one's profit margin. On the other hand, as labor becomes unsettled, as with the end of the Bracero program and the initiation of unionization, the costs of a machine become more justified. This was shown by Friedland to be the case with the development of the lettuce packing machine, the development of which proceeded rapidly during periods of labor uncertainty but slowed during labor peace. Today, little implementation is expected because the recently unionized workers have become stable and their own efficiencies have increased. As Friedland points out, the development of the technology has another social aspect: control over the work force. As uncertainty increases, the prospect of mechanization is used as a threat to the workers (1978: 8):

> All growers look with greater interest to technological development whenever the labor factor obtrudes or threatens to become uncontrollable, that is, the quest for certainty remains a major contributor to technological development in agriculture with labor continuing to be the prime pressure point.

The farmers themselves often experiment with different agronomical techniques including dates of planting, seed depth, irrigation, and the like. But, as Just, Schmitz, and Zilberman (1978) have shown, the farmer is limited by cost and skills to a relatively small number of issues. The second source of innovation is the seed companies, fertilizer and pesticide manufacturers, and other businesses that can make a profit from their innovations. Still, private firms are unwilling to engage in projects like integrated pest management, and responsibility must necessarily fall on the university or other public organizations. In California, marketing boards also do research that is related to the productivity of farmers growing a particular crop (Just, Schmitz, and Zilberman, 1978: 134-5). Sometimes, as in the case of the tomato-picking machine, several of these sources join in the development of a new technology.

The Social Organization of Technological Innovation

The increasing importance of large machinery and the shift from labor intensive to capital intensive farm organization have led to the growth of larger and larger farms and their organization as corporations. Often the owners of the land are stockholders whose purpose is to share in lucrative tax write-offs and loopholes available to farming interests. In most cases the main owners are not located on the farm, but in Los Angeles, San Francisco, or New York. The corporations themselves are often involved in a number of other businesses, and these, increasingly, include the processing of food after it is grown. In short, there is considerable evidence that agriculture in the advanced industrial society is being integrated out of the fabric of local community life into a network of large corporate agribusiness organizations. As a result, decisions making huge differences in the lives of community residents are made on Wall Street, not locally.

Agribusiness is the subject of a great deal of debate we will not enter into here. What is important, however, is the impact of agribusiness on the use of technology. These large corporations are able to gain quick access to the technologies of modern agriculture and, especially, to the capital resources needed to purchase them. Often these farms have highly trained specialists for managing small aspects of the overall operation, and they make efficient use of consultants. For example, it costs nearly the same to have a pest-control consultant examine a large plot as to examine a small one in a rural community. The large farm also may take advantage of volume purchases of supplies such as chemicals, pipes, and seed. Finally, plant varieties maximize the advantage of agribusiness because the varieties most available are bred for the machine-harvested and bulk markets the corporation has access to (Small Farm Viability Project, 1978).

The impact of the tomato-picking machine on the development of agribusiness has been closely monitored. One of the most important consequences of the machine's introduction has been to concentrate production among fewer growers. In 1962 there were approximately 4000 tomato growers; by 1973 that number had dropped to 597. At the same time production increased from 3 million to 4 million tons (Friedland and Barton, 1975: 54). This change came about partly through some consolidation of farm units and concomitantly, by a shift of farming location from San Joaquin County, with its many small and medium-size farms, to Fresno County where large acreage could be turned to tomato farming (59–61).

The impact of the tomato-picking machine on agricultural production and labor has been profound. In the late 1960s the harvester reduced costs by $5.41 to $7.47 per ton (Schmitz and Seckler, 1970: 571) and displaced roughly 91 man-hours per acre harvested. Based on cost estimates the machine has returned an estimated 1,000 percent of the development costs, and the farmers and consumers have shared this benefit. But, as Martin and Hall point out, "the current agricultural mechanization debate centers on the extent of public and private responsibility for farm workers displaced by labor-saving agricultural innovations" (1978: 208). Schmitz and Seckler argue that the savings, or some of them, should go to compensate farm workers unable to find other employment. Friedland argues that the developers of machinery through university-supported research should have to prepare social-impact statements to anticipate the effects on humans. These impacts of technological development thus lead to increased efforts to define responsibility for agricultural innovation.

Farm Worker Skills and New Technology

One of the consequences of increasing technological development on farms is the need for more sophisticated worker skills. Farmers complain about the treatment their machinery received from poorly trained workers, and sometimes the management problems become severe. Much of agricultural mechanization has helped to simplify farm tasks so that poorly trained workers cannot ruin anything. But more and more, farmers are discovering that fewer highly skilled workers bring great efficiencies. Efforts have begun to develop this more highly skilled work force.

Recently, Mamer (1977) has suggested that there are indications larger growers see the importance of developing a more stable work force through the development of more highly skilled, year-round workers. California's total farm employment has dropped significantly since 1950; however, in the last 10 years there has been little further change in the number of hired farm workers. More recently, changes in unemployment insurance coverage have provided farm workers with the benefits other workers have long received. Before this, farm employers were not much concerned with the persons who might work in their fields. Workers had few particular skills and worked for any employer who needed help. Now, under unemployment insurance, Mamer and Fuller report that both parties have a greater interest in staying with a stable labor force: "The employer will want to minimize his tax burden; the worker will want to maximize his unemployment insurance eligibility" (1978: 25). Unionization and other regulatory orders have the same effect of encouraging the employer to work with fewer seasonal employees and more full-time, year-round employees.

In the face of these changes new social technologies are being developed to facilitate the increasing demands for a more rational social organization of farm work. This process aims to develop workers who have greater abilities, can use machinery more skillfully, and can take less supervision, just as the factory rationalized industrial production by organizing the workers socially. Although evidence is still sparse, where it is available it appears that significant labor- and cost-savings are to be had from these social technologies applied along with the mechanical ones in California agriculture.

Mamer (1977) reports that the training of orange and lemon pickers in Southern California resulted in vastly improved wages and working conditions for the workers and improved productivity for the growers. Recruiting and selecting the more proficient workers and employing them for longer periods yielded a higher output with fewer employees on the payroll. As Mamer and Fuller (1978) point out, many similar changing labor conditions were created by new patterns in the social organization of work, not by new machines.

Community developers working with the Rural Economic Institute and the University of California have created a "job ladder" (Baker, 1976) in valley farm work. Researchers coded all farming tasks in a section of Fresno County and, based on these tasks, specified a set of skills arranged in ladder-like steps of increasing difficulty. Workers could then qualify for a job on the basis of their achieved skills, and they could be trained to upgrade these skills in an orderly fashion. Similarly, employers could have a better idea of the skills a particular worker has. This process then leads to more effective training programs and to more efficient use of the labor in the field. The result has been more full-time employment and higher productivity. In turn communities are strengthened by these developments.

Technological Impacts on the Farm Community

Technological change, including the creation of large agribusinesses, has not been accepted happily by many California farming communities. One of the paradoxes of advanced industrial use of technology is that the widespread knowledge base in the society knows that any new technology is not unqualifiedly good, and that alternatives for every technology exist. The debate over technology increases in the advanced industrial society because more informed critics are better able to communicate their own conflicting points of view. Thus, there is no surprise that rural areas have been subjected to debate over alternatives to agribusiness. Following the notions of Schumacher (1973) many of these critics call for a more responsible agriculture based less on chemicals and machinery and more on procedures favorable to the interests of the farm workers.

Stemming from this debate, community developers and other rural development specialists within Cooperative Extension, the State Department of Food and Agriculture, and the Employment Development Department are interested in revitalizing the small farm. Consequently a study has recently been done to take an objective look at the viability of the small farm in California. It was discovered that the major advantage of large farm over small was that the large has greater access to capital, technology, and especially markets. With large integrated purchasing and distribution systems in the state, large producers decrease the uncertainty of the marketing system and get better prices. Small farmers are frequently unable to sell at all and, if they do, they frequently must take a lower price. The general assumption is that larger units achieve greater economies of scale, and that the 1000-or-more acre farm is most efficient for most crops. However, these studies are based on hypothetical farms and imply no labor from the individual farmer. Furthermore, there is a great difference between farms which are optimal and those which are profitable. The Small Farm Viability Project (1978: 46) discovered that "in Imperial County all farms of all sizes were found to be 'profitable' in the sense that income was sufficient to cover costs." The study went on to show that:

> . . . the degree of advantage conferred by large size, even if farms were to behave efficiently, is very small. For example, in Yolo County the advantage of a 600 acre farm in comparison with a 250 acre farm is about 15 percent lower costs, while the advantage of a 2000 acre farm in comparison with a 250 acre farm is about 18 percent lower costs. Given the substantial variation in the performance of farms from such factors as access to transportation and water, soil quality, management, differences in technological costs of these magnitudes . . . may be easily offset.

The debate about the size of the farm and its consequences is closely rooted in a study done by William Goldschmidt (1946) of two agricultural towns in the San Joaquin Valley, Arvin and Dinuba. The two towns were similar except that the first was surrounded by large corporate farms and the second primarily by small family farms. The findings of that study were that corporate farming produced a community structure that was less rich and beneficial to residents—in the community with small farms there were more schools, more local businesses, more cultural activities, and, in general, more social and organizational opportunities and participation. In addition, there was more local wealth. Recently, the comparisons done by Goldschmidt have been replicated by the Small Farm Viability Project (1978) which found that the structure of the communities has changed little in the intervening 30 years and the advantages of the small farming community persist.

As a result of the small farm project the state of California is devoting resources to both the small farms in the state and the surrounding communities as well. The role of the community developer in this effort has been to identify the social impacts of technology and to help the community adjust to (or resist) the changes brought about by the introduction of new technologies. The community developer does this through the coordination of resources from the various institutions that can help local communities. For example, the state is providing loans and credit guarantees up to 95 percent to build small local business enterprises. At the same time, other community development specialists are involved in making and facilitating recommendations related to the local governmental structure and the provision of human services.

While no one of these activities is particularly novel, collectively they represent a new role for the adaptation of social organization to the introduction of sophisticated technologies. Significant community activity is aimed at helping those individuals who have lost jobs or have been exposed to adverse health effects, but the involvement of the community and the state government in the activity represents an important increase in the level of social responsibility for these changes.

THE SERVICE SECTOR AND
RURAL ECONOMIC GROWTH

A second major characteristic of changing economies in the advanced industrial society is the growth of the service sector. As Victor Fuchs (1968: 1) points out, the United States has become a "service economy" where the evidence of service growth is readily available:

> The *increase* in employment in the field of education between 1950 and 1960 was greater than the total number employed in the steel, copper, and aluminum industries in either year. The *increase* in employment in the field of health between 1950 and 1960 was greater than the total number employed in automobile manufacturing in either year. The *increase* in employment in financial firms between 1950 and 1960 was greater than total employment in mining in 1960 (emphasis in original).

Virtually all the net increase in employment in the nation during the last decades has come from growth in the service sector; modest increases in manufacturing and construction have largely been offset by declines in agriculture. The trends of the nation have been seen earlier and more dramatically in California and, as we shall show, have extended to rural parts of the state as well.

The expanding service sector means that persons are employed in jobs where the main orientation is service such as the distribution of goods produced elsewhere; the provision of banking and insurance where money rather than goods are processed; the repair of broken machinery; the entertainment of people during leisure; the assistance of people through professions in health, legal, educational, welfare, and religious service; and the governance of cities, counties, states, and the nation. In addition, services are provided in the form of communications, utilities, and transportation, including trucking and the railroads. It is characteristic of all these industries that their product is not goods such as food, clothing, houses, automobiles, and the like; their product is labor itself.

With its dominantly agricultural base, rural society has not been considered to have much of a service base in its economy, and rural developers have paid little attention to the service component of economic development. This comes in part from the neglect of the service sector by economics in general and from theories of development that argue for the establishment of more traditional industries in poor countries and rural areas first before service industries can grow.

The lack of attention to service functions by economics has changed somewhat with recent studies of the economy by Fuchs and others. Musser and White, in an important article on the character of economic development in rural areas, suggest that much potential for reducing the economic strains of rural areas lies in the promotion of service industries. However, as they point out, "Overcoming the rural disadvantage in service employment presents a serious conceptual problem. Unlike the output of manufacturing, services are largely not exported to other areas. The lag of rural service behind urban employment service therefore results from lower consumption of services by rural residents" (1977: 12). However, with new rural affluence, especially in advanced industrial rural regions, common urban and suburban services such as fast food outlets and communications are finding expanding rural markets. In many parts of the country, tourism and other services for urban residents are also providing a new opportunity for rural service sector growth. Increasing numbers of retired persons in numerous rural communities are also creating the conditions for the growth of many services. Finally, government is channeling many new resources into rural areas and is increasing its own employment levels.

In this section we review data on the growth of service sector employment in rural California and, subsequently, consider the impact of tourism on rural areas and the challenges that service sector growth raises for economic development strategies.

Service Sector Employment

In the United States employment increased 17 million between 1947 and 1967, and virtually all the new workers were in service industries (Fuchs, 1968). Today, over 70 percent of employed Californians are in service industries. Although Daniel Bell (1973) makes much of the fact that the United States is the world's first country to have more than 50 percent service employment, it is notable that California passed this mark shortly after 1920 (LaPorte and Bradshaw, 1977). Data suggest that this process has progressed outside metropolitan areas as much as it has within. For example, Haren (1974: 8) presents data on 1960 national nonmetropolitan employment that show slightly over half of rural employment was in service-performing industries, and during the following decade nonmetropolitan wage and salary service employment increased by an average of 4 percent per year with total nonmetro employment increasing only 1.5, due to a large decline in farm employment. This was the most rapid increase of all broad sectors of the economy in nonmetropolitan areas although somewhat behind the rate of increase in service employment in metro areas (4.7 percent). In spite of this statistical evidence on the importance of services, Haren and others examining nonmetropolitan labor markets (for example, Marshall, 1974) emphasize the importance of manufacturing over service sector employment.

In rural California the process of increasing service sector employment is even more pronounced. Table 2.5 shows the change in employment in the various broad employment sectors in California's rural areas. During the period from 1965 to 1976 total service employment increased from 57.7 percent to 68.0 with the largest growth in trade, personal and professional services, and govern-

TABLE 2.5

Changing Employment in Rural California, 1965–76
(not including self-employed nonagriculture)

	1965	1972	1976	New Jobs 1965–76
Agriculture	128,230	117,010	116,430	(−11,800)
Mining	3,163	2,836	3,348	185
Construction	30,962	28,373	30,910	(−52)
Manufacturing	81,755	96,707	108,503	26,748
Services, total	333,281	446,159	550,415	217,134
(Percent)	(57.7%)	(64.6%)	(68.0%)	(93.5%)
Transportation and utilities	26,762	31,115	36,953	10,191
Trade	106,167	137,350	169,800	63,633
Finance, insurance, real estate	16,990	20,332	25,414	8,424
Service (personal and professional)	50,962	83,462	110,448	59,486
Government	132,400	173,900	207,800	75,400
Total	577,391	691,085	809,606	232,215

Note: Data computed for nonmetropolitan counties in 1965; government data computed by subtracting Standard Metropolitan Statistical Areas from total.

Sources: California Employment Development Department, *Employment and Payrolls*, 1965, 1972, and 1976; California Employment Development Department, *Report 881-x*; and *California Statistical Abstract*, 1970: Table C-8 and C-9, and 1977: Table C-6 and Table C-9.

ment. Presently, these figures for rural service employment are only about five percentage points below the proportion of service employment in the state's urban areas.*

Data in Table 2.5 also show that for the same period (1965-1976) non-service employment grew very little while 93.5 percent of the net new jobs occurred in the service sector. Gains in rural manufacturing were nearly offset by losses in agriculture. Total employment in California's agriculture declined about 11,800 workers but has been relatively stable since 1972, and sharp drops are considered unlikely in the future. Mining declined by a small number of workers in 1972, mostly through the depletion of oil fields, but higher oil prices have stimulated more employment. Construction declined from its 1965 high because of fewer dam and highway projects, but is again increasing its employment share in rural California with the rapid growth of California's rural population and the consequent residential and commercial construction. These data show that the bulk of the economic growth in rural California is coming from the service sector, not from the industries traditionally counted on for rural economic development.

An example of how the services are filling the employment needs of rural areas is provided by the following excerpts from a labor market report on Humboldt County where the new Redwood National Park has eliminated a significant proportion of timber planned for harvest.

> Over the year, the total number of wage and salary workers in Humboldt County declined by 175. Leading the decline, manufacturing payrolls contracted by 450. The catalyst for this decrease was a reduction in the amount of harvestable timber in the county, which caused a drop in the number of workers needed in the lumber and wood products industry. . . .
>
> On a more positive side, healthy employment gains were recorded in the remaining industry groups. Payrolls in the retail trade division advanced by 200, with new and expanding eating and drinking places, drug stores, and general merchandise and apparel stores responsible for over 75 percent of this growth. Services employment rose by 100 as new jobs opened in nonprofit organizations and personal, business, amusement and recreation services.
>
> The next major source of new jobs was government. Within this division, the opening of a California Conservation Corps camp and the expansion of federal job rolls accounted largely for the payroll increase of 75 (Humboldt County Labor Market Bulletin, 1978).

---

*Data computed from same sources as Table 2.6.

These experiences of rural counties have been typical throughout California. Although service sector growth is not always this dramatic, it has generally contributed to employment stability.

Rural service growth in the transportation sector is aided by the completion of the interstate highway system and, in California, by the establishment of distribution points for trucking outside central city areas. Some growth has also come through rural airports for small planes and the provision of flying lessons and other air transport facilities for the increasing numbers of private aircraft in California. The state has over 100,000 private airplanes, one-sixth of all in the nation. These airport facilities are an important resource for businessmen in high technology industries who need rapid transportation for their products as well as for themselves if they are to locate in rural areas. The airport may well become an increasingly important asset in the economic development of many small California communities.

Communications also provide new opportunities for rural economic development. In Ukiah an anesthesiologist has a toll-free telephone number from which he provides information services to his widespread clientele. With such a telephone system it makes virtually no difference where persons locate, and increasingly persons and businesses are choosing rural locations. For example, the National Communications Center chose to locate in the small Sierra town of Shingle Springs (population, 1,000) to provide courteous, reliable message-taking for urban clients who offer free 800-prefix call-in lines. They now boast a $4 million telephone business which is expected to double in a year (Pennington, 1978: 85). Better communications in all forms promise to facilitate further the development of rural regions of the advanced industrial society. For example, conference centers no longer have to be in cities because a rural location provides a welcome change of pace for business executives and at the same time lets them be in close contact with computers and staff if needed.

Finance, insurance, and real estate are also providing some employment growth in rural areas. As migration increases the number of real estate sales persons rises. (Many rural residents in growing areas complain about the newcomers who come, buy property, and then open real estate offices. Growing employment in rural banks and insurance offices is closely associated with the growth of rural areas, but it is also part of the larger shift in the advanced industrial society to increased emphasis on this type of service.

Prior to the advanced industrial society cities were main centers of commerce and trade. While this is still true to some extent, the rural areas are becoming increasingly self-sufficient in trade, facilitated by the growth of more regional shopping centers and better transportation networks. Over 60,000 new jobs were added in retail and wholesale trade in California's rural areas from 1965 to 1976. Based on total California employment, trade is only eight percent less in rural areas than in metropolitan—21 percent vs. 9. This suggests that there is a considerable improvement in nonmetropolitan counties in providing essential consumer services for their residents. Furthermore, many sales services are increasingly sophisticated and draw regional clientele for farming, recreational, and other items. In fact, the *Whole Earth Catalogue* and similar publications among the diverse alternative culture groups in the advanced industrial society have provided a significant trade resource for Mendocino County and similar places where rural living and the types of goods traditionally associated with it are increasingly attractive to urban shoppers (Bradshaw and Blakely, 1979).

Table 2.5 shows that California's rural areas have experienced significant growth in personal and professional services, and government. In each of these components of the service sector there has been a general increase in the skill levels needed for employment. Professionals and semiprofessionals also constitute a greater proportion of the overall personal service group of industries, with fewer persons working in barber shops and more in law and medicine. New paraprofessional occupations in health and law are also being developed. In government, along with the large number of job trainees, an increasing number of workers are technically sophisticated planners, regulators, and the like. The growth of professional and public services in rural California will be discussed in greater detail in subsequent chapters in terms of their role in education, government, welfare, and community development.

The discovery of the rural environment by the service sector is an example of the larger change in location of businesses of all sorts in the nation. In a study of large business headquarters leaving New York City Wolfgang Quante (1976) found that the corporations valued the improved life styles for employees afforded by the move from the city. While the corporations did not choose rural locations for the most part, Blakely (1978: 107) draws from the study a general lesson applicable to the rise of business in rural areas:

> In essence, the exodus in New York is the harbinger of a major socio-economic change. This change is in the direction of human resources rather than physical or communications networks forming the focus of commerce. The basic idea here is that people and in particular their life style choices are bringing about a profound movement away from the city toward a less compact environment. This is all made possible by the fantastic recent advances in communications and related technologies.

Two further issues about the expanding service sector in California concern us here. First, the creation of tourism opportunities presents an example of the way communities can be involved with the emerging life styles of modern affluent residents to create valued recreational touristic experiences. Second, the growth of the service sector presents new challenges for the rural economic development planner.

Tourism and Community Development

Nonmetropolitan communities in regions with attractive physical and geographical features have increasing opportunities to develop resources for tourism. Considerable possibilities for some communities to make economic progress with touristic attractions, although economic change based on developing tourism is beset with problems such as highly seasonal employment, inadequate distribution of community amenities to residents as well as tourists, and uncontrolled growth coupled with a large absentee property ownership. Hansen (1973: 161) notes the limitations of too much emphasis on tourism for economic development.

> There are indications that while tourism and related activities bring undoubted satisfactions to metropolitan populations and profit to many metropolitan-based developers, their positive impact on the local nonmetropolitan labor force is less certain. The tourist industry does not have strong linkages to other industries and usually does not lead to the growth of complementary activities. Moreover, the kinds of skill required by the tourist industry are not those that would be likely to lay the bases for new industry; rather, what is usually needed are low-level skills utilized in retail trade.

Although California and other advanced industrial societies will undoubtedly face many of the problems of a large tourist industry in rural areas, it remains fairly certain that demand for tourist-service amenities will continue, and these new tourist-related services will provide the basis for some continuing economic growth.

Perhaps the most remarkable aspect of the growth of tourism in the advanced industrial society is that it is part of the mass marketing of recreational and entertainment opportunities to an increasingly affluent population. As MacCannell and Meyers (1976) point out, the tourist attraction is not simply a natural occurrence but must be first *"marked off"* from similar objects or spots of worth. Sometimes this is done by governmental bodies, as in the case of national parks or historic landmarks. Sometimes it is done by a businessman recreating an "authentic '49er" lodging and inn. Other times it is a combination of both. Once marked, it is then "elevated and enshrined" by reports in the press and national media. Tourists, after visiting an attraction, bring back souvenirs which attract others as well. In short, this process is becoming well understood and elaborated so that many rural areas are turned into fantasy lands where the mass society can fulfill its dreams.

The use of fantasy fulfillment for touristic attractions is nothing new. As is well known, William Randolph Hearst imported a castle and all its furnishings for himself and friends. The rich often toured other parts of the country and stories of John Muir in California's Sierra mountains attest to the place of tourism, even in the early days of the statehood. What has changed is that the development of the touristic attractions has expanded beyond John Muir showing Theodore Roosevelt Yosemite and urging creation of a national park. Now millions of working and middle-class persons go with their campers and tents to visit the same spot and imagine themselves lucky explorers.

Rurality is now fantasy. Small towns are preserved because they are different and marked as noteworthy. There is a craving for this type of authentic rurality. For example, the small Sacramento River delta town of Locke was recently described in *The New Yorker* magazine as the "last authentic rural Chinatown in California." The real problem for Locke, however, is to preserve its authenticity from those tourist interests that want to make it into a booming attraction with Holiday Inns and souvenir stands. The local Chinese are mostly old and can no longer keep pace with the growing affluence of the Sacramento region, and thus they may die out or be forced out (Trillin, 1978). However, the story of Locke is just one example of the virtually insatiable thirst of modern Americans for authentic rural village experiences. If towns such as Locke did not exist, they would be created, as they have in fact been. Outside of Stockton there is a "Frontier Town" with an artificial stockade where children ride a small train and people walk through small shops selling candy and trinkets. Every half hour some actors "hold up" the train and have an all-out gun battle with other actors falling off balconies as they are shot. As MacCannell (1976: 8) points out, these attempts to authenticate the past and make it available to the mass public are indicative, not of the persistence of traditional culture, but of the successful development of the new:

> Interestingly, the best indication of the final victory of modernity over other sociocultural arrangements is not the disappearance of the nonmodern world, but its artificial preservation and reconstruction in modern society. The separation of nonmodern culture traits from their original contexts and their distribution as modern playthings are evident in the various social movements toward naturalism, so much a feature of modern societies: cults of folk music and medicine, adornment and behavior, peasant dress, early American decor, efforts in short to museumize the premodern (8).

The rural past is thus at the cutting edge of the interests of a modern advanced industrial society that needs to recreate its past in order to assure its future.

Tourism builds on both public and private facilities. Public facilities in California are being used in increasing numbers. For example, during the period from 1945 to 1973 California's population doubled, but the use of the state park system increased 11 times. Although California is an urban state, most outdoor recreation is in rural areas. This requires considerable investment by the public in facilities and amenities in order to make available the outdoor resources for an increasing variety of sport, recreational, and educational interests. In fact, we have argued elsewhere that a significant feature of the advanced industrial society is the increasing importance of "public" facilities for modern life styles. These public facilities, frequently located in rural areas, serve three types of public need. First, expanded resources are needed for traditional activities such as parks, boating access, rural airstrips, and even adult education. Second, the vast number of new activities and interests of the modern affluent society create a need for new types of facilities. For example, hang-gliding, cross-country skiing, mountain climbing, off-road vehicles such as dune buggies, train bikes, and jeeps, are acquiring increasing numbers of interested participants who require public facilities, training, regulation, and coordination. As these types of activity frequently take place in rural areas, the impact is especially great there. Finally, a number of activities that were once mainly private are being subsidized by the public. For example, theater is gaining large amounts of state and federal money— this includes many rural theater companies. These changes in life styles have implications for the growing importance of tourism in rural areas of the advanced industrial society. The state spends considerable money on these activities, providing a logical impetus for rural economic growth (Bradshaw and Blakely, 1979).

At the same time as expansion of public facilities for tourism is affecting rural areas, private investment and construction is speeding. Private commercial recreational facilities were visited over 30 million times in California in 1974 (Security Pacific Bank, 1975: 12-14). In recent decades, *large* vacation resorts, with ski lifts and summer trails and golf facilities, are gaining interest. These projects are only a small part of the total rural touristic development in California, but they are particularly instructive as to the problems that may be encountered. An example is the Disney Corporation's attempts to build two large Sierra resorts. The first, at Mineral King in the area west of Fresno ran into opposition from environmental interests. Mineral King, a high elevation valley surrounded by picturesque peaks of Sequoia National Park, was an early mining area and was excluded from the creation of the Sequoia and Kings Canyon National Parks. There is no mining there now, and environmentalists urged the inclusion of the area into the adjacent national parks. Congress had agreed and Disney's proposed resort was halted. Another proposed Disney project in Northern California is running into a different type of opposition. The impressive size of the project at Independence Lake was startling. The corporation planned to spend $80 million to bring 12,500 skiers daily during the winter and 8,000 swimmers during the summer. Sierra County, in which the project is located, stood to gain some $1.5 million in tax revenue each year; but most of the problems, such as housing for employees would be borne by Nevada County and its growing town of Truckee only 17 miles away; however, Nevada County would gain few tax benefits (Stanley, 1978). The opposition of local residents and others to a development of this scale, along with claims of delays in the permit process, led the company to withdraw their plans for this development as well.

As the Disney projects show, rural economic development for tourism, as for other types of economic change, is increasingly complicated and difficult.

The economy of a region, and the values and aspirations of residents for the quality of life they want in that area, now compete with economic expansion. The touristic development of an area thus calls for the acquisition of new skills for managing these difficulties.

Economic Development in the Service Society

The challenge for economic development in the service society is to apply principles that are not very well understood to an environment which is continuously changing in new and unexpected ways. This is further complicated by the fact that many of the agencies responsible for economic development are federal and state agencies that attempt to implement policy set for urban areas. When there is a specific rural policy, it usually does not take into account the particular needs of regions such as those in California and other advanced industrial societies. The range of economic development efforts that have been generated from conditions such as these stretch from traditional programs to attract industry from the central city to innovative efforts for developing the service sector. The methods vary from the creation of industrial parks with special tax incentives to the promotion of regional integrated planning. In this section we can only suggest that there is a huge variation in these programs and that the needs of the advanced industrial society frequently call for new economic development structures.

In order to learn about the economic development of rural California we conducted an informal study of the development efforts in 41 rural counties in the state. Data were collected from 61 different agencies, commissions, or organizations working on some aspect of economic development. The goal of the inquiries was to ascertain the type of economic development that was being undertaken and how the organization perceived its role in such an effort. Since no list exists of all development programs in the state, we have no assurance that all were covered; nonresponse to about a quarter of our inquiries further limits the overall coverage of the study. Nonetheless, we think that it is roughly representative of the range of economic development efforts in the state and is satisfactory for the general ideas we are presenting. Detailed percentages are not reported in order to avoid overinterpretation of the accuracy of our results.

Economic development efforts in California are of three broad types. The first is federal programs operating on a local basis. Many of these are integrated with CETA and the Community Services Agencies (formerly Office of Economic Opportunity). These constitute perhaps a quarter of the economic development efforts working in California. Half of the agencies are of a second type that we call traditional industrial and agricultural development projects. They include Community Development Corporations and other projects such as industrial parks. Finally, a quarter of the agencies are special-purpose groups oriented around a particular need, such as energy development, small businesses, or farm-worker cooperative farms. In all three types of economic development agency, the majority of effort is devoted to securing federal money and to fitting local needs into federal program guidelines which, all too often, are not attuned to the changing economies and values of a rural service society.

Many agencies are involved in multicounty and regional networks which coordinate development activities. Some of these projects are regional because part of their mission is to serve as a regional planning body for a particular human services project, and some have been set up by legislation on a regional basis. Our survey data estimate that about half of the community development agencies in California are multicounty and statewide in jurisdiction. The provision of a multicounty organization facilitates the optimal use of planning and action resources.

Economic planning is one of the primary functions of most of the economic development organizations, leading some to challenge them for concentrating on too much planning with too little action. We estimate that about two-thirds of the economic development programs in California are involved in planning, but only one-third of the total involved integrated planning covering more than one specialized function. Few of the agencies are set up to do much besides plan, with only about one in ten having a vital action component to complement their planning activities. Thus, the advanced industrial society is not free from the common problem of most other economic development programs.

Furthermore, most effort for economic growth currently occurring in rural California is not being done by chambers of commerce and other organizations primarily oriented toward the interests and needs of business persons but by governmental and quasi-governmental agencies. The governmental planning activities are done through multicounty agencies such as Sierra Planning which integrated the economic needs of several rural counties. Quasi-governmental agencies are for the most part nonprofit organizations which are funded through federal and state contracts to perform vital services. One of these is the California Human Development Corporation in Santa Rosa which conducts training and other economic development projects in northern California. This multimillion dollar organization with 200 employees operates almost entirely by governmental contract; it builds into its programs a special interest in the involvement of low income and poverty level families with far greater vigor and success than purely governmental organizations.

CONCLUSION

Economic development in the advanced industrial society has adopted several characteristics that make it suitable for adapting to the challenges of the high technology and service industries which are becoming more important in rural areas. In particular, there are a number of critical changes in economic development activity. While most are only partially implemented and few are fully successful, the following points show the direction of change:

—The orientation changes from local community to region.

—The economic development objective changes from industrial growth to ecologically balanced growth within community life style goals.

—The techniques change from emphasis on tax incentives and industrial parks to networks of organizations coordinated through planning.

—The emphasis changes from implementing federal programs to developing local capacity to meet the unique needs of a particular economic objective.

These components of economic development give promise of becoming a viable response to the challenges of advanced industrial economic growth in rural areas.

Economic development, however, is only one part of the social changes occurring in the rural advanced industrial society. Economic life is tightly linked to educational opportunities, government, welfare, and to the process of integrating these components to make changes in the community. In the next chapters we will deal with these themes and show how economic development comes as much from the activities of educational institutions and welfare programs, as it does from the direct action of an economic development strategy. Indeed, there are indications that the role of the community developer in the advanced industrial society is moving toward one of integrating and facilitating cooperative efforts among these institutions.

3

New Knowledge Institutions in Rural Communities

CHANGES IN RURAL EDUCATION

Rural areas have long suffered limited potential for economic and social development because of the lack of educational resources of every type, from preschool to adult, from vocational to liberal arts. Rural people have been short-changed and, as a result, lack needed skills and knowledge for modern life. Rural communities have also been hampered by the limited ability of their educational institutions to initiate social and economic development. However, in the rural advanced industrial society, educational and research institutions provide essential tools for socioeconomic change through implementation of high technology industrial processes in agriculture and other industries and through developing local tourism and cultural resources. Furthermore, these communities are linked closer to the urban by far-reaching social and economic ties, increasing the need for persons in rural communities to acquire the knowledge base to interact in productive ways with persons outside their locality. We argue that, unlike most traditional rural areas whose educational resources were limited to one-room school houses, the rural areas of the advanced industrial society are marked by expanding programs of continuing lifelong postsecondary education oriented toward the needs of the community and the life styles of modern rural residents.

Rural education is usually portrayed in the literature in terms of its poor quality, its lack of finances, and its failure to develop the skills of rural residents. B. Eugene Griessman (1969: 13) summarizes the research which supports this conclusion:

> When judged by national averages, education in rural America ranks low in educational achievement of students, average years of schooling, and allocation of resources that go into the system. Rural students drop out sooner and the percentages of those who go to college after completing high school is much lower than for urban youth.

Similarly, Dale Hathaway (1970: 19) argues that education is often the focal point of efforts to provide beneficial services to rural areas but, he goes on, rural school systems are so underfinanced that they are unable to develop innovation programs to help individuals and the region cope with the changing conditions of a new economy. Sher and Rosenfeld (1978: 25, 29) note that while most small schools are in rural areas, the problems of rural schools are not entirely related to size issues. As they point out,

> Rural schools, unlike small schools elsewhere, must contend with unique problems of sparsity and isolation. . . . Rural schools tend to be isolated from the educational, governmental and economic support systems found in metropolitan areas. It also means that sources of assistance to rural schools (from universities, mental health centers, teachers centers, cultural institutions and other potential allies) are notably absent in most regions.

The President's National Commission on Rural Poverty (1967) also noted that the rural education system has "historically shortchanged rural people" in denying them the "achievements of a good educational system and the resources to make it better." As part of its platform, Rural America, Inc., a nonprofit advocate group for rural areas, restated the widely accepted conclusion that the effects of a poorly developed educational system have hurt rural people: "Illiteracy, lack of marketable skills, lost opportunity, low achievement and a limited capacity for self-government have had and continue to have a crippling effect on the society and on the lives and aspirations of rural children and adults throughout America" (Rural America, 1975: 38).

The lack of rural educational facilities and limited human resource development pose problems for economic development. Companies frequently hesitate to expand into rural areas for this reason and if they do, they have to bring in trained workers from outside the area and conduct inhouse training programs. (Milroy, 1970: 44). Generally, the lack of adequately skilled workers means that economic development in rural areas can only take advantage of the lowest-level technology transfer, while local economic development initiative and innovation are practically nonexistent. Also, the low level of human skill development perpetuates significant problems of health, housing, and limited participation in government and voluntary organizations. These problems are exacerbated by the limited opportunities in rural areas for persons who obtain greater skills. They migrate to better jobs in the urban area, creating a "brain drain," leaving an even greater shortage of human resources in rural communities (Luytjes, p. 1971: 38).

While even the most advanced rural areas still lag behind most metropolitan areas in the development of many human resources, advanced industrialism brings to rural areas some significant human resource capabilities which may facilitate both economic and social development.

Knowledge Resources and Advanced Industrialism

There are several reasons "post-industrial theorists" offer for the increasingly important role of education, and its scientific knowledge base, for augmenting human resources in the advanced industrial society; reasons we suspect could apply to rural areas as well. Perhaps the most important one is that high technology manufacturing and professional services demand it. In developing his conception of the technetronic society (used similarly to our concept of advanced industrialism), Brzezinski (1970: 12) shows that the university comes to play a markedly different role:

> The university in an industrial society—in contrast to the situation in medieval times—is an aloof ivory tower, the repository of irrelevant, even if respected, wisdom, and for a brief time the fountainhead for budding members of the established social elite. In the technetronic society the university becomes an intensely involved "think tank," the source of much sustained political planning and social innovation.

Daniel Bell (1973: 212) generalizes beyond the university, presenting his conception of the post-industrial society as a *knowledge society* in a double sense:

> first, the sources of innovation are increasingly derivative from research and development (and more directly, there is a new relation between science and technology because of the centrality of *theoretical* knowledge); second, the weight of the society—measured by a larger proportion of Gross National Product and a larger share of employment—is increasingly in the knowledge field.

Furthermore, because of the increasingly complex social and political issues that face the society, governance and politics raise many new issues that require sophisticated bases of knowledge provided by continuing and advanced education and information services. The relation between these needs and schooling is best articulated by European thinkers such as Torsten Husen who describe it in terms of a "learning society" (1974). The learning society is the logical outcome of the type of changes inherent in advanced industrialism, where education is no longer restricted to the young or limited to basic literacy skills. In America, California has progressed further than any other state toward becoming a learning society. This itself creates a new context for education, with the following features, according to Blakely (1978: 45):

—multiple points of entry for all persons at all ages
—no time or space boundaries to learning activities—persons could learn when and where they needed and wanted to learn
—linkages would be forged between and among all segments of non-formal education

—churches, associations, business and all the current organized non-formal education activities outside the home
—creative links between formal and nonformal systems would be made so that any individual would have access to formal and nonformal education based on need rather than location or personal finances.

O'Toole writes (1977: 139) that the learning society aims to achieve the integration of education, work and leisure, the combination of liberal arts and technical-vocational education, the extension of schooling structures to provide for continuing education and lifelong learning, and the emphasis on goals of learning and individual growth instead of credentialism. With these educational efforts the society will be in a position to avoid domination by the technical elites, as predicted by Bell (1973) and others. The widespread diffusion of knowledge among large sections of society, has given new tools to groups arguing against high technology in society on such issues as the location of nuclear powerplants, the use of chemicals in agriculture, the design of dams planned for earthquake areas, corporate marketing strategies, etc.—which stimulate wider discussion of many subjects than there would be if simply left to technocrats. An informed learning society is thus a political necessity in the increasingly complex and technically sophisticated society of today; it may even be more important in rural areas where urban interests create projects of potentially long-lasting and unforeseeable consequence.

Knowledge Resources in the Rural Advanced Industrial Society

The changes that bring greater knowledge resources to rural areas are multifaceted, but they have the one common theme of increasing diversity of services, forms, and clientele. These diverse characteristics spread away in all directions from the traditional model of education in rural areas, whose mission was to provide basic literacy and functional skills to young persons before they went to work on the farms and in local businesses, or migrated to the city. Advanced industrialism however, provides such a multitude of educational services that formal learning programs are not limited to young persons but are, instead, a knowledge resource for the whole community. Specifically, a model for the expanding educational/knowledge enterprise in rural areas will include five areas of change. These are summarized in Table 3.1.

1. The motivating force for the development of a new educational effort in rural areas is a perceived change in the *mission* of educational institutions. The traditional function of classroom instruction for the young remains, and is in fact improved, in the advanced industrial society, so that higher quality primary and secondary education is available to young persons. In addition the rural school becomes increasingly responsible, through the development of commu-

nity school programs, for coordinating and providing the cultural and recreational resources demanded by the community. Furthermore, the school becomes involved in the definition of community goals and in setting up programs to meet these goals. Colleges take as their mission to serve not only 18–21 year-olds but to become involved in the teaching of adults and the provision of facilities for a whole range of community cultural and recreational programs. Cooperative extension, long limited to agricultural pursuits, becomes involved in a broad spectrum of community programs. In these ways educational aims change from relatively restricted traditional schooling to providing community knowledge resources for technical and cultural development.

2. In meeting this broadening challenge, rural educational efforts become geared to *increasingly diverse groups of clients*, ranging from very young to very old, from full-time to part-time, from training for self-help to training for the trainers. In addition, young persons with high school diplomas nearly always will attend college for some time, making college attendance nearly universal among high school graduates. For adults new programs allow them to keep up with their fields, retrain for new occupational opportunities, and learn new skills for leisure.

3. In order to serve these new clients and provide them the new knowledge resources they want during their entire life cycle, the institutions must develop new *forms of structure and organization*. These forms include location of colleges in rural areas and the use of off-campus locations for many classes. New technologies of instruction and communications make programs available in especially low population-density rural regions. In addition, a new array of private educational efforts provides alternatives in rural areas that promise to be increasingly important in the future.

4. As these institutional structures deliver knowledge to increasingly diverse rural students, new research-oriented institutions for the *generation of knowledge* are becoming important in the rural areas of the advanced industrial society. University and private industry research is no longer restricted to the research labs of central cities. Professional researchers are attracted more and more to remote regions by virtue of their research needs and their own desire to enjoy the life styles of rural living. As this takes place, employment opportunities are developing in rural communities with the new, highly educated resident becoming more involved in community life and politics.

5. Finally, because of the changes in rural educational institutions, a new capacity is developed in schools, colleges, and alternative institutions to effect social changes. This increased institutional capacity in rural areas facilitates the creation of new industries and the solution of many community and individual needs.

These five changes in the availability of education in rural areas are important to the individual, the community, and the community developer. Individuals benefit because they can take advantage of the opportunities to learn for per-

TABLE 3.1

Development of Educational Resources in Rural Areas

Educational Resources	Traditional Society	Industrial Society	Advanced Industrial Society
1. Mission	Literacy for masses and professional training in colleges for few, most of whom will migrate to cities	Vocational training in new white collar occupations	Community service; lifelong vocational upgrading and retraining, and avocational programs for self improvement
2. Clientele	Young persons not yet working	Managerial and clerical training for expanding middle class; high school graduation for most and college for many youth	Nearly universal access by youth to college for specialized training; graduate school for many; continuing "lifelong" education for adults
3. Institutions	Many local primary schools, but few colleges	Consolidation of local schools; rise of state colleges and community colleges	Community colleges and adult schools located in rural areas, offering many courses through media and off-campus sites to most small communities
4. Research and Knowledge Generation	Basic research, not done in rural areas	Rise of agricultural extension and research; new opportunities for other applied research	Research by universities closely related to rural resources and rural needs; knowledge intensive research by many noneducational organizations
5. Institutional Capacity	School source of community organization and pride.	Narrowing of function of school to child-centered effort.	Community development efforts make use of faculty skills, school programs and facilities, and organizational structure to develop change

Source: Compiled by the authors.

sonal improvement, vocationally or avocationally. Communities benefit because of the increased organizational structure provided by school efforts to achieve their new mission of becoming increasingly involved in shaping the fate of their communities. Community developers benefit with increased effectiveness as their role changes from being the most educated, primary knowledge resource for the community to being a facilitator who works within the system to mobilize other available knowledge resources to meet community needs.

The expansion of educational opportunities into rural America is the result of several strong pressures for its growth and of ample resources for expansion and development. As Smelser has pointed out (1974: 15-19), California developed its extensive educational system as a result of pressures for an educational system which combined the competing social values of equality of access for all Californians to college and the development of an educational system of superior quality. The notion of equality was especially important in the development of the extensive community college system. State policy held that all Californians should have access to the first two years of college at an institution close to their home, at no extra cost, without regard to past achievements or social status, and with possible transfer without credit-loss to the four-year state colleges or university system. The policy made no distinction between rural and urban areas and has lead to a large system of rural community colleges. At the same time open access was guaranteed, efforts were undertaken to assure that all community colleges were quality institutions, competitive nationally, while remaining under local control. In order to meet these objectives, the state provided substantial funding for higher education, available through the increasing affluence derived from rapid social and economic growth.

NEW EDUCATIONAL MISSION
FOR RURAL SCHOOLS

As knowledge becomes more central to the daily economic and social affairs of the rural community and to the life styles of its residents, the traditional educational mission of elite socialization and white collar vocational training of youth must expand. There is a need for a new mission which encompasses the escalating demands of society for educational resources to facilitate lifelong human resource development and community improvement. In many ways this notion has made the school or college of today a civic center where activities take place and debates are held, where programs are organized and carried out, and where the character of the community is studied, defined, and elaborated. In the model of the school as it was individuals came to school or college for the things it could offer; now the school and college come to them as activist and advocate for learning new ways to do things.

Schools in rural areas have been typically seen as barriers to social change, perpetuating class structures and economic advantage from one generation to the next. In the advanced industrial society, the role of the educational establishment changes from providing terminal training early in life to providing lifelong resources to meet community goals, acquiring on the way more capacity to respond to change.

The new educational mission in rural areas is most clearly seen in the growing appeal of the community schools movement, the new orientation of community colleges to meeting community service needs, and the greater role of university extension in dealing with community issues beyond those of agricultural development. These components of a new educational mission bring colleges into the arena of facilitating community change. Social action groups use university resources and knowledge, students themselves become involved, and the school becomes a positive contributor to the economic growth of the region.

Community Schools

The improvement of the quality of rural education means that administrative attention and resources are available for a school system to develop new programs—for example, effective community school organizations. The basic concept of community education is to open the schools at night and on weekends to adults and children for recreation, continuing education, and the arts, and to make the schools a resource for community change and development. The pressures for these types of programs are being accentuated in rural areas as new migrants and teachers demand innovative and experimental approaches to education. Earlier concepts of rural schools as the defender of traditional customs and belief systems give way. Rural community schools are now involved in the delivery of health and welfare services, the integration of minorities into community life, and the expansion of the range of community government services.

Beyond offering programs catering to community interests, community schools provide a locus for significant citizen participation and community development efforts. The school becomes the central stable resource for developing new economic and political initiatives. One of the most important ways these activities are coordinated is through the use of community advisory boards and paid staffs to attack community economic and social problems. Community advisory boards are particularly effective for bringing participation into the schools for community purposes. Among the most innovative of these endeavors has been the use of rural community school programs in California's north coast counties as a focal point for training immigrants to rural areas in trades needed locally. Another example is the use of the community school in agricultural areas as a base for the formation of consumer and producer cooperatives. Over 300 such coops have been started in rural California. Santa Barbara County uses the community school program most extensively to link social and educational services in rural areas with those in the city. In other states, such as Oregon, community education plays even a larger role in state rural community development and outreach activities. Community educational mobile units are employed to train the trainers in rural areas on housing, human resource mobilization, and a number of other activities.

College Community Service Programs

The second arena in which we see the changing mission of the educational system in advanced industrial rural areas involves greater participation of colleges in community development. This effort is most clearly manifest in the *community service programs* of the California Community Colleges which serve triple the number of students as the regular day credit program. Until Proposition 13 eliminated much of its funding source, the community service program received ample funding at the district level from an optional 5 percent property-tax levy to support noncredit educational experiences and to make facilities available to community groups.

The community services program was started in 1951 and all districts, even the most rural, had some program in 1976. The following objectives are considered most important in shaping these programs.

1. To become a center of community life by encouraging the use of college facilities and services by community groups when such use does not interfere with the college's regular schedule;
2. To provide community members educational services that utilize the special skills and knowledge of the college staff and other experts and are designed to meet the needs of community groups and the college district at large;
3. To provide the community with the leadership and coordination capabilities of the college, assist the community in long-range planning, and join with individuals and groups in attacking unsolved problems;
4. To contribute to and promote the cultural, intellectual, and social life of the college district community and the development of skills for the profitable use of leisure time.

(California Community Colleges, 1977: 1)

The extensive involvement of Californians in community service programs is indicated by the fact that 18,344,000 "participants" were counted in community service classes, events, and activities in 1976. These are non credit programs making use of college facilities for public purposes—for example, using the auditorium, lecture halls, theatres, gymnasium, tennis courts, swimming pool or similar facilities.

A significant part of the community services program is the provision of cultural events and activities for local residents. In virtually every rural community where there is a college, these programs provide the main source of live cultural performances—including symphony, opera, and folk music, among others. Nearly 4 million attended these cultural activities in 1976. Another three-quarter million participants were counted in actual community development activities, such as associations, meetings, career development, and activities for disadvantaged groups (California Community Colleges, 1977). The ways of financing these activities are now in question, but we have been told that most colleges do not intend to completely eliminate community service activities since Proposition 13's passage.

This type of activity is surely not unique to the community services program in California's community colleges, but it is one of the most important new developments in the expanding program of the community college movement. Furthermore, it is not an isolated program instituted by the state legislature so that school facilities appear to be better used. The spirit of community service has been incorporated into the basic philosophy and mission of the institution. As an example, the five-year plan of the community colleges of California aims to provide services for the whole family on a continuing basis. The report sees the future as being shaped by the following trends:

> This plan anticipates that there will be increased emphasis on individual expression and development. Progress toward male/female equality in education, career, the home, and society in general will continue. There will be increased numbers of young single adults and in general, smaller and later families. Social and employment conditions will result in more leisure time being available to individuals. The importance of education will increase as parents exhibit greater concern for their children's development (Board of Governors, California Community Colleges: 1977: 5).

The community colleges represent perhaps the clearest articulation of the new feeling of community responsibility among the several levels of California colleges. However, in the state colleges and the university, new emphasis is being given to upgrading relations through public service. In eras of financial cutbacks such as the present, colleges attempt to increase their political strength through demonstration of direct contribution to public needs. The faculty and students in many colleges have long been involved in working with small cities in their planning efforts through internship programs and related projects that have brought university assistance to hard-pressed local communities. Blakely and Zone (1976) found these resources to be of immense value to local governments with programs requiring work and information they did not have and could not afford to purchase privately.

A New Role for Extension

University Extension activities for many years have been the principal educational resource for rural areas, but even here the mission of these programs is being altered to reflect the new community-centered emphasis. For over a century cooperative or agricultural extension has been the principal source of technical information to rural communities. The agricultural extension service remains an immensely successful model of technological and economic intervention, especially related to economic revitalization and the introduction of new methods of agricultural production. In responding to the agricultural demands of the advanced industrial society, extension necessarily found itself involved in a larger web of social issues and concerns. The extension advisor in California's most advanced rural sectors is a scientific innovator and, in many instances, is as involved in basic research as his university colleagues. Clearly the level of this research activity varies, but the principal contribution to California agriculture by Cooperative Extension is in direct scientific input. For this reason, new techniques in integrated pest management, environmental toxology, and labor-management are being developed under the guidance of extension experts.

In chapter 2 we detailed the size, scope, and diversity of California agriculture. This diversity and complexity is clearly reflected in the Cooperative Extension service delivery system. Emmett Fiske has shown that extension responds to large, modern agriculture needs, while neglecting other groups in rural areas. Based on a factor analysis of county farming patterns, three types of county farming were identified: modern rational agriculture (agribusiness), traditional family farming, and rustic isolation. Fiske (1977: 8) found that data on county extension programs show

> Cooperative Extension specializations, budgets, and manpower correlate *positively* with the modern rational agriculture factor; they show almost no correlation with the traditional family farm factor; and they have a strong *negative* correlation with the rustic isolation factor. It is not too surprising that, given the trend in California towards larger and larger agricultural operations, Cooperative Extension activities at the county level relate quite positively to the modern rational agriculture factor.

Cooperative Extension, as well as the University of California and State University and College extension programs, provide a rich variety of new, non-agricultural educational opportunities. These are principally of two types: public service and community development. Public service programs offer resources for rural communities ranging from credit courses to technical assistance. Courses are given to rural residents, public officials, and business persons on topics such as how to manage growth or city budgets after Proposition 13, how to evaluate the impact of new tax laws, how to use new materials in the design of roads in mountain areas, or how to provide special care to the elderly. Specialized community assistance is provided as needed by professors, researchers, and cooperative extension advisors. The chief characteristics of these activities are that they are essentially *ad hoc* arrangements which provide flexible resources to persons who know how to use them; in all cases they expand traditional concepts of the role of extension.

Extension's community development programs are preplanned and organized activities conducted by special staff to achieve specific goals in a community through group decision-making. The specialists who work in these activities are mostly from Cooperative Extension, and they deal with community projects, oriented toward the provision of services identified by community groups and carried out by them with extension assistance. The creation of various community development organizations to undertake a particular project, such as a farming cooperative, is an example.

In an advanced industrial society with relatively high access to knowledge, the community development extension specialist must play more than the role of an information source. The more important role is that of mobilizing community opinion and directing it, with technical assistance, to solve community problems. Most rural communities appreciate the need for scientific information in agriculture. The new challenge for extension is to provide the same resources from the social sciencies to solve new problems created by advanced industrialism.

Thus, the mission of educational institutions in rural areas is broadening from narrow programs in training and credit courses to general resource for community enrichment and service. There are a number of organizational forms which have facilitated this change. What is important is not the particulars of the organizational forms—because there is much variety—but the recognition that the community's needs may be met through programs coming out of rural colleges or schools.

NEW CLIENTELE IN RURAL
POSTSECONDARY EDUCATION

The advanced industrial society, with its knowledge-intensive technology and service industries, generates highly skilled workers and informed citizens by expanding access to education on two fronts. First, access to college and other postsecondary educational opportunities is available to a growing clientele that includes virtually all high school graduates at some point in their lives. Second, education becomes in effect lifelong with programs in adult education, continuing or lifelong education, and extension. These two trends have greatly increased the scope of the clientele for educational programs in the advanced industrial society.

Access to College for All

The proportion of California high school graduates enrolling in college sometime during their lives has been estimated at over 80 percent in contrast to a national total of 50 percent (Harris, 1972: 423-4; Benveniste and Benson, 1976: 37). Martin Trow has suggested that for California and other states with wide college availability, college has become nearly a "universal" experience for young persons, much like high school became a universal stage in the growth of young people by the end of the 1930s (1962: 1970). Data collected by the California Postsecondary Education Commission (1978a) show that both rural and urban areas of the state have very high rates of college attendance. Figures presented in Table 3.2 show that in 1977 first-time enrollees in California public colleges and universities, aged 19 or less, included 52.6 percent of all rural high school graduates. Another two to three percent of the rural high school graduate population went to private colleges in California, and perhaps the same proportion went to private colleges outside the state (although this latter figure was not determined by the Postsecondary Education Commission study). College attendance for rural students thus exceeds 50 percent by a significant margin. Urban attendance in California institutions, as shown by the data, includes 56.8 percent of all urban high school graduates, only 4.2 percent greater than rural. From 1974-77 the attendance rate of rural youth has increased at a faster rate than that of urban youth, although one should probably not place too much emphasis on a trend over these few years.

TABLE 3.2

Percentage of High School Graduates Enrolled as First-Time Freshmen in Public Colleges and Universities in California by County of High School Attendance

County	1974	1977
Rural	49.6	52.6
Urban*	54.4	56.8
Total	54.0	56.5

*1976 Standard Metropolitan Statistical Areas.
Source: Computed from California Postsecondary Education Commission (1978a).

These are nonetheless significant differences in the attendance patterns of rural and urban populations. Rural counties without a community college or with a community college only have generally lower attendance rates than rural counties that have a state college as well. Furthermore, counties away from a state university reported a lower transfer rate of community college students to the university. A number of the most remote and smallest counties had enrollment percentages in the low 40 percent range, sometimes even below that. In 1977 rural counties showed a great deal of variation, from a low of 30.4 percent in Del Norte County to a high of 71 percent in Yuba county. The high by Yuba county surely has to do with the number of off-campus locations its community college uses.

Enrollment data for all students, not just those in first-time attendance, at college, are not available, except from the 1970 census. Table 3.3 shows census data for enrollment in school by rural residence, age, and sex for California and the nation as a whole. With the exception of male rural nonfarm groups, California's enrollment exceeds that of the nation during the college years (age 18–22). One of the more interesting patterns in the census data is the difference between California and national attendance for rural farm males: among 19-year-olds, California leads the nation by 22.2 percentage points and by almost 10 percentage points, or more, during the whole period between the ages, 18–24. Presumably the greater availability of community colleges in California rural farming areas and the need for specialized agricultural study lead more men to attend college in California rather than take farm employment, as is the pattern in other rural parts of the country. Women in both rural categories are more likely to attend college in California than in the nation as a whole, and this difference is often quite large, especially in the rural farm areas. For both sexes, by the age of 23 or 24, California's proportion enrolled in school begins to double that of the nation, reflecting the considerable adult training and graduate study in the state.*

The presence of this highly educated population in rural California has two important effects. First, education creates its own demand. The more educated people there are in rural areas, the greater the demand for more education in all forms. Second, the community developer's capacity to function as a resource link is dramatically altered. The presence of a professionally skilled population and educational institutions, particularly at the postsecondary level, means that the developer can concentrate on obtaining, organizing, and transmitting information rather than developing organizations or institutions for this purpose. Further, the development specialist in California can utilize the vast array of educational institutions as the transmission channel and support base for socioeconomic change. As noted above, the community colleges in particular provide a tremendous network through their faculty and facilities for introducing or supporting new community-oriented programs. It is not an accident, for example, that much of the vocational training carried out under the Comprehensive Education and Training Act (CETA) in rural areas is concentrated in community colleges.

In sum, the capacity to extend and expand an educational resource in rural California is nearly unlimited in terms of the types of programs that might be developed to meet community needs. The availability and use of this structure is critical to the developer's success.

---

*Census enrollments for college-age persons may be hard to interpret because they count the location as the place where the person was residing on the day the census was taken. However, the general patterns are still indicative, since most students attend a college near their home.

TABLE 3.3

Enrollment in School by Rural Residence, Age, and Sex: California and the United States, 1970

Age	Rural Nonfarm				Rural Farm			
	Male		Female		Male		Female	
	Calf.	U.S.	Calf.	U.S.	Calf.	U.S.	Calf.	U.S.
3	8.0	3.8	7.9	3.9	8.3	2.6	7.4	2.6
4	17.9	9.7	17.3	9.5	19.5	5.5	16.4	5.4
5	64.3	41.9	65.8	42.2	59.7	36.4	64.4	37.5
6	93.2	83.2	94.4	83.7	92.3	83.6	93.3	83.3
7–15	96.4	95.9	96.3	96.0	96.7	96.4	97.8	96.8
16	92.8	89.4	92.5	89.6	96.9	92.8	95.2	93.3
17	83.1	83.7	84.4	83.2	91.2	88.5	90.1	90.7
18	61.8	64.3	58.1	53.8	78.7	69.6	69.6	65.4
19	37.2	42.3	38.6	29.5	65.1	42.9	57.3	34.0
20	23.3	26.4	21.1	15.6	37.7	25.2	30.4	17.7
21	18.2	19.9	15.6	10.9	29.0	15.8	21.5	12.8
22	18.6	13.2	11.1	6.1	20.7	10.9	21.6	7.7
23	16.4	9.9	8.7	4.1	18.8	7.4	7.1	4.4
24	14.1	7.8	6.0	3.3	13.6	5.3	9.5	3.1
25–29	10.2	5.6	5.4	2.5	6.9	3.0	5.3	2.5
30–34	6.3	3.4	4.1	2.2	3.2	1.7	3.5	2.1

Source: U.S. Census, Table 146, 1970.

79

Adults as New Clients

Equally significant as the growth in enrollment of high school graduates in college is the trend of enrollment of adult students in all sectors of postsecondary education. Whereas traditional college systems focussed almost exclusively on 18-22 year-old students, a rapidly changing society dependent on increasing use of knowledge has created a greater demand for education for continuing training and for personal lifelong enrichment. A significant proportion of California's adult population enrolls in college each year. Salner (1977) conservatively estimated that a third of the state's adults were enrolled in a college or university, in adult school programs, or in educational programs provided by non-academic organizations or agencies. In 1977 California community colleges reported 33.6 percent of its students were aged over 30 (Postsecondary Education Commission, 1978b: 75).

With the expansion in rural areas of technologies in agriculture and industry and professional specialties, continuing lifelong educational programs have significant appeal. Many states, including California, require all members of several professions to take training programs prior to recertification. These programs are found nationally in 11 fields, nine of which are required in California: the fields are accounting, dentistry, law, nursing, nursing home administration, optometry, pharmacy, medicine, and real estate (Watkins, 1977). State requirements for these and other specializations in California's rural areas are mandating educational programs that have not been available or considered necessary in traditional rural areas.

Adult education is also important for job retraining. The rapid pace of social change in advanced industrial rural areas eliminates many jobs and alters many others. Because of such a changing employment picture, the state estimates that during the next five years at least a third of the working population will change occupations; during the next twenty years two-thirds will change. Of the first group half will seek additional education to prepare for their new careers; of the second, 60 percent will seek more education (Board of Governors, California Community Colleges, 1977: 6).

Access to adult education programs in California is easy since they are provided by 320 of California's 370 secondary school districts. Although many of the districts not offering adult education are in rural areas, a majority of rural areas offer such programs through their high schools. These programs provide traditional state and federal mandated courses of basic education for adults who have less than an eighth grade education and prepare adults for high school equivalency examinations; plus special education for the handicapped, disabled, mentally retarded, and older persons confined to rest homes.

The educational resources of basic adult education are supplemented by community education programs in a wide range of vocational, academic, and avocational subjects. During the 1976-77 school year, California's adult education enrolled 2.3 million persons, of which only 275,000 were in adult basic education. The remaining 90 percent of enrollments were in the huge community education program. Data are not available to compare California's enrollment in these forms of adult education with those of other states, but interviews with knowledgeable persons suggest that only Florida, New York, and Michigan have large programs and none is as large as California's.

Table 3.4 shows rates of participation in adult education programs for California's rural and urban areas. Total enrollment in California's rural areas was 126,058 leading to an overall rural enrollment of 80 persons per thousand, compared to the urban rate of 110. Rural areas, as compared to urban, provide relatively little service through the adult basic education program, while doing comparatively well in the industrial/agricultural and civic education categories. Clearly, the rural areas of California lag in the development of adult education; yet, compared to the virtual absence of such programs in most of the nation's nonmetropolitan regions, the California adult education program provides rich opportunities.

TABLE 3.4

Rural and Urban Enrollment in Adult Education, California, 1976–77 (per thousand population)

	Rural*	Urban*
Adult Basic Education	5.5	13.4
Liberal Arts (English, Foreign Languages, Math, Science, Social Science)	10.6	15.5
Fine Arts, Music	5.3	8.7
Business	5.5	10.0
Industrial Education, Agriculture	8.8	10.6
Civic Education and Community Development, Americanization, Recreation, Homemaking, Foreign Series	45.1	52.5
Total	80.8	110.7

*Rural/urban statistics based on SMSAs as of 1976.

Note: Population figures used in computations were 1,559,400 (rural) and 19,954,500 (urban).

Source: Computed from California State Department of Education, Adult Education Field Services, 1977.

Although the adult education program of the state carries the greatest share of adult enrollment, all components of the state educational effort have tried to supplement their youth enrollment with adults attending night schools and weekend classes in areas without a college (Woods, 1975: 286). Thus, Visalia, a small community, has an experimental joint university and state college "Learning Center" where adult students work on their four-year degrees. Other efforts are presently operating in numerous communities. Teacher and educational administration courses are offered in rural counties where there is need to expand local capacity. In remote Angels Camp, for example, Sacramento State University offered a series of master's degree courses leading to the certification of school principals. The orientation toward adults is thus an important resource for rural areas.

Many educational programs aiming at new clientele have goals associated with community development. For example, California adult education is engaged in a program called "La Familia" in several parts of the state where large numbers of Spanish-speaking Mexican Americans live. The goal of the program is to involve the entire family in educational experiences based on the assessed economic, cultural, and educational needs of various individuals in the family unit. The aim is two-fold: to satisfy the desire of migrant farm workers for specific educational programs in such fields as language and occupational skills and to provide the educational opportunities for the special social context of the migrant child. The migrant child is often isolated from his or her family because of new knowledge gained from school. The "La Familia" program assists children directly but also aids the parents so there is a better chance to avoid a breakdown in communication between the child and the school and community. In this way a particular rural segment has been introduced to the programs of adult education (Del Buono, 1978).

In addition, the rural elderly are being assisted by special programs. As a first step the State Department of Education is conducting workshops throughout rural California in an attempt to define areas of need and to provide training for agency personnel who work with the elderly in local communities. One of the suggestions deriving from this effort is the development of schools as centers for the coordinated delivery of social services to older persons. Primary and secondary schools have facilities such as kitchens and nursing stations; with declining enrollments, the schools have the capacity to serve the elderly. Under some circumstances schools can involve the elderly in the educational programs of young children with a net gain to both groups.

These and other examples show how the educational system is becoming involved to a greater degree in the lives of people, virtually from birth to death. Courses are offered in childbirth techniques and breastfeeding, and children are taken care of in day-care centers from an early age. In this respect, as may be seen in Table 3.2, California children at the age of three and four are enrolled in school at over twice the national rate. Then, after the youth period, adult programs continue throughout their lives; "family courses" are even provided (Katz, 1978). Courses for the elderly round out the exhaustive involvement of the school with the life cycle of the individual.

Professional Clients

One of the ways continuing attention to learning processes affects rural areas is through "training for the trainers." A small cadre of professional, full-time community developers in the University of California consult with and teach local community developers in the school systems and elsewhere. This is a continuing process, involving community colleges and state university and college systems as well. City planners and managers, economic developers, and a wide variety of social workers and government officials participate in continuing education programs in most rural areas.

In using these resources, the community developer has opportunities to utilize education as a device for creating social change by providing the means to reach several critical goals (Blakely, 1978: 45):

a. goal setting—participant involvement in determining future objectives for society and for themselves;
b. experimental learning systems—maximizing experiences which provide individuals with successful coping skills and minimizing other adverse educational situations;
c. integration—breaking down the stereotypes and barriers between races, sexes, classes and life roles e.g. home, work, play so that people are freer to learn and become; and,
d. development—providing systems to assist individuals, groups and communities meet their needs and desires to shape their own future.

NEW ORGANIZATIONAL STRUCTURES
AND PROGRAMS

In keeping with the new mission and the new clients served by rural educational programs in the advanced industrial society, innovations in the structure of education are meeting the challenges of providing knowledge services to non-metropolitan areas. Expanding state systems in California have located four-year and community colleges in rural settings with the explicit purpose of bringing together a variety of agricultural and nonagricultural programs. No longer are rural colleges agricultural schools serving the limited interests of traditional rural society. The programs in rural California public institutions are increasingly diverse and articulate, or link to, programs at other colleges. (Other states are following a similar pattern. Thus students, studying at a rural community college for their first two years, may transfer to a senior college for the remainder of their college studies and suffer no academic loss. Outside of the traditional college programs for youth, innovations in teaching programs and alternative institutional structures are used to serve new adult part-time clients and to overcome many of the problems of providing education for widely dispersed rural populations. These new educational structures rely increasingly on such things as learning centers, self directed learning, TV and media centers, traveling class-rooms, off-campus locations, proprietary schools, and a wide variety of alterna-tive institutions. While there is a great deal more diversity than we can illustrate here, it is clear that innovations in rural educational structure have responded to the new challenges of the advanced industrial society.

Availability of Colleges in Rural Areas

One of the first innovations of California's public post-secondary educa-tion system was the establishment of community colleges and branches of the state colleges (later named state universities) throughout the state so that stu-dents could attend close to home. The basis for this was explored as early as 1910 when arguments for a community college near Fresno were advanced—a college that would give students an opportunity to continue their studies at home and then transfer to a four-year college at minimal expense (Smelser, 1974: 17). Since then, colleges at all levels have been located near the center of the population served by it, leading a report on community colleges in 1966 to state with pride that the goal of putting two years of college within community dis-tance of every high school graduate in California had nearly been reached (1974: 18). The philosophy of extensive public college availability to rural residents has been pursued in many states, but California's system was clearly the one copied by others.

Today, California lists 102 public community colleges in 70 different com-munity college districts, encompassing virtually the entire state, although a few rural counties still must send their students to neighboring colleges. There are 14 campuses in nonmetropolitan counties and 20 more serving the primarily rural regions of counties classified as SMSAs. These 34 colleges are a vast resource for rural education and have grown rapidly during recent years. Three new colleges have been added since 1967, and total rural enrollment grew 88 percent by 1976, compared to a growth of 75 percent for the system as a whole.* Rural commu-nity colleges had a total enrollment in 1976 of just under 100,000 students. Four campuses of the State college and University system are located in rural parts of the state, and these enroll some 40,000 students, many from urban areas who are attracted to the rural setting.†

Off-Campus Locations and New Technologies

Although a number of campuses have been established in rural areas and a few rural educational needs have been met by urban campuses, the most effec-

---

*Data are opening fall enrollment in the National Education Association's *Education Directory, Colleges and Universities* (1969 and 1978.)
†Chico State University reports 60% enrollment from urban areas.

tive means of reaching most rural persons is to bring programs to them in their own towns through the use of off-campus locations. This added capacity allows for significantly greater educational coverage for many general courses, though some specialized courses still have to be centralized in larger cities. The use of off-campus locations by community colleges has been expanding considerably in California. In 1960 virtually all courses were offered in campus facilities and emphasis was on building new campuses; only a few hundred off-campus locations were used.* But by 1976 the emphasis on construction stopped and over 3,000 off-campus course locations were used, including storefronts, nurseries, hospitals, machine shops, and local high school auditoriums. Data collected by the California Postsecondary Education Commission showed for 1976–77 that 867 rural off-campus locations were used by 46 different community colleges to reach rural residents. Many of the courses were given hundreds of miles from the central campus location, though most were closer. State colleges and universities also offer off-campus courses but to a lesser extent than community colleges.

In addition to the special off-campus programs for adult and continuing education described earlier, an illustration of the broad reach of these rural off-campus programs is Yuba College in Marysville on the eastern edge of the Sacramento Valley. Serving many of the mountain communities in the northeast, this ambitious college offers instruction at over 60 off-campus locations, almost half of which are 30 or more miles from the central campus. These courses turn virtually any type of business or public facility into an extension of the educational system. Airports, automobile electric shops, state correctional facilities, Air Force bases, and Indian reservations have been used by Yuba College to provide learning in a setting, not only close to rural residents, but appropriate for their learning needs. This example is not particularly unique in California and is likely to be duplicated over and over in rural areas of California and other educationally oriented states.

In particularly remote locations, where population density is so low that courses could not possibly attract sufficient enrollment, community colleges are experimenting with community-based learning centers under a Rural Outreach Program with Title I funding through the California Postsecondary Commission. The Rural Outreach Program advises adults in rural areas about the educational opportunities available in community colleges near them, develops educational programs to meet rural needs, and offers instruction. The instructional program through various learning centers is most indicative of the response of education to the needs of remote areas in the advanced industrial society. Paltridge, Regan, and Terkla (1978, p. C15–C16) describe the program:

---

*Interview, Dr. Storey, California Post Secondary Education Commission (June, 1978).

Groups of twelve to twenty-five adults gather to study a number of different subject areas under the direction of the outreach facilitator, also referred to as a "learning facilitator." The learning facilitators are classroom experienced teachers, generally recruited from the facilities of local high schools, who have concentrated on the learning process rather than on particular academic disciplines. They assist students in their use of self-paced programmed instruction and help create a supportive learning climate. The programmed instruction is augmented by visiting faculty from the community college. The facilitator functions to a certain extent as a broker between community needs and college resources. Classes usually meet for sixteen three-hour weekly sessions and the whole operation is conducted under the supervision of an instructional supervisor from the nearby community college.

One training project for nurses uses live interactive television training sessions in remote centers. Another involves a computerized Regional Data Bank for health manpower which provides names of rural medical persons who are periodically contacted and urged to take courses to upgrade their skills. As these examples show, California's rural areas often make immediate use of new educational technologies even before they find widespread application elsewhere. The use of innovative educational methods and settings in rural areas is clearly near the frontier of this technology.

Private Noncredit Educational Institutions

Although much innovation affecting the educational opportunities in California's rural areas has been provided by public school systems, a large and diffuse private effort is also making a growing contribution to the educational enrichment of the state. Very little concrete data exists on private noncredit educational opportunities in rural areas: only estimates for the state as a whole are available. There are about 1,700 private specialty schools in California. In 1972 about 750 of these were engaged in the occupational training of approximately 200,000 students. Estimates suggest that other schools, largely avocational in program (speed reading, charm schools, flight training, income tax, and drivers training) reach another 200,000 students. Some of the private alternative schools are linked to large corporations; others are "mom and pop" proprietary schools with little financial stability (Salner, 1975: 29). The evidence suggests that these are widely distributed around the state. Rural phone books and newspapers show that there are many serving nonmetropolitan areas, but the variety is considerably limited, in contrast to places like Berkeley and Los Angeles where hundreds of opportunities exist.

A large number of educational organizations make use of rural areas for programs in interpersonal relations, mystical experiences, and for seminars for urban "escapees" (Salner, 1975: 146). A "living-learning catalogue" called *Some-*

where Else indexes out-of-the-way educational ventures across the nation where people can learn without enrolling in college. California has more of these alternatives than any other state: its total is 21.4 percent of the 407 learning experiences listed for the United States. California's share is thus about double its proportion of the national population. Many are located in rural areas as, for example, "The Bridge Mountain Foundation," located in the redwood forests above Santa Cruz and offering programs "covering everything from the void, doing nothing, wilderness tripping, and self-hypnosis to Gestalt, psychoanalysis, breathing, dance, and encounter" (Center for Curriculum Design, 1973). Other programs use California rural areas for offering wilderness "survival" experiences to facilitate self-understanding. Still others make use of California rural areas for specialized avocational interests such as photography, rock climbing and, of course, summer camps. These activities are a form of tourism which in the advanced industrial society has an important educational component. Rural areas are also used for more traditional training conferences for professionals or businessmen who find the rural setting a tool that facilitates learning in a way that would not be possible in the complex and active bustle of urban areas. Rural areas also have conferences oriented to their own needs and interests. For example, seed companies and suppliers of agricultural chemicals hold many conferences on problems relating to the crops grown in a particular region. In addition, conferences are held by irrigation districts, marketing boards, and other links in the agricultural food chain. County fairs still serve a large educational interest for which they receive some money from the county.

Structural Changes

There are four general ways in which educational institutions in the rural advanced industrial society have altered their structure. First, the various sectors of postsecondary education are more closely coordinated with each other. In California many courses are transferable among three college sectors: the community colleges, the state colleges, and the university. Recently efforts to link the assorted adult educational activities as a "fourth sector" to the above mentioned sectors have failed, but other alternatives to achieve more coordination are being studied.

Secondly, educational opportunities outside the traditional primary-secondary-college sequence are increasing. Resources to accommodate alternative lifelong learning are being established, and future assessments of the educational resources of rural areas will have to take these developments into particular account.

Third, efforts are being made to make access to pay and jobs after graduation less related to the prestige of the school one attends. As Wilms (1976: 1) points out, a significant body of literature (Hansen and Weisbrod, 1969; Karabel, 1972; Bowles and Gintis, 1976) shows that students in proprietary and community colleges end up earning less and taking poorer jobs than their university counterparts. The system in California, as elsewhere, remains stratified, and rural areas continue in the main to be served by less prestigeous institutions. Bringing the resources of the university to rural areas remains a challenge.

Finally, tax limitations, such as those recently instituted in California, may inhibit much of the expansion described here. However, there is a strong trend for increasing private alternative provision of educational opportunities; it remains to be seen whether people will increase their use of the private opportunities or will pay public institutions *directly* for services that once were supported by tax funds. In short, future analysis of the educational opportunities of rural areas will have to be more concerned with the availability of financial resources in California that has been the case in the past. As pointed out earlier, the system was able to grow in California because of ample resources; that era may now be over.

INSTITUTIONAL RESOURCES FOR RESEARCH IN RURAL AREAS

Under the traditional model of limited educational resources in rural areas the possibility of research institutions developing outside of metropolitan areas would be quite unreasonable. However, with the increased availability of technical resources in rural areas and the expanding educational system there, the rural area of the advanced industrial society is becoming active in many types of research and development activity. Some research institutions are directed toward problems of unique rural concern, while other research is aimed at problems of the society in general. Although direct evidence on the number of research positions in rural areas is not known, other data may illustrate that rural areas are no longer as isolated as is frequently assumed from the innovation, research, and creation of new knowledge needed to solve rural problems.

One of the most extensive uses of rural areas for research comes from the University. The University of California has 10 agricultural field stations, an experimental forest, vineyard and orchard, and 24 samples of California's diverse natural habitat in the Natural Land and Water Reserves System (see Map 3.1). These research centers only begin to illustrate the reach of university research into rural areas: anthropologists study Indian remains; historians chart the rise and fall of goldrush communities; sociologists study migrant farm workers. Even use of the California desert for research and teaching is increasing to the point that a recent study estimated the desert had been used for over 250,000 person-days of education during the 1975-76 school year (Stebbins et al., 1978: 7). Professors and students doing graduate work have used the desert for many years for research in paleontology, zoology, botany, and geology. This research is important, they report (19), because "the natural lands of the California desert constitute a *unique* teaching and research facility."

There appears to be no other place on earth where such a biologically and historically rich desert environment has been subjected to

MAP 3.1

Teaching and Research Facilities: University of California

★ Campus
⬚-㉒ Agricultural Field Stations, Research
   Stations and Experimental Areas
㉓-㊽ Natural Land and Water Reserves
   System
• Cooperative Extension

1. Arrowhead Conference Center
2. Blodgett Forest Research Station
3. Bodega Marine Lab
4. Deciduous Fruit Field Station
5. Hopland Field Station
6. Imperial Valley Field Station
7. Kearney Horticultural Field Station
8. Laboratory of Nuclear Medicine and
   Radiation Biology
9. Lawrence Berkeley Laboratory
10. Lawrence Livermore Laboratory
11. Lindcove Field Station
12. Mt. Hamilton Observing Station
13. Napa Experimental Vineyard
14. Richmond Field Station
15. San Andreas Geophysical Observatory
16. San Joaquin Valley Research and
    Extention Center
17. Sierra Foothill Range Field Station
18. South Coast Field Station
19. Tulelake Field Station
20. West Side Field Station
21. White Mountain Research Station
22. Wolfskill Experimental Orchards

23. American River Reserve
24. Año Nuevo Reserve
25. Big Creek Reserve
26. Bodega Marine Reserve
27. Box Spring Reserve
28. Boyd Deep Canyon Reserve
29. Burn's Pinon Ridge Reserve
30. Caprinteria Salt Reserve
31. Cheatham Grove Reserve
32. Coal Oil Point Reserve
33. Dawson Los Monos Reserve
34. Elliott Chaparral Reserve
35. Etiwanda Wash Reserve
36. Granite Mountains Reserve
37. Hastings Reserve
38. James San Jacinto Reserve
39. Kendall-Frost Reserve
40. Motte Rimrock Reserve
41. Pygmy Forest Reserve
42. Ryan Oak Reserve
43. Sacramento Mountains Reserve
44. Santa Monica Mountains Reserve
45. Sawyer Trinity Alps Reserve
46. Scripps Shoreline Reserve
47. San Joaquin Marsh Reserve
48. Santa Cruz Island Reserve
49. Valentine Eastern Sierra Reserve

Note: The University of California comprises more than 70 schools and colleges on nine campuses, including three law schools, five medical schools, two dental schools, two nursing schools, two schools of public health, one pharmacy school, one school of optometry and one school of veterinary medicine; some 150 research institutes, centers, bureaus, and laboratories or stations; the Agricultural Experiment Station and nine agricultural field stations; a University-wide library containing over 15 million volumes; the University of California Press; two affiliated units—Hastings College of the Law and San Francisco Art Institute; and 24 samples of California's diverse habitats in the Natural Land and Water Reserves System which serve as outdoor classrooms and laboratories. Although not all the teaching and research facilities are shown, the map illustrates the University's diversity.

Source: Constructed by the authors.

such breadth of study over such a long period by a variety of academic disciplines. . . . Arid lands constitute the largest remaining portion of the planet with possibilities for major agricultural expansion. . . . The potential of wild shrubs for benefitting man is great. Desert plant species act as a genetic bank upon which we can draw to protect and improve cultivated species. The pharmaceutical properties of such plants should be more fully investigated.

This report and others like it document the important contribution that rural areas are playing in the research and development activities of the state of California. But Stebbins also points out that the desert is a fragile ecology and argues that the increasing use of the desert for recreation poses a serious threat to the reserve it has for research. This is already leading to new policy considerations, limiting recreational use to areas where little research is going on.

In addition, many industries have established research laboratories in rural areas. An index of these research laboratories suggests that they are distributed throughout the state. Some are connected with agriculture, including Ferry Morse Seeds, Driscoll Strawberry, and Campbell Soup. Others are oriented to natural resources, including Portland Cement and Forest Products labs. In keeping with the main thrust of the California economy, an impressive number are related to electronics: there is a firm in the Santa Cruz mountains which develops techniques for semiconductor manufacturing; electrical instruments development is taking place in Sonoma; aerospace components are being made in Los Alamentos, and Colloidal products in Petaluma. Admittedly, the majority of these research efforts are not in the most distant rural counties, but they are clearly signs that industrial research does not always require close proximity to urban centers.

One recent development, which permits research to take place at greater distances from urban areas, is the rise of the new profession of "information brokers" in urban areas who gather information from libraries in metropolitan centers for persons located at a distance from the resource materials they may need. Information brokers have been working as independent professionals for a fee in some of the nation's largest cities only since 1970, making use of university libraries and other specialized information sources, including computerized data banks. For researchers in rural areas they may become an institution of increasing importance in the future, providing the link between private research and development activities in rural areas and the information available elsewhere. For example, Finnigan (1976: 102) reports performing literature searches for a physician in Maine who studies various sea animals but lacks access to literature at his rural location. Other cases in rural California involve the information broker providing information to publishers of specialized books in Willits and Bolenas. A person in Gilroy needed information on a plant noted for its high protein content, grown in Japan and Russia; but the only publications about it were in Japanese. A broker got the information and translated it for the rural client. Somewhat similar services are available through public libraries in rural areas at no charge. While these examples of rural research use of information brokers are few, they suggest the emergence of a new institution which may have increasing importance for facilitating research in nonurban areas.

Not all research in advanced industrial rural areas necessitates the use of information brokers. Over 100 *special* libraries are located in rural California (out of some 1100 such libraries in the state as a whole). These libraries cover special—usually technical—topics and do not include recreational reading collections. In addition, the general libraries in rural California areas include many county law and medical collections. Air force and naval bases also have specialized libraries. Of particular interest are the libraries of research units, including four marine research institutes and three astronomical observatories. Libraries are also run by a number of seminaries, museums, national parks, businesses, and nonprofit organizations in rural areas. Thus, a variety of information resources have been developed to meet rural needs.

The presence of this knowledge base is significant in itself. However, more significant and relevant to the developing character of advanced industrial rural communities is the fact that this information system in California is essential to keep large numbers of skilled and educated persons residents of nonmetropolitan areas. These people in turn are resources for the community because of the economic impact they have and because of their social input in defining community goals and programs. The researchers and their staff are highly articulate and trained persons. They have technical skills which are useful to the community, both for getting things done and for making decisions about physical and technological systems. They pressure schools for better programs and want their children to be as well schooled as their suburban counterparts. Finally, they become involved in the planning and development of the community in disproportionate number—whether in official capacity or through participation in voluntary organizations and interest groups. In short, the rural researcher is a cosmopolitan influence in areas long dominated by traditional influence.

THE USE OF INSTITUTIONAL CAPACITY FOR CHANGE

With its unrelenting demand for knowledge resources in rural as well as urban areas, the advanced industrial society has educational institutions playing a significantly larger role in the process of change. A number of case studies in California's rural areas illustrate how this takes place and may permit us to generalize about the role of educational institutions as capacity builders for community development.

Institutional Capacity

The challenge of growth in the advanced industrial society requires interactive processes between emerging educational institutions and economic, governmental, and service organizations. These processes operate in both rural and urban areas but are, perhaps, more evident in the rural where they are not as obscured by the complexity of metropolitan life. At the core of advanced industrial development is the realization that individuals alone do not effect change. They must work through organizations linked to other organizations in institutionalized patterns. The capacity of these institutions to contribute to the development of rural areas lies both in the resources they have to offer and the accessibility of these resources. Increasingly educational institutions in advanced industrial rural areas have the resources and the access needed to stimulate community development.

This new capacity, brought by the educational system to rural areas, goes beyond the function of scholarship; it provides a vehicle to link local government, private nonprofit organizations, and health and welfare institutions to state and federal resources. Whereas large cities have municipal departments to seek the benefits of external resources, small cities have too few employees with too few skills to do this. In particular, higher educational institutions provide a vehicle to conduct studies, do sophisticated analysis, interact with national and international knowledge resources, and to provide legitimization for efforts to alter traditional community patterns. For example, Blakely and Zone (1976) have shown that a prime perhaps central ingredient in rural northern California communities responding to the Housing and Urban Development new community block-grant program was the technical assistance provided by local colleges.

Four Examples

Rural California has met a number of challenges in economic and social development which depended on the capacity of educational institutions. Four cases will be examined. The first shows the involvement of a state university in combining the creation of a salmon-farming project with improved waste water treatment. The second example shows the links involved in getting a far-reaching, Indian pageant project operating. The third involves use of a community college to facilitate development of a locality's geothermal resources for hydroponic farming. The fourth shows the use of multi-institutional arrangements to achieve community development goals.

Ocean Ranching

The city of Arcata with a population of 12,000 is an old lumber and fishing town on the California coast line 400 miles north of San Francisco. It is the location of Humboldt State University which has a department of natural resources with specialists in biology, and fish and wildlife development. From association with the university, federal funds were obtained to construct an "ocean ranching" project in conjunction with efforts to upgrade the local sewage treatment system. The system uses the purified, nutrient-rich waste water in marshes and holding ponds to produce a food chain to support salmon hatched in tanks. The salmon are raised in the outflow from the treatment plant until they are old enough to migrate to the ocean. Salmon return after several years in the ocean to spawn and then die in the stream where they were born. Upon their return the ocean ranching project catches the adult fish, removes their eggs for future hatches, and harvests the meat. This project has had the stimulation and technical supervision of several university professors who worked with city officials, the Director of Public Works, and fishing industry persons. Without the expertise provided by university faculty, this project, based on "state of the art" technology, could not have been attempted (Klopp, 1978).

From this example we may begin to identify the steps in the process whereby the institutional capacity of educational institutions is addressed to local development. The university became involved in local needs and problems through the Marine Advisory Board. When a specific project was identified, the State University then developed, or tapped, an internal organization to coordinate work on the project. Outside funds were acquired and organizational links with community groups and federal funding were created, permitting a continuing organizational effort.

Indian Theater Project

Arcata is also involved in many other projects through the State University's Center for Community Development. The Center has long been involved in getting projects started that aid local residents and Indians in nearby reservations (Parsons, 1977). Over the last decade the Center has developed an alphabet for the Indian language and written down much of the remaining folklore. This institutional capacity is being used in meeting the challenge of our second example, improving the economic base for the Indians, while at the same time preserving their culture. Due to a number of happenstances a French mime retired near the community, and a playwright "dropped out" to live there for life style reasons. Both were interested in Indian legends. The Center has brought these two together and is proposing that they train Indians as performers, acting out legends in the nearby Redwood National Park's proposed amphitheatre as well as going on tour. While this proposal is still in the design stage, it illustrates how the capacity of an educational institution can be translated into social change by creative community development efforts.

From the start, the State University's Center for Community Development has seen its role as a "change agent." While it assists in projects defined by others, its mission includes "to act as a community catalyst, identifying and bringing together harmonious purposes" and "to foster a comprehensive, well articulated grasp of regional community concerns" (Parsons, 1977: 2). With this guideline, resources in the University are identified and linked to resources in the private sector and government through a community developer at the university. In each of the Center's projects, including the Indian theatre, its staff has worked with community groups to help define areas of mutual interest and programs of action none would have thought of by themselves.

Furthermore, the Center was able to act because of a long-term interest in capacity-building and an established experience dealing with funding agents. Its experience includes dealing with over 15 funding sources, such as the Bureau of Indian Affairs, Department of Labor, and various foundations. Furthermore, the director is known by people in Washington D.C. at the National Park Service and National Endowment for the Humanities. The Center's earlier work in languages and in the schools where the languages are being taught provides another type of base.* In short, the Center represents experience, reputation, and resources for change.

Hydroponic Farming

The third example is from Susanville, a small logging community on the eastern slopes of the Sierra, which has suffered economically since technological efficiencies started reducing employment in the timber industry. Recently interest in geothermal resources led to the coordinated development of a new industry for the area. A private developer proposed a project of growing vegetables in hydroponic solutions, using the geothermal resources of the Susanville area to heat green houses on a year-round basis. However, no workers in Lassen County knew anything about hydroponic farming until community developers in a number of state agencies, in cooperation with the community college in Susanville, helped facilitate this project. A new program in hydroponic farming was started at Lassen Community College even before the greenhouses were completed. Students are taking courses in chemistry, soils, and biology, as well as in hydroponics. The teacher of the hydroponics course is the assistant manager of the greenhouses and has had experience elsewhere in hydroponic farming. Through this collaboration, 120 jobs are being created in a highly sophisticated technology.

At the same time Lassen Community College, Chico State University, and the Davis campus of the University of California have formed a consortium to explore the more general development of the area's geothermal resources for electricity generation. Designs are being developed to use waste sawdust to superheat geothermal steam in a power plant, making better use of each fuel. The waste heat from the power plant would then be used to dry wood chips made from currently wasted wood. The multiple uses of this "cogeneration" plan require sophisticated institutional coordinative capacity for development.

Multi-Institutional Consortia

Perhaps the best example of a rural regional consortium is the Northeastern California Higher Education Council, composed of six community colleges, a state university (Chico), and the University of California at Davis. Joseph Cronin notes that there are several types of consortia, of which the regional is

---

*Interview with Tom Parsons, June 1978.

the most complex. They are also found in Pennsylvania, Illinois, and New York (Cronin, 1975: 112). But, unlike other consortia, the northern California one includes institutions of different kinds and vastly different resources. Housed in Chico, the Council is involved in the development of programs to meet the needs of the sparsely settled mountainous region of northeastern California, an area of 30,298 square miles, about the size of Ohio.

The Northeastern California Higher Educational Council has been a focal point for monitoring legislation by state and federal government that affects the interests of higher education in rural areas. The same attention to rural area interests could not be given by individual colleges, and in this way the Council was able to effectively argue that fund allocation formulas of the Vocational Educational Act of 1976 were strongly biased against nonmetropolitan areas. This one action led to a revision of the formula and to an increase of allocation of some $204,069 for the area. The Council was also the central contact agency for the development of a rural advisement system being developed by the state legislature (Northeastern California Higher Education Council, 1977: 2, 12). In this role the consortia are analogous to councils of government and other regional intergovernmental organizations.

The second capacity that multi-institutional organizations provide rural colleges is the development of regional programs that could not be done on campus-by-campus basis. This is illustrated most vividly by the Council's efforts to develop programs to improve nursing and health service delivery in the rural areas. A special program of live, interactive television training programs was designed and implemented for 121 rural nurses at six different sites. The cooperation of the various colleges enabled the development of the television network and the creation of special modules for specialized training. Funding was obtained from several different sources for this collaborative effort. Additional activities of the coordinated programs include the development of a regional health data bank, the establishment of rural health fairs in small towns, and the organization of community advisory task forces.

Furthermore, the Council provided the potential for rural areas to respond to a new state-mandated program, originally designed for urban areas, of regional coordinating councils for vocational education programs. It furnished the rural areas with staff assistance—men and women who had experience working in the rural counties—that could not have been obtained elsewhere. In this way the Council's capacity was tapped as an existing resource to meet new mandates for regionalization. As it responds to more such efforts, its area of expertise grows, and in turn can contribute increasing resources and capacity to adjust to new challenges.

The third function provided by the Council is to help articulate the needs of students in rural areas and to develop programs within the individual colleges that better serve local needs. The Council serves as an information conduit for program interests of the state and federal government and, in so doing, calls attention to local problems and offers special programs which can only be done with council sponsorship. For example, the Council has become interested in the problems of economic development in the rural communities in the northeastern part of the state. Faced with a region of high unemployment but un-tapped capacity, the Council assisted one community college in getting a grant from the California Council for the Humanities and Public Policy to present a conference on economic development and job creation, and the humanistic im-plications of it. In many ways these efforts legitimize a new role of the colleges in economic development. As a result of these and other projects to define the job creation mission of the community colleges, the colleges in a whole region have changed from being passive responders to economic stagnation to being active advocates of new knowledge-intensive development responding to com-munity goals.

In spite of this promise, multi-institutional consortia lead a fragile exist-ence. Proposition 13 has cut much of the discretionary funding that many in-stitutions were using to sustain the Council, and only time will tell the degree to which this consortia will suffer because of funding limits. Moreover, it is a volun-tary collaboration, and internal politics may endanger the ability of the organiza-tion to survive.

Educational Resources as Capacity for Change

From these examples we may identify a number of resources provided by educational institutions in advanced industrial rural areas, that build local capacity.

Technical expertise. Many of the development projects in the advanced in-dustrial society require skills not widely available but found in research facilities, colleges, or universities. In the Arcata Center for Community Development, for example, these skills are both scientific and humanistic.

Legitimacy. One of the most important roles the colleges play is protect-ing and encouraging early dialogue and legitimizing the endeavors of unknown community groups and ideas. Many such "state-of-the-art" projects were able to survive with the assistance of faculty who believed in their potential. Further-more, the collaboration of university and college personnel helped gain funding and other related assistance.

Community education and training. In each program workers for the de-veloping industries were trained in new skills, ranging from proposal writing to highly technical and scientific information to run the new project. This builds local leadership capacity through the institution.

Cultural Climate. The presence of a college in many areas is a force for change in itself. Through community programs and assistance to groups repre-senting various special interests (such as seniors or consumers), the college serves as a catalyst by recognizing needs and translating them into concrete programs. Furthermore, there is a momentum of change created by intellectual inquiry of faculty and students, and this diffuses from college to community, as college personnel become involved in the primary schools, in city and county politics, and in social programs. This college brings in ideas that go beyond local boundaries, and college personnel get involved in professional networks. As Lauderdale and Peterson (1971: 5) state, knowledge is a resource beyond a fact or formula: its impact is from "a whole system or culture of trained persons, supportive institutions, and a special corps of managers."

Our examples also allow identification of some of the steps involved in the process whereby the capacity of educational institutions is addressed to local development.

1. Identification of relevant participants. In each case the first step is that individuals and/or organizations become aware of each other in order to solve some general type of problem. The simple fact that a college is in Eureka does not lead to an "ocean ranching" proposal. Rural colleges in many northeastern states have not engaged in development activities because there has been no outreach. On the other hand, agricultural extension everywhere provides a means to identify an entry point to institutions for agricultural development.

2. Increasingly specific definition of a plan of action. The second step in each case involved making a general assessment of a need to be met by a collaborative project and a strategy for meeting that need. The fish farming proposal was experimental whereas other projects are based on proven technologies. At this point proposals can come from three places: from the university or college in its role as a "change agent;" from private or governmental groups; or from a collaboration between university and other units.

3. Tapping wider institutional capacity. In the case of the ocean ranching proposal and the hydroponics training program, new internal organizational capacity had to be developed, whereas the Indian Theatre projects tapped available organizational facilities.

4. Community input. Wider participation from involved organizations is stimulated, and in many instances advisory groups are established.

5. Enhancing of funding and other resources. This step involves a joint effort to link local projects with resources and activities going on at the regional, state, and national levels. Funding is frequently the impetus for expanding collaborative networks, though almost any resource may lead to distant contacts.

6. Ongoing structures. The final step is the establishment of an ongoing collaborative organization for a project. Perhaps equally important, this ongoing structure becomes a resource, like the Center for Community Development, for assisting future developments. Thus institutional capacity is further expanded.

The process described above is simply a variant of the community development process given by Daniel Schler (1970) and others. Schler described four general stages: organization of resources for development; engagement (linking) of the resource organization with a community change unit; activation of the system to define the problem and implement a plan to achieve goals; and the establishment of a permanent ongoing social change oriented program. Our analysis suggests that this process is not likely to differ greatly from simple to complex social situations. Instead, as the development challenge becomes greater, more emphasis will be on creating specialized organizations to provide technical skills, on designing flexible organizational structure, and on providing wide ranging linkages. In our analysis, organizational capacity grows throughout the project and provides potential for continuing resource capacity.

SUMMARY AND CONCLUSIONS

The role of educational institutions has undergone significant transformation in the rural advanced industrial society. Where education as a good or commodity in rural areas was deficient or totally absent several decades ago, it is now available in nearly every form. Clearly, increasing the general educational level, as we have seen, improves the options and opportunities of rural people both individually and collectively. The presence of highly skilled human resources in rural areas provides new opportunities for rural communities to stabilize and increase their population base; although it may sometimes lead to more growth than the local area might want. At the same time the institutions themselves are becoming major catalysts for socioeconomic change. At the elementary and secondary school level, community school programs funded by the Mott Foundation or by state and federal grants intervene in local community economic development. Similarly, the network of community colleges, state colleges, universities, and Cooperative Extension resources improves the capacity of local governments to engage in economic and social problem-solving. Three conclusions can be drawn regarding the impact of increased educational and related knowledge resources in rural areas in relation to community development practice.

Ignorance, Poverty, and Education

While a correlation between lack of formal training and poverty remains in rural settings, ignorance resulting from inferior or nonexistent education is a diminishing problem. However, more access channels for a large number of the poor are needed. The role of the community developer in this context is to alter the access systems to make them more available and useful to the poor, the disadvantaged, and the under-represented. This is done through programs such as Indian culture, migrant children summer camps, etc. The community developer's educational mission in the advanced industrial society is not to create educational resources but to orient these resources to particular group needs.

Building Information Resources

There is little question that the lack of fundamental knowledge regarding agricultural productivity, industrial technology, community resource development, and governmental programs have traditionally impeded rural economic growth. This problem has been and continues to be addressed through the provision of technical assistance from cooperative extension and other educational services. However, in response to increasing criticism that these services are targeted for traditional clientele and miss those groups who have long been excluded from rural educational programs, improved information services are being directed to the needs of the Mexican Americans, new small farmers, rural back-to-the-land groups, dropouts, recent retirees, and others. As these groups become more organized, their demands for information will rise.

In addition to the need for better individual knowledge and information resources, new mechanisms are required for communities. Community development specialists in California and throughout the nation are attempting to bring more up-to-date information on economics, demographics, and community attitudes to rural communities. Recent experiments with university-developed information systems for community developers in California and elsewhere have met with considerable early success. The community developer now combines useful data on federal grants, foundation funds, and state regulations with actual data on the community he is helping.

Institutional Capacity and Linkage

The education system is the core of the entire rural human service network. The earlier rationale for using the schools was simply to reach the parents *via* the children. Today, in spite of tax cuts, the schools remain the most stable and largest local bureaucracy. Community developers, working both within the schools and in other organizations, are enhancing the capabilities of the schools and higher education institutions to act as brokers for social change. Schools may be used in combination with health, welfare, transportation, and regional coordinating bodies as a resource for developing a community's economic and social future. Developers are no longer the sole community experts but operate within a system of expertise in which they are often the principal link.

4

Rural Government
in an Interdependent Society

SOCIAL INTERDEPENDENCE

One of the most important characteristics distinguishing an advanced industrial society from a traditional one is the extent of social interdependence, that is, the increasing degree to which actions in the society impinge on other actions. The networks of influence link isolated rural and urban areas through social institutions and businesses; communications and transportation link communities which previously could ignore each other; and local government agencies establish new means of regulating and controlling businesses and citizens at the same time that they are being regulated and controlled by even larger units of government. Rural communities are no longer isolated; their policies and actions influence other communities and vice-versa. In an interdependent society government has the added task of trying to manage these new relations. Consequently rural communities in the advanced industrial society now face the challenge of trying to increase their capacity to manage these new interdependencies.

In traditional society local rural governments for the most part dealt with easily managed and thoroughly local issues. Sokolow (1968) tells of a typical autonomous and amateur government in a small rural town for which one meeting's action included adjusting the price of cemetery lots, purchasing parts for the township power mower, fixing the pump on the cemetery well, replacing wooden voting booths, and having a stopped-up toilet fixed. He goes on to report that the meeting was adjourned and reconvened on the cemetery grounds so the board members could see what parts the mower and pump needed. In the proceedings more than discussion was involved; individual board members volunteered to repair the mower and the well (44).

It is against the framework of government requiring few specialized skills that the meetings of a local government in the advanced industrial society might be juxtaposed. A typical meeting of such a government might now include debate on the level of cooperation to be given to the regional council of governments in preparing a general plan for the coming years, its opportunity to get a block grant for economic development, and an evaluation of a report about the technical problems involved in the community sewer system's failure to meet federal environmental standards. Board members often do not have the skills to handle these issues individually but seek the advice and cooperation of professionals through their staff or private consultants. As one small town manager put the issue (Davis, 1976: 1):

> City management and city business has become more and more complex in recent years. The role of city government has changed in the last decade. No longer is a city or city manager concerned only with the physical improvements in the city. We now must address the social and people needs of the cities. We can't just pave the streets—we must also concern ourselves with those who use the streets.
>
> The increasing demands placed upon local governments by federal and state agencies further complicate the problem. Air and water quality regulations, insurance problems, environmental impact reports, coastal zone legislation, employee relations, mandated general plan elements, O.S.H.A. regulations and federal grant programs are a few examples of the problems that complicate the local government process.
>
> These problems are particularly difficult for small cities. Many of these small cities lack professional staff and do not have the financial resources to employ such staff. They must rely on part-time private consultants to fulfill this need. Often they cannot take advantage or lack the staff capability to prepare the necessary applications.

In this chapter the impact of increasing interdependence in the advanced industrial society will be shown to have altered the character of government of rural areas. Interdependence will be conceptualized in terms of four components that increase together as the network of shared impacts extends. The first involves rural governments increasing relation to larger and larger social units such as state and federal governments. The second involves rural governments in actions that require more steps to get things done and more complex paths of influence. In the third, actions themselves become increasingly complicated, involving coordination and planning rather than simply a transfer of funds or provision of a service. The fourth involves consideration of issues over an increasingly long span of time. Government in the modern society responds to these four components of interdependence by expanding where it can and by doing new things if the community wants or needs them and will pay for them.

This chapter, however, is limited to analysis of the character of the functions performed by government, not to the electoral process that determines how the government is selected or to the social processes that place power in the hands of one class or another. Similarly, we are not concerned here with the patterns of political action in meetings or the personalities of political leaders as they affect the operation of the government or its programs. These topics are interesting and informative, but they do not directly relate to the role rural governments play in meeting the special new challenges of interdependence in an advanced industrial society.

The Concept of Interdependence

Social interdependence means the way two or more people or groups are linked together for the purpose of acquiring or providing something that is needed by the others. The concept of interdependence has been inadequately elaborated in the social science literature; although it is acknowledged to be linked to concepts of complexity, it has remained poorly developed (LaPorte, 1975: 7).

Recent research by Bradshaw on the changing functions of California state government has pointed to four changes in the interdependencies to which government must respond. Interdependence is defined by Bradshaw (1978: 4) as follows:

> Interdependence is found whenever a network of two or more social units are connected by dependencies for resources or performances of any sort. The intensity of the interdependency network increases when dependencies involve larger social units linked through more complex patterns involving more extensive coordination with greater perceived long run consequences.

All the intricacies of the concept of interdependence need not be detailed here. The attributes of the concept are useful for an analysis of rural government by focusing attention on these questions about the character of the interdependence relationship: Who are involved (individuals, governments, organizations, etc.)? How are they linked (directly, indirectly)? What do they need from each other (things, coordination)? How long is the relationship important (now, forever)?

Interdependence and Society

Many writers have noted that increasing interdependence leads to a number of problems for government. James Thompson, for example, noted that "civilization seems inescapably to bring with it the expansion of interdependencies" which themselves become the source of problems for the organization of effective government (1967: 156; 1974). Similarly, Stanley Scott (1978) reported that a sample of community leaders favored the growth of regional governments because the regions, counties, and sub-areas were perceived to be highly interdependent with each other and becoming increasingly so. The impact of interdependence on large governments is particularly salient (Elgin et al., 1974: 93):

> Large systems are generally interdependent which, in turn, implies the need for a broad focus of regulation and control. Interdependent systems are generally more vulnerable and this reinforces the need for more effective regulation and control. . . . [They] are also increasingly rigid since no part can be changed without affecting the other components of the system.

Finally, Rufus Miles (1976) claims that "there are limits to the human capacity to design and manage, by the political process, huge, complex, interdependent human and ecological systems" (170) and that "the complexity of human interdependence has reached the point within the United States where system break-downs occur as fast or faster than any combination of problem solvers can overcome them" (182). Surely one of the most essential characteristics of the advanced industrial society, as we have described it, is the growing interdependence which creates new problems government must face.

Rural areas have been slow to acknowledge that interdependence is a problem, though the classic study, *Small Town in Mass Society*, showed how the linkages of rural communities with the outside society brought new pressures and demands on the local area that were not present in a traditional society (Vidich and Bensman, 1958). Yet, even the external pressures of a mid-century rural community in upper New York state were small scale in comparison to the pressures faced today by rural areas in California and other advanced industrial states.

Table 4.1 shows some of these relationships. In the first column the components of the concept of interdependence are shown with a number of steps indicating increasing levels of dependency for that kind of relationship. In the other columns it is shown how government has responded to interdependence during development, with traditional society characterized by low, and the advanced industrial society by high, interdependence. We have not attempted to specify the conditions of society which characterize a low or high level of interdependence but have looked at the way government has viewed the actions needed to solve a problem. When a government creates a program some "worthy" group usually needs something (that is, a dependency), and the government has the responsibility and capacity to try to provide resources, regulation, or coordination so it can get what it needs. In the case of many traditional government programs the dependencies are clearly seen: individuals need streets, schools, and police and fire protection, which are provided by the community in the interest of the collective good. However, with problems of growth management, resource preservation, social change, and federal programs, the character of interdependence demands major new types of governmental response.

TABLE 4.1

Changes in Rural Government with Increasing Interdependence

Component of Interdependence	Traditional Society	Industrial Society	Advanced Industrial Society
Scale of Group Involvement 1. Individuals 2. Groups 3. Community 4. Region 5. State, Nation	Local citizens more or less isolated from external forces	Formally organized government with roles divided among state, county, and local, but considerable autonomy by each. Media link local community to mass society	Increasing impact on local government by state and federal, with special districts and regional organizations playing new roles. Multinational corporations link rural areas to world wide influences
Pattern of linkages 1. Pooled 2. Indirect-sequential 3. Indirect-matrix	Direct from government to citizens	Federal and state programs operated through counties and cities	Complex patterns of indirect linkages between multiple organizations
Major activity 1. Transfer 2. Regulation 3. Coordination, Planning	Service delivery	Regulation and setting broad policy goals	Coordination and planning
Time span 1. Short 2. Generational 3. Long-term (nearly irreversible)	Short-term needs and problems	Some problems demanding governmental attention perceived to require attention up to a generation in the future	Long-term concern with the perceived growth patterns and physical consequences of development that may be nearly irreversible

Source: Compiled by the authors.

Specifically, four types of interdependence-changes affecting rural advanced industrial government are discussed in detail (see Table 4.1). First, the problems of government involve larger scale groups such as regional, state, and federal governments, and even multinational corporations. Second, the solution of problems involves complicated, long-linked efforts to work with other organizations and, thus, requires that most things must be done indirectly. Third, the major activity of government increasingly is not the delivery of money, goods, or personal services such as welfare or fire protection, but the coordination of regional human services efforts or multicounty mutual aid fire districts. Fourth, the increasing concern for developments with a long-time impact is only briefly mentioned. These components of interdependence are separate but correlated aspects of the growth of linkages among social units. As interdependence increases new levels of connectiveness and activity are reached, but the lower levels remain. In this sense the concept builds "Guttman-like" scales for each component.

SCALE OF GOVERNMENTAL INVOLVEMENT: FROM AUTONOMY TO FEDERALLY MANDATED REGIONALISM

The first type of interdependence that local governments in the advanced industrial society have to deal with is their involvement with an increasing scale of units in the organizational environment. They are no longer autonomous but linked closely in regional, state, and federal programs.

Vidich and Bensman (1958) portray the response of a small town to the discovery that it is actually part of the larger social environment. The experience recorded there has taken place all across rural America—few rural communities remain isolated from mass society today. At the same time there have been changes. The traditional small town experience was one of change brought about through media and trade; the advanced industrial society, however, engulfs rural towns through large-scale governmental policy, social service and postsecondary education institutions, and technology. The local government is required to take on increased responsibility as part of broad societal mandates in fields it never considered before, such as economics, health, recreation and culture, and the overall quality of life. These responsibilities represent more than mere lip service to some national goal; they create a significant change in the character of the governing process in rural advanced industrial communities. For example, the Rural Development Act of 1972 set national government policy for the improvement of the social and economic conditions in rural areas and the provision of viable rural alternatives for those anticipating migration to the cities. Just as the act was passed, however, the rural-to-urban migratory flow reversed, and rural areas stopped losing population. Nonetheless, the lagging social and economic conditions of rural areas had been brought to attention, and strong pressures remained to try to do something for the rural areas.

A number of levels of organization are interdependent with local government. These start with the simplest grouping, a few individuals, and expand to a national and international scale:

1. Individuals in a neighborhood or community;
2. Particular organizations such as business, schools, special districts, special interest groups;
3. Community government, which provides services for or administers services in category 2 above;
4. County governments, and regional governments and business organizations; and
5. State and Federal agencies, programs, and businesses which cut across a variety of regional interests.

Rural governments have long been involved in programs which serve individuals and organizations but were only weakly linked to the larger scale of governmental organization. Roland Warren (1963), in describing the "Great Change" in American communities, emphasizes increasing systemic relationships of small communities to the larger society. He suggests that, as communities have become more differentiated internally, their differentiated parts have come to be more interlinked with state and national systems. Organizations such as churches, labor unions, gas stations, PTA organizations, and state welfare offices all have strong ties outside the community. "Viewed this way," Warren suggests, "the trend is toward a community which is less and less a locally-oriented and co-ordinated aggregation of functional units, more and more a sort of way-station for the location of various branches of national organizations" (1963: 63). In the advanced industrial society the numbers of extra-community ties are so large that they are the source of new problems with which local governments must deal. Regional organizations and state and federal governments are two types of larger-scale organization rural with which advanced industrial communities must be involved.

Regionalism

Developments in communications and improvements of roads and cars have linked rural communities to each other in ways not encountered even a decade ago. With people no longer hesitant to drive from their rural community to another in order to shop or do other business, the location of facilities becomes an important issue for rural areas. In many towns the placement of a shopping center is the source of considerable conflict because of employment and tax implications for all the surrounding communities. A similar type of impact comes from the development of recreational facilities such as ski areas or vacation resorts, since a new resort has an effect on communities along the way and in the general area. Government also has regional impact, for example, fire protection in many rural communities is based on volunteer districts, but the communities now share in the cost of professional administrators in order to coordinate and train the local volunteer forces. In this and many other ways we see the increased pressure for regionalism in rural areas.

The disparity of revenue collections for the various units of government involved in such regional ventures is due to a revenue policy that originated in the last century when a person used to live, work, attend school, shop, and seek recreation all in the same community. Thus taxes, generated from a locality's businesses and property, would pay for the services the local residents needed. Today, as people tend to do those things in different towns (and this is increasingly true for rural areas), the tax structure no longer makes sense. Towns with factories or shopping centers have ample revenue while others, having nothing but residential property, shoulder the bulk of expenses (California Office of Planning and Research, 1976b: 86). Various attempts have been made to deal with this, including interjurisdictional revenue-sharing formulas built into regional plans; but, more often than not, competition between communities for development results with ultimate harm to both parties.

Another pressure toward regionalism is the move to consolidate and centralize the provision of governmental services. The closing of rural school districts is the best example of the process of centralization that has affected nearly all rural areas (Sher, 1977). Welfare and other offices have been consolidated for purposes of greater administrative efficiency. The same process has extended to the courts, with many counties closing their court system entirely. In California this has been mitigated by the use of traveling judges who "ride circuit" (Stott, Fetter, and Crites, 1977: 15).

In many rural areas there has been a significant trend toward the use of more consolidated special districts. As Hogan (1978) points out, there has been a significant increase in the number of special districts in rural California. The greatest has been in the new "community service districts" and "community service areas," which are set up to provide one service but many provide others at a later time if needed. The increase in these districts from 1970 to 1977 is remarkable—counties in the mountain areas of northern and eastern California registered a 120 percent rise in community service districts and a 87.5 percent increase in community service areas. At the same time population rose by only 29.3 percent. Although it is not clear what impact the tax-cutting of Proposition 13 will have on funding special districts, there is every indication that special districts will consolidate to provide better services with greatly limited tax-generating ability.

One of the most significant developments in regional government is the large number of Councils of Government (COGs) that have developed. Although they were originally designed to facilitate cooperation among urban counties (the San Francisco Bay Area, the Los Angeles Basin), they have been important in rural areas in the 15 years since they were first used in California. One of the most important is the Sacramento Regional Area Planning Commission (SRAPC), which includes the counties of Sacramento and five surrounding rural counties which are significantly affected by its influence. The association of Monterey Bay Area governments includes three counties and parts of two others, most of which is rural. Other counties in rural California have established formal regional organizations including the four-county Sierra Economic Development District. In 1975 California had 20 such Councils of Government, serving primarily rural areas.

Regional organizations come in many forms and serve many explicit functions, but their activities reflect three pressures that stem from regional interdependence. First, they must provide mechanisms for combined growth management and must furnish planning capacity and coordination activities that cut across the boundaries of individual jurisdictions. Second, they serve as a catalyst for the economic development of communities. An individual town does not have the resources to engage in meaningful economic development activities; but, in cooperation with others in the region, a sensible plan may be enacted. Third, the regional organizations provide a structure for the implementation of many mandated social services which individual communities or counties could not provide on their own. For example, programs for the aging population are in many ways a luxury for remote counties, but programs may be developed through a regional organization. Many regional agencies include a large urban center and surrounding rural communities, reflecting the substantial scale of many California counties (Fujimoto and Symonds, 1971: 5). Programs developed by regional agencies for the urban areas in such organizations sometimes have productive spillovers for rural communities.

Regional governments, however, have a precarious existence in both rural and urban areas because they lack broad-based grass roots support. Small towns fear that regional government will take too much power from them; thus they oppose the emphasis on regionalism in such programs as the Community Development Act of 1974 (Blakely and Zone, 1974). Others are dubious of the ability of the regional government to deal successfully with the mix of programs and problems it is supposed to coordinate (Fujimoto and Symonds, 1971). Too often, rural areas report feeling neglected if they are in a regional government with a large city, as Blakely and Zone noted (1974: 30), in regard to two rural counties in the Sacramento Council of Governments. Nonetheless, the COGs have been useful in many rural communities where they have in fact helped solve some multicounty problems.

State and Federal Impacts

While rural government has recognized mutual interests with regional neighbors, the process of working together has usually been mandated by state and federal programs. One of the most important changes in rural areas of California and other advanced industrial states is the expanding role of state government in setting standards and developing programs that are either mandated for local counties or are optional for which funds or leadership are available. Clear evidence of the extent of state and local involvement is provided by Jones, Magleby and Scott (1975) who analyzed the 1975–76 California Budget and identified 386 references to 40 different types of state-local relationships. The most common were advice and assistance, technical services, coordination, collection and distribution of information, field inspection, and research on local problems, each of which had 20 or more budget references (79–81). Many of these aspects of state-local process carry no distinction between rural and urban areas.

Since statehood, California government created 672 agencies, boards, or commissions to carry out the programs of the government (Capell, 1977). Many of these are advisory committees, like the California State Fair Advisory Commission; others implement programs with great social and economic implications for rural areas. The new agencies responding to recent problems are, increasingly, involved in relations between the state and large organizations rather than unorganized individuals. For example, the California Agricultural Labor Relations Board is charged with the task of facilitating collective bargaining agreements between the state's farm workers and growers. This governmental agency is part of state government with its actions particularly relevant to rural communities and community developers, and it may intervene if local labor conditions warrant it. Yet its actions frequently mediate among groups which are state-wide or national in scale, such as unions, multinational corporations, and producers organizations. For the most part, its primary business does not involve individuals receiving a service from their state government; in this way it is unlike older governmental agencies, such as police and schools, that traditionally have dealt with individuals.

More and more social services such as education are controlled by the state with increasingly large amounts of state and federal funding coming through the state's department of education. Whenever there is state money, the influence of the state is felt, and this extends to rural areas as well. One of the most pervasive requirements by the state is that regional planning be undertaken before the allocation of social service funds. Many communities and rural counties complain that this has caused an enormous burden on them: they do not have the resources to complete a plan in the way that more urban counties can. Nonetheless, the feeling is that these planning requirements are statewide in impact and must be followed by rural counties as well as urban (Waldhorn and Blakely, 1976).

There have been a number of rural areas involved in multistate relations. In California, these have for the most part centered around problems of water, one of the state's most persistent problems. Compacts have been made to divide water among the states of Oregon, Nevada, Arizona, and other states in the Colorado River Drainage. Lake Tahoe has seen interstate efforts to control resort growth, efforts involving the Federal Council on Environmental Quality.

New energy policies will increasingly involve states in decisions having significance for the rural areas. Thus, broad interstate dependencies are creating pressures for governmental involvement in rural areas. The needs of other areas have
long affected rural areas in technology, transportation, and resources. Today
these impacts are increasing and are perceived as problems for rural governments.

Federal funding has become increasingly important to the development of
communities in the United States. Since at least the mid-1960s, however, there
has been increasing concern that federal funds are being distributed ineffectively
and with too many conditions attached. Sneed points out (1975) that categorical grants-in-aid increased from $7.1 billion in 1960 to $29.8 billion in 1972.
The number of programs offering this funding increased from 100 in 1960 to
500 in 1972, making it very difficult for local communities to get funding for
their priorities of projects. Furthermore, Sneed reports that "the increasing
complexity of the funding system has required local public agencies to have
many different planning, budgeting, and accounting systems, requiring additional staff capacity and resulting in significant time lags in program implementation" (1-2). In response to these and other problems the federal Block Grant
program was developed to facilitate the funding of local projects. While this has
improved matters the federal presence remains in local communities, and small
rural communities are not much better able to get adequate federal funding even
with the help of professional community developers as staff or consultants.

Even when federal funding is available, small rural communities are often
unable to take advantage of it. For example, tiny Port Costa has been involved in
a dispute with the federal government over its sewage treatment system that
currently dumps a small amount of inadequately treated sewage from its 250
residents into San Francisco Bay. The government will pay virtually all the cost
of constructing a new treatment plant, but the operation of the plant will cost
individual householders about $300 more per year than they are currently pay-
ing, an increase of more than four times in their bill for sewage services (Tracy,
1977). Thus, they are resisting a federal program that was not designed to help
small communities but set a universal mandate based on the understanding of
the problems and capabilities of large metropolitan communities.

The increasing interdependence of the advanced industrial rural society
clearly leads to new problems for local governments. There is a significant difference between fixing the community lawn mower or pump and settling with
the federal government over a half-million dollar sewage treatment plant. But the
complication is more than who is involved; it is also the complex interconnec-
tions of the involvement, a theme we turn to next.

NEW PATTERNS LINKING RURAL AREAS

As the society gets more complex, the patterns of relations between agencies become more intricate, and these patterns form the second component of
interdependence affecting rural areas. James Thompson, in one of the most

useful analyses of interdependence (1967), described it in terms of three increasing levels of connectedness. In the first, *pooled* interdependence, an individual unit relates in the same way to a number of others in the exchange of things each needs. In the second, *sequential* interdependence, the relations involve a middleman who mediates relations between units. The third, *reciprocal* interdependence, is the most complex and involves multiple relations among sequences of units with feedback and adjustment. Rural government could be informal in previous eras (Rohrer and Douglas, 1969), but today it is increasingly bureaucratic and formal, involving local government increasingly as middleman in a large maneuver designed by someone else. As Luther Tweeten argues (1974: 78), programs of development in modern society should be seen "as a part of a comprehensive system with interaction and linkages," rather than as isolated direct actions. Local governments and community developers in advanced industrial society get things done by mobilizing others, including businesses, schools, and the federal government. They do this by getting together on a regional basis with neighboring communities.

A set of diagrams (Figure 4.1) shows how the three patterns of interdependence work in the context of local government. In the *pooled* type of interdependence the government provides a service to a group of persons who are

FIGURE 4.1

Diagrams of Three Patterns of Interdependence

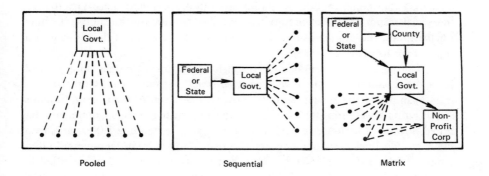

| Pooled | Sequential | Matrix |

Source: Constructed by the authors.

treated roughly the same, as in schools, public protection, or welfare. In the second, *sequential* interdependence, the service is provided to one unit who then provides it to another, as in federal programs for communities to help poor individuals. Community development programs, which support groups in order to help individuals, are also sequential in nature. The most complex pattern is the third, which we call "matrix," and is composed of alternative sequences and multiple linkages. Whereas sequential interdependence involves several links, each outcome has only one path; matrix interdependence is found when outcomes have multiple, overlapping, and interconnected paths.

The interdependence of rural governments in the advanced industrial society, with linkages to larger social units, involves more matrix-type patterns of action. The bulk of new problems for rural government involves either matrix linkages, imposed from outside the local community, or the creation of matrix linkages in community-based organizations. Even within existing programs of small governments in rural areas, the pooled patterns of getting things done are being changed to sequential or matrix.

An example of the operation of matrix interdependence and its impact on rural government is the creation of the California Coastal Commission. Enacted by voters through a state ballot initiative in 1972, the State Coastal Commission and six regional commissions were designed to plan for and regulate development along the 1,000 miles of California's Pacific border. While there are many precedent-setting characteristics of this new form of regional government, our concern here is limited to examining the pattern of relations through which it operates in rural areas.

The problem of controlling the development of the coast can only be solved by indirect means. Local jurisdictions along the coast are not willing to give up control over zoning and development within their own area, even though admitting that compromises among localities in the region are necessary to meet the social responsibility of preserving a unique resource for the state as a whole. Furthermore, the political success of the Commission requires that it gain local support for its activities.

The need to work indirectly through other organizational units necessitates the creation of *sequential* interdependence patterns. The permit process is an example of the sequential nature of the operation of the Coastal Commission. During an interim period of plan preparation, the Coastal Commission has broad powers of land-use control in a "permit area" extending 1,000 yards from the high-tide line. Developments which create "any substantial adverse" effect on the environment or ecology of the coast can be prohibited or modified by commission action. Thus, individuals or builders who wish to do any development along the coastal area have to secure their normal permits and then get approval from the regional Coastal Commission. The process requires visiting a number of permit offices, more or less in a sequence, to acquire needed permission to begin construction. Note that this is different from traditional community zoning where a person only needs to get a zoning permit, which is issued in a *pooled* manner by a zoning board.

The objective of the Coastal Commission, however, is not issuing permits for every construction project along the state's coast, and this is where the matrix structure comes in. The primary effort of the Coastal Commission is to create a "comprehensive . . . enforceable plan for the orderly long-range conservation and management of the coastal zone." The plan is to be based on "detailed studies of all the factors that significantly affect the coastal zone," and in conducting these studies the Commission is required to engage local participation to a significant extent (Scott, 1975: 2-3). The local plans provide an alternative method of regulating growth along the coast by having the Coastal Commission's influence felt through approved general guidelines at the local level that carry *de facto* Commission approval for local projects that meet plan objectives. In order to complete these local plans, the coastal cities and counties must follow "guidelines and policies by the state Commission, subject to review and certification by the state Commission, and with a tight set of deadlines" (2). Since part of the current permit process is for the Commission to evaluate a project in light of local goals, the interaction between these two means of controlling coastal growth is clear.

The impact of the Coastal Commission on local planning has been to involve local government in a complex web of relationships it never had to deal with before. Scott (1978: 5) notes this increase in relationship:

> Previously, local governing bodies had been accustomed to dealing with their own local constituencies. Each local unit planned and zoned to meet the interests and concerns of those who could effectively make their influence and preferences felt in the local halls of government.

The coastal planning effort, of course, made these local plans part of a complex pattern of submission, approval, and integration with other agencies. As Lenard Grote (1978: 2) observed, "Until the coastal law came into effect, state government had never established regulatory agencies or other machinery to monitor the contents of local general plans." Now they must be delivered to federal agencies in the region for comments and review, then submitted to the Secretary of Commerce for approval. In turn, a significant amount of federal money is provided for the completion of the plans: The federal government pays 80 percent of the costs with the state matching the remaining 20 percent share (Scott, 1978: 2). With this money goes another path of accountability.

Coastal planning has responded to the increasingly frequent involvement of the Sierra Club, the Friends of the Earth, the Natural Resources Defense Council, and other environmental and adversary groups. The role of these groups has been institutionalized by the appeals process. If a commercial developer is awarded a permit by a local city or county, it is still possible for an interested party to challenge that permit before regional and state coastal commissions who hear appeals on permits made at lower levels. This is yet another path to the control of growth in rural communities.

The California Coastal Commission is only one example of many similar complex interdependencies affecting rural areas. Energy planning districts, agricultural land preservation plans, waste management regions, water purification plans, recreation districts, historical regions, and the like all engage in a similar process involving complex organizational linkages. It is likely that many of these complex patterns of interdependence will be simplified over time as certain parts of the effort become less problematic; but the net result is that many individual community members become confused about the role their local government plays. Because of long linked connections, individual influence is not clearly seen and may be lost sight of in the process. Thus, interdependence creates the bureaucratic problem of red tape for the governments of small communities.

The role of the community developer also changes under conditions of increasing interdependence. In each type of interdependence, the community developer is likely to be the person involved in relationships of an increasingly complex pattern. In early community development efforts, the developer worked in a pooled fashion, advising and organizing groups. Today, most community developers think of themselves as interpreters or facilitators in a sequential process of helping the local community gain resources from the federal or state government. In the advanced industrial society, the developer is also a coordinator and evaluator, working between governmental and private organizations.

When the community developer works in government with complex patterns of linkage to other organizations, the critical issue becomes one of helping to create alternative paths that allow the community to get something they cannot get for themselves. The community developer has to become an expert in organizational dynamics having a subject specialization in planning, health, or other policy analysis. The techniques used by the community developer to identify community leadership or power structures must be much more sophisticated than those used by earlier developers because there is not just one power structure, but a network of powerful influences on the community.

PLANNING AND COORDINATION
EFFORTS FROM INTERDEPENDENCE

The third characteristic of interdependence is a change in things for which people depend on government. The government in advanced industrial society, dealing as it does with larger social units and involved in complex patterns of action, engages in activities of planning and coordinating, instead of straightforward delivery of some valued object or service. Communities have always provided services and collected taxes, simple transfers of resources from the government to individuals and vice versa. Furthermore, communities continue to do these activities even when provided with additional money, acquired through complicated grant processes. In rural communities everywhere there are problems of poor roads, decaying public buildings, and the like. Parks may be built and other amenities in the field of social services provided, but the fact remains that these services represent a transfer of resources from the government to the citizens. The importance of these activities cannot be overstated, for they provide the basis for the existence of government—it provides things for people collectively which it does not make sense to obtain individually.

Another type of traditional government activity involves the use of regulation to achieve some governmental purpose. In this case the government tells people what to do, or not to do, for the betterment of all. Zoning and traffic regulations are the most common regulatory acts of small town governments but, instead of working to achieve a desired policy goal through direct action, the regulatory effort works indirectly. In this case the interdependence is greater because it takes a more complicated course to achieve a result.

A third type of government activity, reflecting even greater interdependence, is new for the most part in rural areas. This involves the specification of plans and the development of coordination to get things done. It is clear that this type of function involves local officials in a type of activity different from simply deciding to pave roads. The development of community and county plans in California is largely in response to the observation that a community's development should not be left entirely to chance or uncontrolled forces. Waldhorn and Blakely (1976: 3) suggest that "the complex and increasingly social, fiscal, growth, and conservation problems facing cities and counties of all sizes in the state have increased the need for more effective local planning and decision-making processes." Thus, when the problems are perceived to be so difficult that the imposition of regulations is no longer adequate, the effort goes toward planning which, in effect, provides the context for rationalizing and legitimizing regulations or transfers by governments (Ross, 1955: 135).

Planning in the advanced industrial society is increasingly necessary (see Webber, 1969), though the demands placed on it are often greater than can be met by the techniques available to government or professional planners (Huntington, 1974). Expectations for public policy achievements are often met by failure as LaPorte and Abrams point out (1976: 40-45). In rural areas much planning is hampered by the use of urban models, insensitivity to the small scale of rural areas, too much focus on economics, and reliance on standard solutions instead of innovations (Cohen, 1977). Similarly, many rural plans focus on only one component, that is, land use, with little attention paid to the conditions that might make different land-use options attractive. Thus, effective planning requires an attempt to coordinate among competing interests, leading to a general improvement in the social conditions of all (Webber, 1969: 294-5).

California law mandates all cities and counties to complete a general plan consisting of nine elements. These mandated elements include land use, circulation (transportation), housing, open space, conservation, noise, seismic safety, safety, and scenic highways. As of 1975 the cities and counties varied in their rates of completion of the various elements. Virtually all small cities completed plans for land use, circulation, open space, and conservation elements, while less than two-thirds have met noise, safety and scenic highway requirements (California Office of Planning and Research, 1976a). Among small counties a similar pattern has been followed. It appears that the communities generally chose to focus on general plan elements most interesting, salient, or relevant to them. They argued that the other areas were largely irrelevant and meaningless (Waldhorn and Blakely, 1976: 19-23), even though the low completion rates often reflected inadequate staffs and limited budgets rather than lack of cooperation (California Office of Planning and Research, 1976a: 21).

Along with general plans, however, small communities and counties in California are involved in a larger web of planning activities such as planning under the Federal Housing and Community Development Act of 1974. This Act aimed at joining a number of categorical grant efforts in an integrated effort to meet the multiple needs of communities. In doing this, communities were required to prepare comprehensive development plans to determine local needs, set goals, and devise programs to meet the goals. In addition, program management and evaluation capacity was to be established. The problem with these objectives, however, was described by Blakely and Zone (1976: 26) in a detailed study based on 21 California nonmetropolitan cities:

> Our analyses point in one direction: The largest, best staffed, and frequently the least needy non-metropolitan communities are in the best position to compete for resources under the latest community development grant strategy. The communities with the capacity to attract greater resources are those that already have them. . . . This is not to say that larger cities in metropolitan areas are not in need. It merely suggests that small cities with significant need are not equally attractive public investments.

Thus, in order to carry out the management of rural affairs in an increasingly interdependent world, the old amateur government has to give way to professionals who have the technology and training to provide resources for more complex patterns of government action.

A number of innovations have been tried in rural areas where government is not large enough to provide effective local service. One of the best examples is the use of "circuit-riding" teams whereby planners work for several cities in a region. This experiment was first developed in 1975 for five of California's north coast communities that needed planning and community development assistance. Through the Humboldt County Association of Governments, a planner and assistant planner developed goals and plans for five communities, ranging in size from 300 to 500 persons. A circuit-riding city manager was also employed to assist the cities in administrative services. Initially, these cities received federal funds—U.S. Housing and Urban Development "701" planning grants—and have used CETA and other subsidized employees. As the "701" funds have ended and local revenues have been cut by Proposition 13, the cities have taken up sharing the circuit team's costs on the basis of the proportion of use of services. However, in spite of the difficulties of sustaining the program on their own, the cities continue to use the team for a variety of programs. Perhaps the most significant change in the cities has been that they are now linked to programs and are getting aid they never even applied for in the past. The circuit manager told us in an interview that before he came, program announcements were routinely thrown away. A major achievement of the circuit team was assistance in the completion of the Coastal Commission Plan by the city of Trinidad, the first city plan in the state to be approved by the commission. While proud of this achievement, the local people remain puzzled, as the circuit planner put it, as to "why zoning decisions in Trinidad have become a state concern." Clearly, even rural planning is linked to the development of the state at large.

Growth management is a planning issue motivated primarily by local interest in nonmetropolitan areas. As rural populations increase, many rural areas want restrictions so that their low population density is not altered. A planning survey by the State Office of Planning and Research identified growth management as the second most frequently cited planning issue faced by jurisdictions (California Office of Planning and Research, 1976a: 8). The case of Petaluma in northern California is well known for precedent-setting efforts, sustained in the courts, to restrict community growth by a combination of zoning and building-permit restrictions (Clapp, 1975: 42-50). Many other communities are now implementing similar controls on growth and are doing it through the planning process.

CONCLUSION

This role of government in rural areas has changed due to the increasing interdependence of the advanced industrial society. We have provided a set of concepts about how the role and structure of government has been altered. We have also suggested that the community developer must play a different role. Indeed, to an increasing extent the community developer works within government in a variety of positions, ranging from planner to program facilitator. Furthermore, community developers working in state and federal agencies are increasingly important to the local rural community. In the next two chapters the roles and practices of the community developer will be examined in detail.

5

Poverty and Welfare in Rural Communities

INTRODUCTION

Poverty in rural America has been the subject of much research that has focused on its nature and extent, and its economic, political, and social origins. The accumulating research findings have done little, however, to help rural governments solve the problems faced by the poor. A major attribute of the advanced industrial society is the rise of public responsibility for many aspects of modern life, especially of assuring security and stability for individual citizens through an expansion of governmental welfare programs. While much poverty is concentrated in those communities with the fewest advanced industrial resources, innovative new programs are bringing a measure of well-being to many who have previously been left out. At the same time, these programs are affected by as many of the conditions of interdependence as are the governments of which they are a part.

In this chapter we examine first the problems of poverty in the advanced industrial society. While poverty possesses many of its old characteristics related to class, race, and education, it has taken on new dimensions as resources to alleviate some of the most obvious rural problems have come available. The second part of the chapter will examine the response of welfare and human service agencies to these problems. In that discussion we report on the growing availability and increasing diversity of the new welfare and human service efforts, and we describe the organizational responses to conditions of increased interdependence.

Table 5.1 summarizes the changing conditions of rural poverty and public welfare response. Rural poverty has been a common and pervasive plight for centuries. In traditional society it was largely related to shortages of agricultural production caused by weather, pests, and other "natural" causes. Industrial society created, in factory life, man-made conditions whereby poverty became less

TABLE 5.1

The Changing Public Role in Rural Poverty

	Traditional Society	Industrial Society	Advanced Industrial Society
Conditions	Few resources to handle severe problems of housing, health, food, caused by natural events	New poverty conditions from industrialization, leading to massive migration to cities	Conditions remain due to low income, poor skills, and race; expectation for reduction of problems
Institutions for Welfare Response			
Service Availability	Limited availability; some assistance locally	Institutions for severely distressed	Extensive programs available to large proportion of the needy
Program Diversity	Only most minimal needs	Aid to insane, disabled, aged, and increased aid for economically disadvantaged	Vast array of specialized programs covering diverse groups throughout the life cycle, providing broad human services
Organization	Community-based private	Government and private groups share responsibility, with charities organized into "funds"	Large-scale government "welfare state" responsibility with programs increasingly interdependent; rise of professionals and coordinated service programs

Source: Compiled by the authors.

a condition of one's will or strength than a function of one's place in a social structure. Advanced industrialization—as a stage in the industrialization process—seems to place further responsibility for poverty in the hands of social organization. As Christopher Lasch points out (1972: 37), poverty in the "post-industrial" society is changing. No longer a general and pervasive condition of masses of people, it is found in *pockets* as, for example, in particular rural communities and inner cities.

> Wherever it has penetrated, the industrial system tends to eliminate poverty. In post-industrial society therefore, poverty is the lot of those whom the industrial system has failed to absorb: migrant and seasonal workers, the chronically unemployed, and workers in the shops of petty capitalism. The fact that poverty is increasingly identified with certain racial and ethnic differences contributes to its marginality and isolation.

The response to poverty conditions in the society have changed as well. Severe resource shortages in traditional society have been mitigated by new amounts of public support directed toward the poor. This has been channelled through public institutions along with private charities, and the institutions themselves have become increasingly interdependent.

Through these channels the advanced industrial society has at its disposal a number of resources to counter the problems of poverty in rural areas. It has the affluence, for example, to spend significant sums of money to improve housing, to correct health deficiencies, and to upgrade support systems for young families, the aged, and the disabled. It employs large numbers of persons in service industries. There are, in addition, changes in the overall value systems favoring increased welfare expenditures. Rapid communications and social commentaries provide information that further stimulates public actions and governmental response.

THE PROBLEM OF POVERTY IN RURAL AREAS

Poverty is both an objective condition and a social definition. In rural areas real depressed conditions have existed for a long time; yet only recently have they been defined as a "poverty problem." The most influential effort made to define the problem was by the President's National Commission on Rural Poverty. Their report, *The People Left Behind*, spells out the grim picture (1967: ix-x).

> This report is about a problem which many in the United States do not realize exists. The problem is rural poverty. It affects some 14 million Americans. Rural poverty is so widespread, so acute, as to be a national disgrace, and its consequences have swept into our cities, violently. . . .

The total number of rural poor would be even larger than 14 million had not so many of them moved to the city. . . . Rural poverty knows no geographical boundaries. . . . Hunger, even among children, does exist among rural poor. . . . Disease and premature death are startlingly high among the rural poor. . . . The poor have gone, and now go to poor schools. . . . Most of the rural poor live in atrocious houses. . . . Many of the rural poor live in chronically depressed poverty-stricken rural communities. . . . The community in rural poverty areas has all but disappeared as an effective institution. . . .

For all practical purposes, then, most of the 14 million people in poverty areas are outside our market economy. So far as they are concerned, the dramatic economic growth of the United States might as well never have happened. It has brought them few rewards. They are on the outside looking in, and they need help.

Academic research "discovered" rural poverty before the President's Commission, but even there discussion of rural areas in terms of their lack of social services was only occasional. Benson Landis (1949) noted that rural conditions offer limited opportunities for economic survival and are often overlooked by social legislation. Because of the great need and the limited social effort, Landis (9) comments that social welfare service of rural communities has been called "the last frontier of social work."

Nonmetropolitan areas throughout the nation lag behind the urban and suburban in the provision of the basic amenities that constitute a high quality of living. Many rural regions are beset with substantial pockets of intense poverty— in farm worker camps, unproductive ranches, declining small cities, dilapidated lumber towns, Indian reservations, and communities bypassed by freeways. In many cases the poverty stricken are recent ethnic arrivals, chiefly from Mexico, but also from China, the Philippines, and Vietnam. They join minorities already settled in a community of poverty, forming part of a growing underclass with slim options for economic improvement. These conditions are aggravated by poor health, work-related accidents, and criminal exploitation. The condition of the rural poor, even in an affluent state like California, is dismal, but in California it is exacerbated by its proximity to the overall wealth of the urban and suburban populations.

The Extent of Rural Poverty

Nationally, over a third (38.9 percent) of the nation's poor—that is, families with incomes below the poverty level—live in rural areas, although these areas include only 27.5 percent of the total population. In California, rural areas contain only 12.9 percent of the state's poor; these areas have only 9.2 percent of the state's population. Although it is not surprising to find less rural poverty in California than in the nation as a whole, the proportion of rural poverty comes out roughly about the same, when the state's population is corrected for its urban bias: if California had the same proportion of rural persons as the nation as a whole, rural poverty would be 34.5 percent for the state as compared to 38.9 for the entire U.S. Although the relative distribution is not very different, the actual number of persons below the poverty level differs dramatically. California's rural areas have an overall poverty rate of only 12.7 percent compared to a national rate of 16.4, reflecting the state's greater affluence (see Table 5.2). These figures, however, should not be taken at face value: The state has a higher cost of living, and other factors as well make family income a less than optimal indicator of the poverty level.

TABLE 5.2

Percentage below Poverty Level, Rural and Urban, in California and the United States

	Rural	Urban
California	12.7	8.8
United States	16.4	9.8

Source: U.S. Bureau of the Census, 1970 Census of Population: Table 207 (California Detailed Characteristics); Table 259, (Detailed Characteristics, U.S.).

Another measure of the extent of income deprivation in rural areas is the average per capita income for counties in the state. These data, based on accumulated salaries, personal income, interest, and capital gains are averaged to reflect the overall accumulation of money in each county, not its distribution. Eight of California's counties have incomes below $5,000, and they are all rural. Only ten rural counties have incomes averaging above $6,000, while 15 out of the 20 urban counties go above that level. Thus, in terms of average personal income, most rural counties are below the $6,000 level; most urban counties are above it. The range of income in rural areas is huge—tiny Alpine County being the lowest with an average income of only $3,750, Glenn County the highest, with over $12,000 per capita from its rich farm land.

Inadequate housing and health in nonmetropolitan areas continue to hamper the desire of rural inhabitants for a quality life. Nationally, over 55 percent of all substandard, deficient, overcrowded, and "excessive cost" housing is in nonmetropolitan areas with only a third of the population. There are nearly three times as many rural housing units lacking complete plumbing as urban units. Mobile homes are the only housing option open to many nonurban families. The same conditions found nationwide exist in rural California. In the state's nonmetropolitan areas it is estimated that 17.4 percent of the housing units need rehabilitation and 11.7 need replacement; thus, nearly 30 percent of rural housing is clearly substandard. In contrast, the state's urban areas have just over 10 percent of their housing units in need of rehabilitation or replacement. In rural California mobile-home use from 1970 to 1976 increased by 62.5 percent, while total housing increased by only 17.2 percent (California, Department of Housing and Community Development, 1977).

Health problems continue to be severe in rural counties with limited access to medical care and greater incidence of some health problems. The infant mortality rate is higher in rural areas of California, and especially among minority groups like migrant Mexican farm workers a number of other severe medical and dental problems persist. In both health and housing, the social service programs that aim to reduce the problem are largely operated through traditional systems of limited utility to the poor. But new strategies for providing adequate help to persons in rural areas promise to be more effective.

Poverty and Disadvantaged Groups

One of the characteristics of rural poverty in the advanced industrial society is its concentration in groups largely outside the institutional structure of modern economic development and social services. Minority farm workers constitute one of the largest of such groups in rural California. Lumber towns also have their minority poor, sometimes with many blacks among them. The aged and disabled are other groups in rural areas with significant social and economic needs.

In rural California, and the Southwest in general, rural poor are not black, as in most studies of rural areas, but Mexican or Spanish-American. Blacks constitute less than 2 percent of the population of most rural counties, while census counts show the proportion speaking Spanish at home, or having a Spanish surname, is about 15 percent. San Benito County is the leader with some 45 percent having Spanish-language or Spanish surnames. Other minorities that make up large proportions of the population of some rural communities are the Chinese and other oriental races.

The history of exploitation of the minorities in California is a long and bitter one. Carey McWilliam's classic *Factories in the Field* (1935) presents the outlines of a continuing saga of the state's ethnic farm workers who are hidden from public view, but suffer nonetheless. McWilliams notes that the "exploitation of the farm laborer in California, which is one of the ugliest chapters in the history of American industry, is as old as the system of landownership of which it is a part." Calling it a "strange army in tatters," McWilliams chronicled the plight of the migrants, their housing, and their work. "It is an army that marches from crop to crop. Its equipment is negligible, a few pots and pans, and its quarters unenviable. It is supported by a vast horde of camp followers, mostly pregnant women, diseased children and fleabitten dogs. . . " (8). Along with

Steinbeck in *Grapes of Wrath*, McWilliams gave the plight of California's minorities a sympathetic interpretation, which led to some governmental efforts to correct the situation. But conditions improved little during the next 30 years. Today, the numbers of people involved are smaller. With the end of the "Bracero" program that brought Mexican workers directly to the fields, housing, health, and work conditions improved. Yet, in farm counties, minorities remain the dominant poverty group.

Today it is not known how many minority, ethnic, or "third world" persons are in California, let alone how many of them live in rural areas. Census data are available on nonwhite races, but the number of Mexican-Americans was obtained by counting persons who spoke Spanish or had a Spanish surname, instead of asking about Mexican origin. Furthermore, there is considerable evidence that the census missed many persons in minority communities who either simply did not get counted or who avoided being counted. Most state efforts to update the census have been pegged to the census base, and so they merely repeat earlier errors. Recently, the number of minority Californians emerged as a controversial political issue with the Lt. Governor of the state arguing that minorities constituted over a third of the state's population and were growing at such a rapid rate that by 1990 the minorities would constitute a majority. While we have criticized these projections for the year 1990 elsewhere (Bradshaw and Blakely, 1979), the fact of a growing, and politically important, minority population in California is not to be overlooked. In many rural California communities, minority populations are now in majority, and the number of minority communities will continue to grow.

While many of California's ethnic poor are left unemployed in rural areas through changing farm techniques, a new contingent is coming into the state from Mexico and the orient, perpetuating the marginal existence of many rural farm workers. Perhaps as many as 1,700,000 illegal Mexicans, willing to work for very low wages, are in the state of California today. As has been often pointed out, this number includes a significant proportion of persons who are currently "illegal," but who are in the process of obtaining the necessary papers and should not really be counted as such. Nonetheless, a steady and persistent pressure of ethnic migrants has continued to shape the character of poverty in California. In view of the desperate lives these migrants led in their original towns, it is understandable that they are willing to put up with horrible conditions in California and other border states. While many of them go to urban areas, in disproportionate numbers they seek the heavy and hot farm work which takes them to rural areas, away from the services of the city. They are still seen stooped over fields, living in mini barrios on the back corner of a farm.

Poverty Conditions and Society

Indexes of the need for, and provision of, social services all show that rural areas lag behind the urban areas. A large part of the explanation is the loss of an economic base in many rural communities. Most rural extractive industries have experienced dramatic technological changes which have curtailed much of their economic contribution to rural populations. Further, many of the industries that process raw materials, such as lumber milling, have concentrated their facilities in larger communities. Long periods of limited safety regulations in many resource industries—and traditions of limited social services—have created serious problems for the rural poor. The economic growth associated with the knowledge intensive technologies of the advanced industrial society will probably bypass many of the people who formerly worked in extractive industries, perpetuating a racial underclass and other disadvantaged groups.

The migration of people to rural areas has increased the pressure for some services, especially among the retired, who are attracted to the many rural retirement communities, and the urban "dropouts," who seek meaning in a "return to nature." In some counties there is opposition to these newcomers, and welfare benefits mandated by law are available only after much persistence. Nonetheless, innovative programs are coming into rural areas which offer the potential to cushion the effects of poverty. In spite of rural spatial and psychological isolation, community development activities are increasingly able to bring welfare services to the rural needy.

THE DELIVERY OF RURAL WELFARE SERVICE

The considerable problems of rural communities, related to overall low levels of income and the presence of poor housing and health conditions, are being cared for by an extensive and far-reaching welfare system. The welfare program in rural areas is part of a national effort often called the "Welfare State;" it not only provides assistance for the most poverty stricken but includes a growing number of social services—for example, day care centers, dental programs, legal assistance, and the like. We cannot review all these developments here, but we will show that there have been at least three major changes in the delivery of human services to rural areas. First, the quantity of these services has increased so that they are available to increasing numbers of people. Second, the diversity of the programs has increased so that a much wider scope of services are included. Finally, the services are provided through integrated organizational structures which reflect increasing societal interdependence.

The growth of modern welfare systems (see Table 5.1), stands in marked contrast to the institutional structures in traditional society. The history of social welfare shows clearly that poverty was initially responded to by private charities and individual, neighborly efforts. Industrial society saw the first organized efforts to provide for the less fortunate through public institutions. Trattner (1974: 244-5) reports that the early history of public welfare assistance, still referred to as "poor relief," was the responsibility of the locality and was—to the extent of its availability—restricted to the provision of institutions for the very poor young or very poor old, or for the mentally ill. Private agencies or charities took primary responsibility for providing temporary assistance to families who fell upon hard times, but even this was generally limited.

> Finally, by the end of the decade [1930s] social work was not only an acknowledged obligation of the federal government and every city, village, and hamlet in the nation, but its scope had greatly expanded. It no longer meant providing financial relief to the destitute, or even case work to the emotionally disturbed, but both of these and much more. Social workers were now involved in social insurance schemes, park and recreation programs, agricultural resettlement projects, slum clearance and relocation plans, and numerous other similar activities; in fact, all efforts to make America a better and more secure place in which to live. Social work, in other words, was no longer viewed as an emergency profession, but as an accepted part of the machinery of the state, an important everyday function of a modern urban industrial society.

Community developers have been involved in this evolution and have helped to bring these social services within the larger network of programs, aimed at assisting the poor in rural communities to share in the affluence provided by the society of which they are a part.

Availability of Social Services

The extent to which social services are available in California is truly remarkable. One measure of the pervasiveness of such resources is the number of children receiving Aid to Families with Dependent Children (AFDC). In 1975 nearly a million children in California were receiving some benefits with about 65,500 of them in rural areas. Based on estimates of the number of children in rural and urban areas, the data show that in rural areas one in every seven (14.0 percent) were receiving aid, while in urban areas only a slightly higher proportion (14.9 percent) were receiving aid.* Since 1965 the number of children receiving aid in California has increased three-fold; in the previous decade the number had doubled (California Department of Public Welfare, 1975: Appendix A).

Food stamps provide a major source of aid in rural California as elsewhere. Over 103,000 rural residents of the state received food stamps in 1975—about

---

*Calculated from data in *California Statistical Abstract*, 1976 on the number of children per county receiving AFDC. Ratio based on 1975 U.S. estimate of 30 percent of the state's population are 0–17 years old. (*U.S. Statistical Abstract*, 1976). No better age data for counties are available.

6.6 percent of the population. In contrast, food stamps were issued to 7.2 percent in metropolitan counties, presumably reflecting the greater ease of obtaining assistance in urban centers. Similarly, rural areas lag behind the urban in receipt of general relief benefits. Although overall poverty is greater in rural counties, only 1.3 percent of the population received these benefits, while the rate receiving them in urban areas was more than double (2.8 percent). However, these relative lag rates should not detract from our main theme that increasing numbers participate in the programs that are available.

Money provided to rural poor through the extensive welfare programs exceeds $100 million. In 1975 over $77 million was spent on AFDC programs, and another million went to general relief programs. Food stamp bonuses came into rural California at a rate of over $2.3 million, and Comprehensive Social Services added another $23 million to these annual totals. Counties pay less than a quarter of the total welfare bill for AFDC and general relief, though they have policy control over the latter program only. It is unclear how this funding will be handled in the future, since Proposition 13 tax cuts have reduced county revenues. The state will probably pick up most of the financial burden in the future.

The general availability of social services for the rural poor constitutes a major quantitative change in that it has permitted those who fall on hard times to remain in rural areas rather than leave and seek employment elsewhere. It brings money and some stability to rural communities. It is a statement of hope for some; a political problem for others. Nonetheless, the major impact of the increased availability of services lies in the increasing differentiation and variety of programs offered in rural communities.

Welfare Program Diversity

In the advanced industrial society the definition of welfare need has been broadened to include many more classes of service than the limited food and shelter support of previous welfare systems. Two kinds of differentiation of welfare programs have occurred. In the first place, combined welfare programs have been divided into specialized ones to treat problem areas that were once combined. Special programs, for the disabled, aged, health, and housing, are differentiated from the overall program. At the same time new programs have been developed to provide completely new services to rural residents such as day care centers and prisoner release programs. The growing number of specialized programs together cover virtually every stage in an individual's life from prenatal to death, and they cover in detail nearly every group of persons in the society with special needs.

Public Social Service Programs

Significant amounts of federal funding through Title XX of the Social Security Act have supported increased levels of general social service welfare programs for rural residents. These programs constitute one of the major ways of meeting the wide-reaching needs of the rural poor. Federal law has mandated that all states provide services in response to certain goals, including economic self support, self-sufficiency, protection of children and adults, community/ home-based care, and institutional care. Each state has responsibility for specifying services to meet these goals, and California has mandated 10 in particular programs to be provided in every county.

> Information and referral to public and private resources to help alleviate social and health problems.
> Protective services for children at risk from abuse, neglect, or exploitation.
> Protective services for adults who are unable to protect their own interest.
> Out-of-home care for children, including placement in cases where child's home is not healthy, safe or stable.
> Out-of-home care for adults who cannot safely remain in their own home.
> Child day care services provided so parents or caretakers can work or meet other needs.
> Health information, referral, and transportation.
> Family planning information, coordination, and technical assistance.
> In-home supportive services for disabled, blind, or aged who reside in their own homes.
> Employment planning referral and assistance.

These services are intended to provide a minimal welfare effort that includes a variety of programs designed to meet increasingly specialized needs. Each of the programs is developed locally with great variation in the extent of services available and in the professional and financial resources allocated to it. Some services are provided by a contract with a public or private agency; others are provided by the county.

In addition, thirteen optional programs have been established to furnish a range of other services, including special-care services for children in their own homes, home management and other educational services, employment training, housing and legal referral, and similar programs. The employment training program has gained the greatest acceptance among counties, with some 19 choosing to have it. The least used is one that provides diagnostic services for children residing in a specialized residential care facility. It is available only in Los Angeles. Seventy-seven specialized optional programs are offered by California's urban counties, 43 by rural. Urban counties offer about 24 percent of the possible programs in contrast to the rural, which make available only 10 percent of their options. Yet it is significant for rural California that at least two counties make every program available (except the diagnostic services for children). Thirteen rural counties offer at least one optional program, with the remaining 20 tendering none.

These social service programs offer a major frontal attack on a wide variety of social needs in rural communities. But additional services are also provided by private and public agencies which supplement and, sometimes, overlap state-sponsored efforts. In fact, federal, state, and county agencies all operate special programs to improve the welfare of rural areas. There is no listing of all such programs, although many counties have compiled nearly exhaustive lists.

Rural Health Care

The diversity of rural social services in the advanced industrial society may be illustrated by efforts in rural California to improve the delivery of health care. The major problem has been that the low population density in rural areas cannot support adequate numbers of physicians nor such supports for their work as hospitals and ambulances. To complicate matters, the medical profession has been undergoing a number of changes which are themselves altering the provision of services—for example, increasing specialization, and the development of paraprofessionals. Roemer (1976) notes that "in the rural areas of America, as elsewhere in the world, the supply of physicians and other health workers is much lower than in the city. . . . The increasing specialization of medicine has encouraged the traditional tendency of most physicians to engage in practice in urban centers, where medical facilities and other technical resources are most abundant" (74). To bring improved medical care to rural areas an increasing variety of social services has been developed.

New Group Practices

Doctors and other health-service providers are, increasingly, forming group practices based in clinics or medical centers, while fewer and fewer solo professionals are practicing in rural communities. Group practices provide more attractive working conditions for physicians, who do not like unrelieved responsibility of being on call during off-hours, and they allow each team member to develop a specialized practice as well. However, this trend means that some sparsely settled rural areas are going to be without a town doctor since group practices tend to locate in the more-or-less centralized areas that can afford to support several physicians. Several years ago the little town of Happy Camp engaged in a statewide search for a doctor, receiving statewide publicity. However, the town is now being served by centralized facilities in Eureka, with local clinics for emergencies only.

Service by Paraprofessionals

As part of the team approach, physicians and dentists are being assisted by paraprofessionals, also called the "new health professionals" (Clarke, 1975; Scheffler and Kushman, 1978). These new professionals include nurse practitioners, physician's assistants, and dental assistants and hygenists, all of whom play an important role in the newly organized rural health effort. Scheffler and Kushman (1978) have shown that significantly more physician's assistants are used in rural areas than might be expected, considering rural population figures. One of the most promising ways they have been employed is in clinics, where they see many patients, provide diagnosis and treatment if they can, referring complicated cases to appropriate doctors. A doctor reviews all records during periodic visits two or more times a week to the community and sees those patients needing his or her attention. So far, rural public acceptance of the new health professionals has been good, though their use is complicated by high cost malpractice insurance and other institutional problems.

Ambulance Systems

Ever since doctors stopped making house calls, priority has had to be given to improving systems for getting the ill to a hospital or clinic for proper and, often, emergency care. This is especially true in rural areas where adequate ambulance service is frequently unavailable, expensive, and sometimes poorly trained. An excellent example of efforts to improve ambulance service is the Northern California Emergency Care Council which has worked to meet five goals for improved rural emergency health care: 1) communications between ambulances and medical facilities so that patient and doctor arrive at the same time and place, and hospital facilities are prepared; 2) improved on-the-scene care before the ambulance arrives; 3) well-equipped ambulances with adequate medical care during transit; 4) better hospital emergency room service; and 5) the dissemination of information to the public.

Much is being done to meet these goals in rural areas. Since emergency service is often provided by existing public agencies, such as police or fire districts, the greatest improvement in care can often be effected by increasing personnel training. Ambulance drivers (often firemen) are given courses, and sophisticated radio communications systems are established to link the drivers and the medical establishments. Air ambulance services are set up through local airports. In addition, service is improved by expanding the number of qualified part-time drivers. This is especially important in tourist areas where accidents during vacation season create a disproportionate need. Forest service or utility employees, and even taxi drivers, have been trained to provide emergency service with great success. For all these programs substantial training is required, and courses and programs at the community colleges are used to provide necessary instruction (California Assembly Health Committee, 1974: 136, 176).

Alternative Health Systems

Government programs, health insurance, and the major developments of private medicine all perpetuate significant barriers to the rural poor. Cultural and language barriers among many poor in rural areas will lead to low use and inadequate care (Reul, 1974: 585–606). In rural places these barriers are made even more formidable because of the many programs which are designed with city-hospital medicine in mind. Rural areas, which on the whole have less accessible facilities, lower volumes of service, and higher costs, find such programs less effective. One response to access barriers in rural areas is the establishment of clinics—mostly nonprofit organizations—which operate on gifts, volunteer labor, and dedicated personal efforts. Many alternative health clinics serve rural California, including La Federacion Rural de Salud de California (The Rural Health Federation). In 1974 the Federation was composed of 18 programs throughout the state, treating about 150,000 individuals. In Elk, a small coastal town, volunteers set up a dental clinic, using cooperative students from university dental schools to provide health services. In Mendocino County, North Coast Opportunities is involved not only in providing health care but in coordinating the delivery of all social services to those in need.

As these latter examples show, health care is increasingly involved in integrated systems. In rural California and other advanced industrial areas, the problem facing community developers wishing to increase the delivery of social services is not a lack of institutions for helping individuals in the community; rather, those available must be mobilized to provide a more comprehensive package of services to new groups of individuals. The community developer's role involves identifying the need and assisting the organizations to obtain funding and begin the new service delivery.

Integrated Organizational Structures

One of the consequences of the increasing diversity of welfare programs is that a duplicative, contradictory, and confusing array of programs has evolved. The programs have their own mandates and often their own network of information and recruitment. Thus, a major problem faced by a person in need is to discover the programs that are available to meet his or her needs. One of the innovations of successful welfare programs in the advanced industrial society is new ways of integrating welfare delivery.

Welfare Integration Through Nonprofit Corporations

Many efforts by federal, state, county, and private agencies to provide integrated programs have recently been made. In spite of such efforts, Gans and Horton (1975: 5) state that "the integration of services is not great, even in the projects recommended as being successful projects." One of the more common strategems is creating neighborhood service centers where different agencies voluntarily locate. However, those agencies within the center were found to use it primarily as a shelter and not as a means of developing a single, coherent service delivery system. Informal linkages, however, were provided and offered some means of coordination. Perhaps the most surprising means of achieving integration is through clients. Gans and Horton (1975: 58) point out how this works.

Clients have caused the integration of services by identifying problems, soliciting local contributions to finance remedies to the problem, supporting responsive agencies within the delivery systems, lobbying for the availability of existing service to new clientele, changing service provider attitudes, acting as a countervailing force to the establishment of a conservative consensus by participating agencies in the development of project policy, and establishing service legitimacy in the view of potential clients by virtue of their involvement. In many cases, unfettered by traditional definitions of feasibility, clients have achieved positive, creative solutions to service delivery problems.

We have found that the most successful projects for the integration of social services to the rural poor in California have taken a strong orientation around the needs of a particular segment of the client population, such as the farm worker or the rural aged. Under these client-centered mandates, community-based organizations are able to coordinate a repackaging of programs for their particular clientele so that an integrated service delivery is achieved.

One of the best examples of integrated service delivery is Westside Planning in Fresno County. It is a nonprofit community development organization, furnishing an integrated set of economic and social services for low-income persons in the California central valley. Designed to provide, within a single institution, a set of welfare support services, health programs, and economic stimulation, its aim is to turn farm and other low-income workers into landowners and operators. The organization is made up of a number of coordinated units, including a credit union, health clinic, occupational training program, and similar services.

In Monterey County a not unsimilar program, Central Coast Counties Development Corporation, offers an even wider array of services, ranging from basic education to creating cooperative strawberry farms. Acting as an interface for its clients with the welfare agencies of the state, it does much more besides. Housing loans are packaged, training in farm ownership is provided, and a whole range of manpower training programs, funded through CETA and other sources, is managed. The clients themselves have considerable control over the organization.

Similar projects in California and other states have been organized through nonprofit corporations that have the potential of facilitating service delivery to particular groups, with assistance from community developers and from state and federal agencies.

Rural Housing

The integration of service delivery programs in the advanced industrial society is a complex process. As the society becomes more interdependent, welfare programs become more complex themselves. The character of this process was examined in a demonstration project in rural California. While many programs in California and in other states make use of some or all of the techniques we describe, the case history below provides a particularly rich illustration of the way a successful project manages a wide variety of resources to solve complex local problems.

The Demonstration Project

The Demonstration project is a joint effort of federal and state agencies: the Department of Housing and Urban Development and the Farmer's Home Administration, with the California Department of Housing and Community Development. The Cooperative Extension Service of the University of California also participated as an advisor and evaluator. The objective of the Demonstration was to determine if and how rural communities could be assisted in obtaining funding for housing rehabilitation and construction. In particular the task of the Demonstration project was to implement a comprehensive community development strategy that included the construction and rehabilitation of housing, the development of new community facilities, neighborhood revitalization, and economic development. A significant amount of money was set aside by Farmer's Home for the purpose of housing improvement in rural areas, and the Demonstration team was expected to get through the red tape and deliver the money in the form of grants and loans to needy individuals.

The needs of the four rural counties in the Demonstration project are great. The counties are large mountain areas with scattered small communities, mostly of less than 5,000 population. There is a scarcity of acreage for housing development because corporate and national forest land holdings surround most communities. Most of the communities have poor water and sewer systems, and available lots are not connected to city systems. The area was largely unorganized for such a project, though it shared in the advanced industrial capacity of other rural areas in California.

Regional Mobilization of Specialists

Organizationally, the Demonstration was designed as a multi-county effort with teams of community development specialists mobilized to work throughout the entire region, moving from one community to another, as their services are needed. The organization of the project, thus, is not the traditional work group organization, handling tasks in a hierarchical bureaucratic arrangement but is a flexible matrix-like organization. The work group itself is constituted on the basis of the particular requirements of the tasks to be performed. Four community development specialists are available to the project: a single-family housing rehabilitation and construction specialist, a rental housing specialist, a sewer and water specialist, and an economic development specialist. The four make up a "circuit riding" team which travels from project to project, as needed, throughout the entire region. They even have a small budget for aircraft rental to facilitate the travel.

At the same time the project is locally based. It hires persons from the local communities to package loans and carry out the daily operations. For most of its activities it develops local advisory groups. To conduct various projects, a nonprofit corporation, with community officials on the board of directors, is established. In addition to the professionals, the local community is strongly involved.

The organizational innovations have helped rural areas overcome the handicap of low population density and other widely diffused problems. A regional basis becomes critical in the allocation of specialists to the solution of many problems because no small community can afford to hire persons with highly specialized skills to work only occasionally; yet, clearly, generalists do not have the skills to adequately handle the complexity of many problems.

The regional design has another benefit since the solution of many problems has repercussions beyond the county line and requires action in other counties as well. For example, senior citizen groups in Plumas and Lassen counties wanted to construct a housing project for the senior citizens of two small towns about 20 miles apart but in different counties. Neither town had enough resources nor a population large enough to justify an independent project, but they were able to join together to form a joint nonprofit corporation to obtain loans and construct one project with assistance from the Demonstration team. Other regional efforts requiring intercommunity cooperation are sewer and water projects that cut across many political boundaries. Furthermore, many resources from the federal government may be advantageously obtained by multi-county organizations.

New Emphasis on Organizational Brokering

The increasing interdependence of the project in rural California has made it necessary for project members to spend a greater proportion of their time in efforts to coordinate their activities with those of others. This has led to a new emphasis on organizational brokering, three different aspects of which may be seen in the project. The first is the provision of technical assistance in the form of expert advice on the construction of housing and sewer and water systems. The second is financial assistance through loan processing for federal agencies. The third is political troubleshooting with the leaders of the local communities. Each of these components is an important means of assisting a local rural community to better deal with large regional or national organizations.

The *technical* role is seen most explicitly in project efforts to link several programs available to solve local community housing needs. It does no good to go around town and help people fix or install interior plumbing if the community sewer system is not working; similarly, it does no good to fix the sewer if septic tanks, not hooked to the sewer, are the cause of pollution. Thus the programs must be coordinated to achieve results.

The *financial* role is seen in the project's aim to find ways to increase the options of a person to build or rehabilitate a house. For most persons there is a small range of assistance available for such a project, depending on the person's total income. The Demonstration project helps secure additional funding and provides other assistance, such as facilitating do-it-yourself projects for some or all of the required construction where the client has the skills. Programs are being developed to have a "self-help housing" group work in the area to teach low-income persons how to build their own house. By reducing costs or by combining resources, the project is able to maximize their financial leverage. Another example involves a community which worked, through the Demonstration, to achieve a sewer project otherwise unavailable. Federal and state governments pay 87½ percent of the cost of sewer projects, requiring only a small local match. However, for this poor community the local match was too great, and they were unable to qualify for the funding. The Demonstration overcame this block by granting the community enough to afford its share, facilitating the completion of that project, and many more.

Furthermore, coordination efforts become more essential as the number of agencies with something to contribute to housing programs increases, as it surely does in the advanced industrial society. For example, the Demonstration coordinated the development of a county weatherization strategy in Plumas County that involves the federal Department of Energy, Farmers Home Administration, the Department of Labor with CETA workers, the County of Plumas, the Plumas Sierra Rural Electrification Coop, the Pacific Gas and Electric Company, and other private financing. It is anticipated that this multiagency effort will lead to the weatherization of many homes of the elderly and will significantly reduce the fuel budget of homes in that county.

Often the provisions of federal and state projects are threatening to local interests. The *political* role of the Demonstration project is to coordinate efforts to overcome these problems and avoid a confrontation or misunderstanding with local governments. The larger perspective or vision of this approach makes the political effort significant. The project director stated it clearly: "The project aims to show that things can be done in the local communities. This is a process of increasing the sophistication of the community leaders so that they can break out of the blocks which up to that time have prevented them from improving the quality of life in their community."

Building Linkages

A third response of the project to the increasingly complex environment within which it works is to build linkages, that is, place more emphasis on creating longer-linked and more complex relationships. While brokering and building linkages are related, this latter category refers more particularly to the pattern of networks the project develops as a facilitator of continuing cooperation among organized groups. One function of the project is to provide an intermediary for linking rural housing needs with the organizations in Washington and elsewhere that can help rural communities meet these needs. Such a linkage was provided by the Demonstration and it multiplied the effectiveness of community efforts. We will cite one example. The Small Cities Community Development Block Grant program made available some money for projects in rural communities. The project assisted local governments in obtaining $1.5 million, a quarter of the money available for small towns in the entire state. This disproportionate allocation was in part due to the technical assistance of the Demonstration and in part due to work by the staff to link Demonstration efforts with Block Grant projects.

The Demonstration project does not do everything for a community in the way of housing. Local banks still play an important part with the financing of other projects. What the project does do is develop projects local banks are not likely to be willing to finance because risk is too high or because they have no experience in such projects. Once local successes are seen, banks or other private corporations can come in for the long-run benefit of all. Thus, linkages between the private and public sectors achieve much that neither could do alone, or in one single effort.

One of the important linkages of the Demonstration is with the Northeastern Higher Educational Council, which we described in the third chapter. The Council is facilitating training sessions for community officials in sewer and water financing through local colleges. Another program with the same institution will provide training conferences in evaluating the impact of the tax cuts from Proposition 13 on the financing of sewer and water projects in rural areas. Training for homeowners desiring to undertake self-help construction, already mentioned, was also facilitated through the Council with project stimulation.

Another kind of linkage comes from the fact that the project itself is in a network of resources that stretches throughout the country. The individuals in the project are drawn from a national personnel search, have for the most part worked in other states, and have ties with others doing a multitude of projects. These ties are easily activated—for example, for information about a specific problem—simply by picking up the phone. In terms of resources, then, the Demonstration has proven that there are multiple resources in remote places which may be brought to bear on local problems.

A major result of the Demonstration, thus, has been to enhance local capacity to respond to the housing needs of the community so that, after the Demonstration ends, processes will continue. The aim of the project is not to create basic community organizations which already exist but to link the local organizations so their effectiveness can be increased.

As an example of rural welfare delivery organization in a rural advanced industrial society, the Demonstration Project in California has shown that regionalization, specialization, coordination, and building networks of information and interaction are essential ingredients for a successful service delivery program in an increasingly complex environment.

6

*The Rural Community
Development Profession
in the Advanced Industrial Society*

INTRODUCTION: EVOLUTION OF THE PROFESSION

The capacity of rural communities to determine their own future in the advanced industrial society will depend upon the quality of the policy structures and the skills of professionals assisting them. The interdependence of economic, social, and political institutions in rural areas requires more responsive community institutions and practitioners to mediate competing physical, economic, and social goals. This will be complicated by changing migration patterns; increasing pressure on the rural landscape for oil, minerals, timber, and other natural resources; improving transportation, which increases tourism or sprawling highway strip development; and increasing racial, social, and economic friction, as rural communities are swept up in events affecting the broader culture.

Yet, in most rural communities, the institutions and professions involved in responding to these changes remain deeply intrenched in historical assumptions designed for an agricultural and industrial society. The procedures and professional practices of most rural programs are inadequate for coping with emerging social conditions. Such practices usually cost more to employ than they are worth, and may not result in the construction of desirable policy alternatives or the organizational forms necessary for their implementation. The rural advanced industrial society needs new policies to meet its changing social and economic conditions, along with new responsibility for the rural community development profession. In earlier chapters we examined aspects of changes in rural California's communities and specific activities important to community developers. In this chapter we look more systematically at rural community development practice and its practitioners in the advanced industrial society.

Community development, much like other new or emerging professions, uses a set of practices that are only now being systematically articulated and codified. Community development is increasingly professional in its recruitment, training, and action, but it also has the characteristics of a movement, process, and set of techniques engaged in by a number of different professionals. No fine line separates community developers from many other professional and subprofessional groups and occupations presently working to alter socioeconomic conditions in rural communities. Professionals involved in and identifying with community development constitute only a small proportion of workers in rural communities using community development techniques. For example, community development work is carried on as a full-time profession by planners, community resource specialists, rural specialists, community educators, and others. Many other professionals, including social workers, adult educators, public administrators, and city managers, use community development techniques to carry out responsibilities as a secondary portion of their job.

As Sanders (1964: 310) describes it, the concept of community development sometimes is used

> . . . in the sense of *process*, with the stress upon what happens to the people and their social life; on other occasions it is used in the sense of *method*, or a means by which agriculture can be improved or health standards raised; or, it may refer to a formalized *program*, such as the various national community development plans . . . and, finally, it may be viewed as a *movement* to which people are emotionally committed, a cause to which they are dedicated.

The evolution of the community development profession illustrates how practitioners have consistently altered their approaches to meet the needs of rural communities. An examination of this change will help inform an assessment of current pressures facing community developers and how their professional activities will be altered by future trends.

The Evolution of Community Development Practice and Profession

Community development had its origin not as a special field of emphasis but as a technique, or set of methods, used by some professionals to introduce or induce change in agricultural communities. During industrialization the profession became increasingly interested in applying its techniques to urban problems and declining rural areas faced with changes brought about by new techniques in both agriculture and manufacturing. As the industrial period gives way to the advanced industrial, community development in rural and urban areas is taking on a new dynamic with more technical, complex, and professional methods of effecting change. For the community developer the major activity involves social technical planning that leads to regionally integrated change programs. These changes are shown in general outline in Table 6.1, which delineates the evolution of the community development profession and the way

TABLE 6.1

Evolution of the Rural Community Development Profession: 1860 to Present

	Agricultural Society 1860–10	Industrial Society 1910–60	Advanced Industrial Society 1970–Present
Socioeconomic Program	Westward movement; and lacking information	Agri-industrialism with people not able to share in benefits. Unorganized communities	High technology service society with projects needing coordination
Basic Model for Community Change	Individual leader model	Peer identification and development of groups and leaders.	Social technical planning
Development Goals	Improve agriculture	Modernize rural areas and improve disadvantaged neighborhoods or communities	Integration of socioeconomic policy structures in region
Community Developer Roles	Technical transfer: advisor and counselor	Group organizer	Increasingly skilled and professional planner/developers

Source: Compiled by the authors.

the basic goals and methods of the profession have changed from the agricultural tradition to the advanced industrial.

Origins of Community Development in Agricultural Society—The Westward Movement

The westward movement was an immense social experiment. As Senator Thomas Hart Benton, one of its chief proponents, proclaimed, the westward movement for him was "a boundless field, dazzling and bewildering the imagination" (Smith, 1957: 38). The critical belief in the migration was that common men and women could build their own social order and political institutions. Congress supported the movement by adopting a "safety valve" theory which asserted basically that impoverished Eastern families could reduce economic distress and relieve class conflict by moving west. However, some critics of the approach, like Representative Howard of Texas, argued that free land was not enough. "It is a great mistake," he said (quoted in Bailey, 1965: 561), "to suppose

> that you will materially better the conditions of man in the old states, or Atlantic cities, by giving him 160 acres of land in the Far West. The difficulty with him is not that of procurring (sic) land, but to emigrate himself and family to the country where it is, and to obtain the means of cultivating it.

Howard and his colleagues were not merely concerned with economic means for western emigrees. They knew from first-hand experience that few of the new Westerners had ever farmed before or, if they had tilled the soil, had ever managed a farm. A large and better social infrastructure had to be created if the experiment were to succeed. California's growth was stimulated, not by agriculture and free land, but by gold. Gold mining in California was a high technology extractive industry. As agriculture developed in California and replaced gold, it too took on the same highly technical orientation.

The most important, significant, and successful intervention by the government in support of farmers was the development of the Land Grant College system. The new colleges "became the headquarters not so much for the training of farmers as for the training of experts to advise farmers" (Hicks, 1955: 93).

As part of the land grant college system, the University of California pioneered in expanding the basic concept of the advancement of scientific agriculture (Farmers Institute Papers, vol. 40, 1896).

> This effort [was] a serious one on the part of the Regents of the University [California], who are well informed broadminded men, to make use of the University which the people pay for the direct benefits of the people themselves . . . bringing the farmers of the State into direct close touch with men whom they employ to find

out things for them and to maintain conditions year after year, is a very important thing.

A regular course of instruction in the University of California Agricultural Extension was instituted as early as 1896 "in which all methods and phases of the efforts are expounded and discussed to influence the farm community" (Hilgard, 1901-03: 21).

The orientation of rural development in California was, from the outset, developmental in character. The amassment of highly technical and scientific agricultural information within the University provided the impetus to create relatively sophisticated farm organizations in California to absorb and utilize this information. A network of agriculture experiment stations was established throughout the state. The University recognized very early that "in rural communities, there are not only business or economic institutions but there are also educational, political, social and religious institutions. . . . The purpose in organizing this [Rural Institutions] division of the College of Agriculture was to determine by scientific investigation to what extent rural institutions have been outgrown by modern conditions and where necessary to propose more effective forms of organization" (Fiske, 1976).

This strategy was so effective that the governmental, social, and political organizations and institutions in rural California were substantially strengthened. Community development practice in the state continues to emphasize building local capacities. The farm adviser's role in California from its inception had a community orientation. As Dean Crocheran in a 1916-17 report noted, "Only a man of great physical endurance can stand the work that the farm adviser is called upon to do. In addition to working all day, answering inquiries and visiting farms, the farm adviser must attend three night meetings on a definite schedule, from which he does not usually return until the middle of the night" (Hunt, 1916-17: 9). These earliest community change strategies focused on individual and small group techniques, techniques which continue to be observed in much of rural community work even today.

Agri-Industrialism

The rapid expansion of agricultural technology and growth in many manufacturing industries altered rural life dramatically in the late nineteenth and early twentieth century, and the expansion of agriculture contributed to the severity of the Great Depression. Subsequent to the crash in 1929, agriculture drifted into a long and difficult slump. Farmers abandoned the land by the millions to crowd into the cities. However, as credit was restored through national institutions, farm communities began to receive additional assistance from the College of Agriculture.

The Depression and, subsequently, the Second World War ushered in an era of modernism with a cadre of rural modernizers. These new professionals identified themselves as Agricultural Extension Specialists. Their expertise was essentially in organizing groups, organizations, and institutions. Thus, the specialists used the networks devised by the farm agents and formed them into self sustaining institutions. The modernization of California agriculture had the unintended consequence, as Walter Goldschmidt (1946) has demonstrated, of reducing the quality of community life in some rural communities. This and similar findings stimulated further research on the impact of agri-industry on communities.

The era of the specialists continues. The new specialists in rural areas are in health, energy, pest management, economics, and planning. In fact, in states like California, the Cooperative Extension program is so specialized by crops and various control specialists, as Fiske (1977) points out, that the integrating and planning framework for the extension program is based on available specializations, almost without regard to local client needs. For this reason small farmers and small communities find it difficult and sometimes impossible to use the resources of the system which was originally designed to serve them.

Community Development in the Advanced Industrial Society

The end of the Second World War brought in another era of national prosperity. Technological advances improved rural life, and cities and factories prospered, or so it seemed. It was true that the middle class was expanding and more young people in farms and cities were experiencing new opportunities; yet a new type of rural poverty emerged. In the affected areas it took two principal forms. In Appalachia and much of the rural south, extractive industries replaced agriculture and enjoyed a brief relative prosperity. Technological advances in lumbering, coal and other forms of mining (Blaustein, 1968: 21) displaced the rural labor.

> [These industries] invested little of (their) profits back in the region and allowed . . . communities to maintain schools of only the most rudimentary sort. It created an environment almost totally dependent upon the employers for bread and leadership, then provides only a small measure of the former and practically none of the latter.

Mechanization of crops led to equally distressing and disturbing conditions. Paul Jacobs described the deplorable situation in one small farm town (Blaustein, 1968: 128).

> The park on the border of the Skid Row area in this California farm town is filled with men and one or two women sprawled out on the grass or sitting under the few trees. Some of them are sleeping, their mouths open, their stubbed faces pressed into the ground; others are merely staring off into space.

This portrait of rural America was a re-presentation of a similar malaise in the metropolitan areas. After the Watts, Detroit, Birmingham, and Chicago riots of the 1960's, new strategies were devised to attack national poverty, with rural areas being only a small component of the national strategy.

In rural areas the focus of community organization efforts was on civil rights for American Indians, poor whites, and Mexican Americans. Out of this political base, economic institutions were altered with the formation of unions, consumer, small farm and craft cooperatives, and the like. On the political front their efforts were directed at changing the racial and income composition of school boards, city councils, county boards of supervisors, and a host of appointive positions. The urban scene was, and remains, more active in these areas. Rapid changes such as these in social and political institutions represented the first signs of the institutional shift toward an advanced industrial society.

A new wave of professionals were trained in community strategies during this period. Blakely's *Training People for the War on Poverty* (1972) describes this new cadre of professionals in California—and several other states—who were no longer found in Cooperative Extension or agriculture but in social welfare institutions, government agencies, and even private organizations such as public utilities, chain department stores (Sears), and banks (Bank of America). These new professional community workers found themselves at odds with established social workers, agricultural extension agents, and rural development specialists. They seldom came from the same economic or social background. The new professionals in community development received specialized education and training to perform their roles, not as an adjunct activity to another profession but as the core of an emerging human services profession.

Community development professionals are concerned with the means to influence or direct change through altering institutional structure rather than through changing particular individuals or groups. Many of these professionals are engaged in a variety of contexts where the concern is for integrated socioeconomic problem-solving in contrast to single approaches involving, for example, simply employment, health, or education. The contexts where these opportunities are flourishing is in multicountry or regional planning and coordination organizations; these are the best example of where the new community development efforts are being experimented with and worked out.

In summary, our analysis shows that the community development profession has significantly changed its emphasis. First, community developers recognized the importance of individuals with peer support as the impetus for community change. Later, communities, groups, and organizations were recognized as important, and more vital organizations were designed to perpetuate certain socioeconomic goals utilizing a specialist as the catalyst. Finally, the bureaucracies themselves became the central focus of the development process with the community developer an actor having the particularly important job of linking organizations with others to effect institutional changes. The result of this historical evolution is a revised set of responsibilities for community development, which considerably expands traditional roles, and a set of new directions for the profession.

NEW RESPONSIBILITIES FOR RURAL COMMUNITY DEVELOPERS IN THE ADVANCED INDUSTRIAL SOCIETY

One consequence of increasingly rapid social and technological change in rural areas has been to render much of current professional rural development practice ineffective. "It is not simply," as Biller says, "that the procedures no longer work well. It is rather that to employ them may be counter-productive as well as ineffectual" (1973: 36). As a consequence we need to reexamine the rules and assumptions of current professional rural development practice against the background of the new complex and uncertain environment of the advanced industrial society. Table 6.2 summarizes some, but by no means all, of the differences discussed in this and earlier chapters. These conditions affect the context and definition of current community development practice and challenge its traditional conceptual framework. The table shows what significant changes have been occurring, including increasing opportunities found in rural society, improved human resources, ample rural social institutions, and new policy responses. These changes are detailed in the following sections.

Opportunities for Development

The first major development with a significant impact on rural community development in the advanced industrial society has been that rural society has become more receptive to change. Now rural areas are looking to community developers for assistance in articulating more comprehensive goals and planning their implementation. The change is one of degree, with the community developer taking more responsibility for new activities since many of the traditional programs have already achieved their intended goals. For example, traditional development programs have included projects that are appropriate for an agri-industrial society—industrial parks, building roads, developing water and sewer systems for industrial processes, and the like. While these are beneficial and needed in many rural areas, as we noted in chapter 2, the lack of additional programs going beyond these efforts prevents many rural areas from fully participating in the most viable and growing aspects of the economy.

For some time traditional social pressures slowed the process of change in rural areas. Changes were something external to most rural areas, and they tried to avoid it. This has been true in spite of the fact that rural areas have had access to the products and technology of the society as a whole, and some areas of rural life have been subject to considerable change. In rural advanced industrial areas there is a growing awareness that change is needed in such vital places as energy conservation, environmental protection, land use, and the like. In fact,

TABLE 6.2

Changing Rural Community Development Responsibilities in the Advanced Industrial Society

	Traditional and Industrial Society	Advanced Industrial Society
Opportunity for Development	Rural society is backward and resistant to change, needing considerable outside help but not able to get it or use it	Rural areas are a new frontier affected by pervasive change, needing technical and organizational help to manage and coordinate it
Rural Human Resources	Rural people are undereducated and require upgraded human resource skills	Rural people have ample talents and capabilities but need help developing programs which use available skills
Changing Patterns of Participation	Formal participation is underdeveloped and needs more effective leadership	New highly organized groups make new demands on community, requiring new methods of conflict resolution
Rural Institutions	Rural institutions for effective change activities are unavailable and must be created	Rural institutions are successful and vital, while remaining responsive to local needs, but require coordination with resources of regional economic, social and political organizations
Policy Structure for Rural Development	Policy is developed within existing governmental structures and needs to overcome traditional limited capacity	Policy is developed in response to federal and other external pressures. New organization is needed to implement policies within framework of local needs and interests
Focus of Development Strategy	Self-help strategies through the introduction of outside technologies are needed to build local human and physical resources, aimed at integration of community into wider social order	Rural organizations and institutions need coordination and information-sharing networks on a wider basis to provide needed services

Source: Compiled by the authors.

in energy conservation, for example, rural people seem more ready to alter their behavior than do other groups in the nation (Blakely and Schutz, 1977).

Thus, as opportunities in rural areas become less restricted by lagging industries and depressed economic and social conditions, a need emerges for professionals to assist in the planning for growth, the management of fiscal resources, the attraction of federal sources of funds, and the development of the appropriate mix of industries to provide for overall community stability. In order to do this, coordination and planning has to cut across many sectors of the local economy and has to involve government, commercial, social service, and volunteer organizations at multiple levels—from neighborhood to city, county, multicounty, and even multistate organizations.

Human Resources

An historic assumption has been that rural people are somehow backward, underskilled, and undermotivated. This notion has less and less validity, as was shown in chapter 3. The human resources of rural areas have been dramatically improved through the growing availability of educational facilities in rural communities. In addition, new migrants are bringing to rural areas increasingly sophisticated skills and capacities, which were found primarily only in urban areas.

As a result of the changing capacity of rural dwellers, community developers no longer need focus primarily on means to improve the local human resources but must put their efforts into establishing means whereby people can better utilize existing talents and resources. Many small communities now have a surplus of well-trained persons, including many with technical and professional skills. The new responsibility of the community developer is the more effective use of these persons and their resources for community growth and an improved quality of life. Relative to the people in a rural area, the community developer role changes from one that is bringing capacity to one that is mobilizing it.

Changing Patterns of Participation

The role of citizens in the development process up until recently has been restricted to a few powerful groups in the community. Participation structures have been limited in their capacity, and large numbers of groups were not involved. Racial and class structures have been important in rural areas for a long time, but these structures have limited citizen involvement. The responsibility of the community developer has been to increase the involvement of the various interests that had been outside the community development process, a prospect formerly made difficult by the limited human resources of rural residents.

The arrival of new migrants in the advanced industrial society has altered community structure so much that the traditional groups with primary access to community power have been challenged. New countercultural groups and racial minorities wish to be involved in rural economic and social programs. Some bring with them a tradition of social and political involvement, which is translated into demands for greater access to the political and economic structure in rural areas. For example, senior citizens in many rural areas of California are organized and demanding facilities and programs that have, until now, only been available in urban centers. Communities are thus faced with increasing pressure from a number of social groups, organized around a basic demand for rights shared by the rest of the society. As we have argued elsewhere (Bradshaw and Blakely, 1979), the increasing diversity of life styles in the advanced industrial society leads to new policy pressures. In rural areas, the policy issues faced by the community developer have changed from an initial stimulation of disadvantaged groups (so that they could press for their rights) to a new goal of facilitating community action designed to meet those demands.

Community developers, faced with this wider array of groups desiring participation, are also learning to develop new participation structures and strategies. The old techniques of small meetings and coffee clatches do not reach important segments of the community. Recently the media and new information-processing techniques are being used to reach a broader segment of the community. In one small community in the Sierra foothills, for example, a dispute leading toward a strike was settled when a debate on the issue separating the school board and the teachers union was broadcast over cable television, reaching most families in the area. Citizen participation *via* the broadcast led to a softening of positions by both groups and a reasonable settlement. In these and other ways the community developer must work to maintain the maximum public involvement in decision making and conflict resolution as new groups become increasingly active.

Rural Institution Building

Another change in the social structure of rural areas affecting the responsibilities of the community developer is the development of effective institutions for economic and social service delivery. A consistently important theme in much of rural sociology and community development has been that rural areas need to build a broad social and political institutional base, because such an organizational structure has generally been missing. As we have shown in chapters 4 and 5, these concerns continue but are being transformed in the advanced industrial society. The development problem increasingly is no longer one of creating viable institutions for effecting social change but is one of linking these organizations and institutions into a more effectively coordinated system.

A second change in rural institutions created by the process of advanced industrialism is the growth of regional organizations, which have developed increased and sophisticated capabilities. Community developer goals are now to provide private and public institutions with very sophisticated, computerized data for use in local decision making about regional land use patterns, tax rates, school locations, and economic planning. The traditional role of the community developer as institution builder is being supplanted; more and more he is being perceived as a new prime resource for information assembly and transfer. The developer in rural areas no longer is thought of as the single person in the community with information but as the one who knows how and where information can be obtained, and how processes for sharing information within the community should be developed.

Policy Structures for Rural Community Development

In traditional approaches to rural community development the policy structure for reaching community change goals was not specialized. Changing policy directions had to be implemented within the context of the existing policy-making institutions such as local and county government. However, such institutions are far too limited to meet contemporary needs. Political decision-making process restricted to local governmental boundaries cannot meet the requirements for areawide manpower planning, economic development, health systems, or human service delivery.

The policy structure for an effective community development process in the advanced industrial society builds on a well-designed and comprehensive organizational structure, which consists of a number of components: 1) an information and data base available for effective problem definition and fund acquisition; 2) community development efforts organizationally integrated with other government agencies, especially welfare and housing agencies; 3) community-based decisions structures, which are recognized and have important channels of influence to the development agency; 4) an organizational unit, rather than a single specialist, which coordinates the activities of the development effort; 5) ongoing evaluation and assessment, used to alter institutional structures and to improve the quality of life for rural people. In these ways the community development agency becomes institutionalized in an effective policy structure for change that will continue beyond a single program, individual, or community government decision.

Focus of the Development Strategy

The net result of these changes is a new focus of development strategy. The traditional focus of much community development activity has been individual or community self-help programs. The fundamental assumption has been, and remains, that the people themselves can collectively solve their problems with minimal transfers of external resources. This strategy has led to such rural community development programs as self-help housing, rural small farming and marketing cooperatives, and a whole variety of public service and public works projects. The focus on mobilizing community resources for collective action is and continues to be one of the most important goals of the community developer.

However, today the issue is not whether combining resources can and should be done to effect a cooperative venture; it is, rather, the question of which resources in what combinations can lead to the most beneficial results. Community developers may take for granted that community pressure will lead to a variety of cooperative ventures; the challenge for the community developer in the advanced industrial society will be to help the community develop the right configuration of organizations, institutions, and individuals to achieve a desired result. Sometimes it means merely getting the local welfare office to cooperate with the school district to start an early childhood education program or to offer free lunches. In other cases, such as Title XX social service planning, it requires a major structural reorganization of a vast network of public and private agencies to deliver improved human services. The community developer's responsibility is as a facilitator and, to some degree, innovator who can assist community groups in getting together to do their jobs more efficiently and effectively. In sum, the challenge is to effect cooperation among organizations within the community, and among communities within the region, so as to achieve more effectively common goals.

A wide range of changes are affecting the responsibilities of the community developer in the advanced industrial society. Communities need less basic help in organizing *themselves* and laying the groundwork for social change. Communities in the advanced industrial society are more likely to need help in balancing opportunities and in carrying out projects whose implications stretch far beyond community boundaries. The aim is to use or refine existing organization and to alter traditional ways of doing things. In the next section we explore—in two case studies—the way the design of community development projects is affected by the advanced industrial society of which they are a part. The first case involves the creation of state small-farm policy as a community development issue and is what might be called "macro" design since it deals with statewide, and potentially national, policy within a community development context. The second example is the more typical: a "micro" development process, involving the design of a project affecting a single community.

The Small Farm Viability Project

The debate over small farm versus large corporate agriculture has taken on special dimensions in California. where agriculture has been highly technological and capital-intensive for many years. The combination of scarce water resources and land requiring irrigation, large scale mechanization, and scientific agriculture has led to the development of extremely productive large-scale agriculture. Questions have been raised for several decades as to the social and economic policy implications of large scale agriculture. While this issue continues to be debated, the state of California has recently joined in a community development project of designing local community options to large-scale agricultural ventures. Regardless of whether this is a wise statewide economic policy, it has been embarked on for technical and social policy reasons of broad community development significance.

The state officials who were responsible for examining these issues viewed them as community development issues. The problem was not one of the economic development of a lagging area but of an experiment with new social patterns interacting with traditional agri-industrial economic forces. They recognized that the questions of small-farm viability are related to the topic of contribution made by a variety of community institutions and support systems, ranging from advisers to local markets and feed stores to branch banks and savings-and-loan institutions. The state pursued a strategy that involved existing local-level community institutions in a process of setting goals and outlining the kinds of programs required to meet those goals.

The California Employment and Development Department was given the responsibility to design the small-farm program. Its first act was to involve a statewide network of community developers out of existing state agencies, the University of California teaching and extension faculty, regional Councils of Government, and with the local organizations. The community developers in turn, through an elaborate system of task forces and committees, enjoyed the help of numerous local individuals with experience on small and very large farms; they also had the help of local and statewide lending institutions, and a variety of social service, technical assistance and private commercial organizations. From this massive consultation process emerged a set of clear goals for a state small-farm policy which recognized certain economic realities. In addition, a state plan to provide assistance for the individual small farmer at the community level was developed in light of the goals established. Finally, the goals formulation process itself brought together a number of people of divergent views and shaped a new network of persons working toward an agreed-upon end before state policy was promulgated.

The rural development process in this case illustrates how community development assumptions and process are being reformulated. In this project it was assumed that adequate resources—physical, technical and social—could be assembled within the local area to meet the project goals. As a result individuals, organizations, and institutions were brought together by the community developers through a variety of new participation structures to form a new network of institutions capable of supporting the small-farm efforts.

Community Goals in a Small City

Another example is provided by Yuba City, California's community goals project. This case better illustrates the new social techniques and technologies that community developers are employing as they assist rural advanced industrial communities to meet current growth pressures.

Few cities of any size set long-range community goals. City governments are primarily reactive entities, and there are several reasons for this. First, city governmental functions are fairly well-restricted to public service functions (for example, police, fire, public works, and parks). This leaves few areas for genuine planning or decision making by public officials. Second, city officials often and justifiably complain that most of their decision-making authority is usurped by federal or state mandates. Finally, in the very areas that local city have jurisdiction for making decisions, the problems are well beyond local capacity to resolve; for example, employment, air quality, and land use.

Small cities face even more difficult circumstances since they do not have the staff resources to engage in goal-setting or planning. Nonetheless, many small cities are facing issues that require very sophisticated planning systems capable of balancing the requirements of growth with the need or wish to maintain a small town atmosphere. In the case of Yuba City, a small California town, it was decided to attempt to engage in community development goal-setting, in spite of the obstacles cited above. Yuba city officials recognized the need to embark on a program that would take into account growth pressures. The limitations of the decision-making parameters were also taken into account, but even within them city-elected officials felt they had some latitude. Further, the recently passed Housing and Community Development act of 1974, combined with general revenue sharing, provided them with certain assets and the needed push to engage in goal-setting for a citywide community development plan. The central question was: what kind of community do the residents want? And related to that, what current or future programs can assist in attaining that objective?

In order to conduct this program, Yuba City requested assistance from the Sacramento Regional Area Planning Commission and the council of government in that area. The Commission in turn enlisted the aid of the University of California at Davis. In addition, the city administration designated a top aide as city community development coordinator. The city, GOG, and University worked together for over a year developing and administrating an in-depth community-assessment and goal-setting program. The goal-setting project used a variety of tools, ranging from personal and mail interviews to radio and television communications, and meetings. The result was a community-planning and priority-setting document that could be linked to the local budget. This system was designed to encourage and stimulate—on the part of all city departments—greater accountability, and public contact with local residents.

Data from the study did provide detailed information on the types of public policies local residents preferred, as well as indication of which services should be made available and which should not (at least without charge) by the city. Neighborhood planning based on the community goals grew out of the more general city-wide goals process. City parks, public works, fire and public works departments utilized the goals data to determine how they might reassess their service and delivery systems. As a consequence of engaging in the goal-setting process, groups formed with a special interest. Acting as a cadre within the community, they were instrumental in facilitating changes based on the goals.

The methodology utilized by the community development team was innovative in as much as it captured qualitative and quantitative dimensions of the community. Local capacity was developed in community planning and decision-making analyses, as a result of the project. More important, the city had a concrete set of goals, and plans for implementation. In sum, these examples show that the goals of community development can be set by integrating resources over a regional basis so as to provide a more effective means of gathering and expressing community opinion and creating responsive policy.

NEW DIRECTIONS FOR RURAL COMMUNITY DEVELOPMENT PROFESSIONALS

Community developers have been described in the literature as encourager (Biddle, 1965), advocate (Alinsky, 1971), facilitator (Cary, 1970), and planner (Rothman, 1974). While the nomenclature changes, the central role of the community developer as an "agent" remains central. By agent we mean an intermediary for others. Essentially, community developers, no matter where they perform their task, provide linkages and assistance in obtaining resources for communities attempting to achieve a goal.

While the literature is by no means definitive on the role of community development professional, Ecklein and Lauffer (1972: 12) offer the following condensation from it:

> . . . in community development the organizer's [agent's] main target is always the consumer of his services: the resident, the member, the recipient. His goal is to overcome the individual's or the group's ignorance of the possibilities open to them. People are organized to facilitate education and communication, to nurture hope. An intermediate goal, if selected, is always considered by the organizer as a means toward another goal: the establishment of "community" and the ability of people through cooperative and collaborative ventures to face their common goals.

In this book and especially in this chapter we have stressed the way changing social conditions have affected the responsibilities of the community developer and have changed his or her method of achieving change in rural communities. In this section we examine the methods used by the community developer in three different ways. We examine the development professional from the point of view of the skills and activities needed to effect change, the organizations in which the developer works, and the profession of which the developer is a part. These changes are summarized in Table 6.3.

TABLE 6.3

Changes in the Community Development Profession: 1860 to Present

	Agricultural Society 1860–1910	Industrial Society 1910–1960	Advanced Industrial Society 1970–Present
Required Techniques and Skills	One-to-one client orientation	Variety of social- and community-action techniques designed to build group solidarity	Sophisticated policy methods designed to broaden participation
Typical Positions and Institutional settings	Adviser in College of Agriculture	Community organization/development specialist in College of Agriculture and/or other social welfare agencies	Planner/developer in regional planning organizations and institutions
Professionalization	Adjunct to other professional roles	Specialists with emerging sense of professional potential	Quasi-professionals linked with planning, public administration, and related policy-oriented fields

Source: Compiled by the authors.

Techniques and Skills for Community Development

The professional community developer has become increasingly specialized in the techniques and skills brought to the job. No longer can the community developer effect change by working primarily on an one-to-one basis; he or she must increasingly interact with complex organizations on a complex and technical basis.

The new community developer acts as a manager and facilitator of the participatory process (Kaplan, 1973), using a variety of methods to assist groups in decision making. The community developer assists in shaping and modifying the human environment which in turn helps create a genuine sense of community.

Human Resource Skills

Many community developers are primarily involved in community service delivery and must be skilled in the administration of human services in order that community services are effectively delivered to those in need of them and in order that community needs are effectively assessed. Regional economic planning skills are needed for determining the potential for economic change in the community available to meet the employment and industrial development objectives of local businesses and citizen groups. Social planning skills are also needed since economic development is so closely linked to the character of the delivery of social services in the community. Social planning skills are necessary to effectively alter the existing and developing social-service mix provided by local communities. Further, the community developer increasingly is required to have significant skills in organizational behavior to understand the impact of change on workers in organizations and how to encourage their commitment and increase effectiveness in implementing change.

Management Skills

Within the organization in which the community developer works there are increasing needs for new management skills to effectively coordinate the organization that is set up to achieve some community goal. (Such an organization offer has limited resources, conflicting organizational goals, and short time perspectives.) The skills required include the ability to develop management information systems to obtain meaningful data on community needs and desires. Further, the community developer will need to have skills in budgeting and fiscal administration to link resources from local sources with federal and state grants, and other funding. These skills must be combined with other general quantitative methods for decision making, important tools for assessing and determining the variety of options available to meet community goals. Finally, the ability to be successful in bringing about effective change in community organizations requires skills and knowledge in organization and management theory.

Public Administration Skills

As the community developer becomes effective outside his local organization, he will have an important influence on policy as it is made in community, county, state, and federal governments. This requires training in public policy and administration so that the developer knows of actual changes and the best way to effect new programs. Research tools and evaluation methods further aid in deciding the possible consequences of different policy choices. Finally, familiarity with intergovernmental relations is a cornerstone of rural community development in the advanced industrial society, especially for the design of effective long-range planning.

Most of these new skill requirements reflect the knowledge-intensive orientation of the advanced industrial society, particularly in the special use of efficient information and data systems. One of the most significant factors that affects the quality and effectiveness of the planning process in rural areas, is the character of the data and information employed by community decision makers. Good data are rarely available in meaningful or useful formats for community residents. An excellent example of this problem is the extreme difficulty rural researchers like Eberts (1978) and others have had in the creation and use of data files and systems in rural New York. Rural planners and decision makers constantly complain about this problem, yet little is done.

The macrosocial accounting methods, aerial photo methods and similar techniques used by MacCannell (1979), the Youngs (1973), and others provide helpful guidance in this area, along with the use of unobtrusive source data on community processes and community institutions. In addition, Blakely and Schutz (1979), Dilman and Dobash (1972), and Christenson (1974) have described how primary data can be formulated into useful social indicators for decision making. In each of these studies the critical component is a description of the goals-formulation process, using social economic data in order to aid small cities (Blakely and Schutz, 1979) or regions and states (Dilman and Dobash 1972; Christenson, 1974). The developer and the community must agree on the data-gathering strategy, the proper interpretation of the data collected, and the policy options which will be informed with the data. The community developer must be able to identify the causes and consequences of various actions with the aid of the data and, thus, must have sophisticated skills for the analysis of a variety of data sources. These analyses become especially important when they are presented to funding agencies.

The Institutional Setting for Professional Community Development

Community developers are employed by a variety of public and private organizations. These organizations fall into three basic types. First, extension or technology transfer organizations are principally public and quasi-public agencies.

The classical example of this institutional setting is cooperative extension. But the cooperative extension model has been adopted to other institutional settings as well. For example, consumer cooperatives employ field workers to assist in organizing local residents into the cooperative scheme or method and, thus, introduce a set of new social technologies into the community. Similarly, public utilities employ community developers to assist in community analyses and planning for the introduction of new technology in the community. The model has been used by public agencies that range from an "energy extension" program to organizations to improve rural health delivery.

The second institutional form is advocacy organizations. These attempt to bring about social change through mobilization techniques and power politics. While this type of organization is not as visible in some respects today as in the 1960s, it remains as a major component or subcomponent of some organizations. The mission of these organizations is to alter political relationships, to transfer power in the community, and to share it with under-represented groups, for example, minorities, handicapped, etc.

In the advanced industrial society community developers working in this context have shifted their interest to advocacy not only for the underprivileged but for particular groups that advocate such social issues as consumer and environmental protection. Advocate organizations range from environmentalist, such as Green Peace, to feminist groups such as NOW, the Farm Workers Union, and other active sociopolitical organizations. The emergence of such issue-oriented organizations increases the ethical questions within the profession as to how issues are to be formulated and as to who controls the strategy—the technician (community developer), or the community.

Finally, community developers in the advanced industrial society are now found most frequently in so-called planning organizations. Until recently most community developers were employed by social planning and human service delivery agencies operated by local government, the United Way, and so on. In the advanced industrial society the need for this type of activity continues and has been extended. Community developers—in both rural and urban settings—are involved in planning organizations of the type described but also in new multijurisdictional and statewide agencies, such as health systems organizations and regional councils of government.

In summary, the institutional settings and roles are altering for the community developer within the original framework. The current trend of community developers to move into new public policy organizations concerned with the widest range of socioeconomic problem-solving is the most fundamental change. This pattern has led to community developers becoming associated with a variety of agencies in both the public and private sphere. For the most part, however, traditional neighborhood or community service organizations are no longer the primary location of community developers. Developers, particularly in rural areas, are most frequently associated with new area or regional organizations. Their principal activity has shifted away from mobilizing small groups of people for the purpose of correcting a neighborhood or community problem to linking institutions and designing meaningful participation strategies that deal with broad questions of socioeconomic policy.

Community Development as a Profession

The skill areas described above are the building blocks, in our opinion, of the community development profession. As curricula begin to reflect these types of aptitudes, professional community development training will be increasingly shaped by professional issues.

Professions or quasi-professions of all types are increasing in number and importance. In many respects, the total society is becoming professionalized. However, as Wilensky states (1964: 138): "Any occupation wishing to exercise professional authority must find a technical basis for it, assert exclusive jurisdiction, link both skills and jurisdiction to standards of training, and convince the public its services are uniquely trustworthy." More importantly, Wilbert Moore, in his careful work on professions, states, "To have one's occupational status accepted as professional or to have one's occupational conduct judged as professional is highly regarded in all post industrial societies and at least the modernizing sectors of others" (1970: 3).

There is little general agreement as to whether community developers are professionals or whether the community development process or movement is something in which one set of professionals can engage. Duane Gibson, a past president of the Community Development Society, argues (1977: 37) that ". . . from a pragmatic perspective, the field is not yet clarified enough, and it may never be, to provide a basis for determining who's 'in' and who is 'out'." But Tom Parsons, a board member of the Society counters that

> "community development projects are of many shapes and that probably has inhibited definition. Even programs within a single agency may (and probably should, over a period of time) vary in appearance as widely as there are potential client-groups and client problems in its service area. But it is precisely this programmatic diversity, this superficial appearance of dissimilarity or heterogeneity that professional practice of community development—in whatever guise—finds its identify and its essential definition" (Parsons, 1978: 7).

For community development to be described as a profession requires that it meet generally accepted and rigorous standards. These standards for professional status have been stated by Moore who defines a professional in terms of six criteria. (1) A professional is one who works in a full-time occupation that requires full commitment to it rather than amateur involvement; (2) A professional is *called* to his or her service, requiring the meeting or fulfilling of various normative and behavioral expectations; (3) A professional possesses identity through a set of symbols with some formal *organization* which usually articulates the previous standards; (4) A professional must obtain *education or training* in a specific body of knowledge that forms the core of professional accreditation; (5) A professional is oriented to *service*, to perceive or diagnose the needs of the individual or collective clients; (6) A professional must have a high degree of individual *autonomy* in determining what the client requires and how to deliver it.

Community development is increasingly done by full-time, dedicated workers, yet there is little agreement that it must be this way. Herein lies the debate, the doubt, and the troublesome issue among community development practitioners. As Sanders points out, the current volunteerism is so strong in the community development philosophy that there is an "insist[ence] that local people should not merely decide what should be done but that they should be active participants in the implementation of the decision" (1964: 313). The dichotomy between volunteerism and career or professionalism is apparent. Clearly there is a need for skilled practitioners to act as catalysts in the development process. As professional change agents, community developers meet many of the tests of professionals. Articulating the basic tenets, however, of this profession is difficult.

The community development profession, as we have seen from earlier discussions, is not based on the knowledge of a single discipline or professional organization but a composite, drawn from a number of applied social and behavioral sciences. The range of disciplines and subdisciplines that comprise community development is as broad as the full range human services. Community development techniques are drawn from such diverse professional areas as adult education, public health, public administration, and social work—in combination with the disciplines of sociology, economics, and political science. Thus, Chenault and Burnford's description (1978: 46) of human service professionals as having a knowledge base derived from a cross-field or a number of academic disciplines and professions is particularly true of community developers. Nonetheless, there is a growing sense of identity among rural development practitioners. This is best illustrated by the formation of the national rural caucus as well as by creation of numerous statewide and regional nonmetropolitan and rural organizations.

Finally, community development as a profession is concerned with autonomous community service in the interest of influencing or directing social change. Many professionals are engaged in this activity and operate in a variety of institutional contexts. The unique feature of community development professional practice is the broader concern for integrated socioeconomic problem-solving, in contrast with single approaches (for example, health, employment, etc.). Community planners are now most frequently found in multicounty or regional planning organizations. While they are not completely autonomous agents, they do exercise a large measure of independent judgment in assessing needs with local communities and in developing options.

It is our contention, therefore, that rural community development is in some important ways a professional field, but it still lacks full professional status. The skills required for these professionals are being fashioned out of continuing involvement with the preservation and enhancement of rural life and culture. The specific techniques will require further elaboration by practitioners.

POLICY DIRECTIONS FOR RURAL COMMUNITY DEVELOPMENT AND DEVELOPERS

This book has attempted to define and describe an emerging socio-economic trend—advanced industrialism—and its particular impact on one segment of the nation: rural areas. This difficult and complex task was further elaborated in terms of the impact these changes have had on the community development profession and on rural policy in general.

It is our contention that rural America is undergoing a fundamental and long-term socioeconomic change but that rural policy, for the most part, does not reflect this change. In the past, national policy focussed on basic agricultural production and either bypassed or neglected rural communities and rural institutions, since the decline of small towns and nonmetropolitan counties seemed to be of little consequence to the nation. This is no longer the case, as James Zuiches (1978: 12) argues.

> Now this new growth [in rural areas] is bringing changes in rural land use, infrastructural development, social and medical services, and impacts on rural environment and ecology. The changes and their attendant problems and opportunities are linked to population dynamics and particularly, to the migration flows into and out of different kinds of geographic areas.

Some of the growth Zuiches discusses is linked to the notions of advanced industrialism, which we have described as a central process of social change in the nation as a whole. It is one of the many important changes affecting rural areas, described variously as urbanization, suburbanization, or the new rurality. Using California as a prototype, we have shown that a whole series of basic social and economic changes are affecting rural areas and that the change will alter the policy strategies used to improve community quality of life.

There continues to be little understanding of the genuine need for a well-thought-out and workable rural policy aimed at rural people and communities. The issues involved in such a policy are suggested in the book and involve an integrated attempt to develop economic and social institutions that can take advantage of new possibilities. While many rural community developers are applying inappropriate policy options, we are encouraged by several initiatives underway in the communities we have studied, and in similar communities throughout the nation. We are also mindful of the national efforts by the United States Departments of Agriculture and Housing and Urban Development—with the active support and encouragement of Rural America, Inc. and similar organizations. Nonetheless, the conceptualization by which a more reasonable policy strategy can be worked out is only now emerging.

Furthermore, we are concerned that most of the professionals who work in and with rural communities have not yet recognized the need to alter their practices. While traditional practices of individual-level counseling still have an important place, the most significant present and future role of rural community developers is in the arena of policy and inter-organizational analysis. Community developers should see their role increasingly as looking out for the community, as it is galvanized by successive changes brought about by advanced industrial developments—including new economic opportunities, changing educational demands and knowledge delivery patterns, and expanding and new welfare and governmental roles. The community developer will have to be aware of the problems of increasing societal interdependence and how to help organizations cope with them. These challenges of the advanced industrial society are ones that are faced in a unique way by the community development profession with its emphasis on interorganizational relations.

Finally, we believe that the key for formulating useful public policy and practice for rural communities is to understand the nature, type, and direction of the changes affecting them. We suggest that the concept of advanced industrialism provides a useful framework for this process. While such a framework has been explored here, considerable work still remains to be done to amplify the range of useful insights this conceptual framework provides. We are convinced that the policy formulating process will be greatly enhanced when detailed studies in other areas are completed. We feel that both scholars and practitioners can make significant contributions to this process. We hope the concepts advanced here will stimulate them.

BIBLIOGRAPHY

Alinsky, Saul. 1971. *Rules for Radicals*. New York: Random House.

Anderson, Charles W. 1971. "Changing Concepts in Development Theory." *Growth and Change*, July 1971, pp. 29–35.

Bailey, Thomas A., ed. 1965. *The American Spirit, U.S. History as Seen by Contemporaries*, vol. 2. Boston: D.C. Heath.

Baker, B. Kimball. 1976. "Boosting Workers up Farm Job Ladders." *Worklife* 1, no. 6: 2–7.

Beach, Kelley J. 1977. "Economic Development Attitudes in Siskiyou County." Chico: Center for Business and Economic Research, California State University. Mimeographed.

Beale, Calvin L. 1975. "The Revival of Population Growth in Nonmetropolitan America." Economic Research Service Publication 605. Washington D.C.: U.S. Department of Agriculture.

——, and Glenn V. Fuguitt. 1976. "The New Pattern of Nonmetropolitan Population Change." Center for Demography and Ecology: Working Paper 75–22. Madison: University of Wisconsin.

Bean, Walton. 1968. *California, An Interpretive History*. New York: McGraw Hill.

Beck, E. M., Louis Dotson, and Gene F. Summers. 1973. "Effects of Industrial Development on Heads of Households." *Growth and Change*, July 1973, pp. 2–9.

Bell, Daniel. 1973. *The Coming of Post-Industrial Society*. New York: Basic Books.

Bendix, Reinhard. 1956. *Work and Authority in Industry*. New York: Harper and Row.

Bensman, Joseph and Arthur J. Vidich. 1971. *The New American Society*. Chicago: Quadrangle Books.

Benveniste, Guy and Charles Benson. 1976. *From Mass to Universal Education: The Experience of the State of California and Its Relevance to European Education in the Year 2000*. The Hague: Martinus Nijhoff.

Biddle, William W. and Loureide Biddle, 1965. *The Community Development Process: The Rediscovery of Local Initiative*. New York: Holt, Rinehart and Winston.

Biller, Robert P. 1973. "Converting Knowledge into Action: Toward a Postindustrial Society." In *Tomorrow's Organizations: Challenges and Strategies*, edited by Jong S. Jun. pp. 35–40. Glenview, Illinois: Scott, Foresman and Company.

Birnbaum, Norman. 1970. "Is There a Post-Industrial Revolution?", *Social Policy* 1: 3–13.

Black, Kelly J. 1977. *Economic Development Attitudes in Siskiyou County*. California State University at Chico, Center for Business and Economic Research.

Blakely, Edward J. and Howard Schutz. 1979. "A Policy Systems Approach to Community Development Research and Action." In *Community Development Research: Concepts, Issues, and Strategies*, edited by Edward J. Blakely. New York: Human Sciences Press.

Blakely, Edward J. 1978. *Community Development Research: Concepts, Issues and Strategies*. New York: Human Sciences Press.

——, ed. 1974. *Curriculum Essays on Professional Education in Community Development*. A publication of the Community Development Society of America.

——. 1975. "Prospects for a Learning Society." *Adult Leadership* 24, no. 1: 34–44.

——. 1978. "Review of *The Exodus of Corporate Headquarters from New York City* by Wolfgang Quante." *Journal of Community Development Society* 8: 107.

——, and Howard Schutz. 1977. "Energy, Community, and Quality of Life in California." *Journal of Energy and Development* 2, 2: 224–38.

——, ——, and Martin Zone, with Peter Harvey, Pamela Baird, and Gala Rinaldi. 1978. *Goal Setting for Community Development: The Case of Yuba City, California*. California Studies in Community Policy and Change no. 4. Davis: Institute of Governmental Affairs, University of California.

——, and Martin Zone. 1976. *Small Cities and the Community Development Act of 1974*. California Studies in Community Policy and Change no. 1. Davis: Institute of Governmental Affairs, University of California.

Blaustein, Arthur and Roger Woock, eds. 1968. *Man Against Poverty: World War III*. New York: Vintage Books.

Booner, William S. 1975. "Pluses for Regionalism." *Journal of the Community Development Society* 6: 30–35.

Bowles, Samuel and Herbert Gintis. 1976. *Schooling in Capitalist America*. New York: Basic Books.

Bradshaw, Ted. K. 1978. "Interdependence and the Growth of Government in the Advanced Industrial Society." Berkeley: Institute of Governmental Studies, University of California. Mimeographed.

——. 1976. "New Issues for California, The World's Most Advanced Industrial Society." *Public Affairs Report* 17.

——, and Edward J. Blakely. 1979. "Policy Implications of Changing California Life Styles." Berkeley: Institute of Governmental Studies, University of California.

Brembeck, Cole S. and Timothy J. Thompson. 1974. *New Strategies for Educational Development*. Lexington, Mass.: Lexington Books.

Brunner, Ronald D. and Garry D. Brewer. 1971. *Organized Complexity*. New York: Free Press.

Brzezinski, Zbigniew. 1970. *Between Two Ages: America's Role in the Technetronic Era*. New York: Viking Press.

California, Assembly Health Committee. 1974. *Interim Hearing on Rural Health Care, Vol. III*. California Assembly: October 18, 1974. Sacramento.

California Community Colleges. 1977. *Community Services Composite Report, 1976–77 Data Survey and Fiscal Report*. Sacramento. Mimeographed.

California Community Colleges, Board of Governors. 1977. *Community College Five-Year Plan 1977–1982*. Sacramento.

California, Department of Finance, Program Evaluation Unit. 1975. *Social Services in California*. Sacramento.

California, Department of Health, Social Services Division. 1977. *Annual Statewide Social Services Plan, 1977–78*. Sacramento.

California, Department of Health, *Vital Statistics of California*. 1975. Sacramento.

California, Department of Housing and Community Development. 1977. Mimeographed. *California Statewide Housing Plan, 1977*. Sacramento.

California, Department of Housing and Community Development. March 1978. *HUD/USDA Cooperative Rural Housing and Community Development Demonstration State Quarterly Progress Report*. Sacramento.

California, Department of Housing and Community Development. June 1978. *HUD/USDA Cooperative Rural Housing and Community Development Demonstration State Quarterly Progress Report*. Sacramento.

California, Department of Welfare. 1975. *Public Welfare in California, 1974-75.* Sacramento.

California, Governor. 1976. *Economic Report of the Governor, 1976.* Sacramento.

California, Office of Planning and Research. 1976a. *Local Government Planning Survey, 1975.* August, 1976. Sacramento.

California, Office of Planning and Research. 1976b. *A State Role in Community Development.* June, 1976. Sacramento.

California, Postsecondary Education Commission. 1978a. Prepared by Dorothy Knoell. *Access in A Broader Context: An Analysis of College-Going Rates for Recent California High School Graduates.* Sacramento.

——. 1978b. *Postsecondary Education in California: Information Digest 1978.* Sacramento.

California's Health. 1973. "Elk: Dental Care in a Coastal Village." *California's Health.* March 1973, pp. 4-5.

Capell, Elizabeth. 1977. "The Growth of California State Government, 1849 to 1975." *California Data Brief* 1, no. 2: 1-4.

Cary, Lee. 1976. *Community Development Education and Training Programs Throughout the World.* A publication of the Community Development Society of America.

——, ed. 1970. *Community Development as a Process.* Columbia: University of Missouri Press.

Center for Curriculum Design. 1973. *Somewhere Else.* Chicago: Swallow Press.

Chenault, Joann and Fran Burnford. 1978. *Human Services Professional Education-Future Directions.* New York: McGraw-Hill.

Christenson, James A., n.d. "Priority and Consensus in Public Goals." Mimeographed.

Christenson, James A. 1978. "Three Themes of Community Development: A Review of Articles in the Journal of the Community Development Society of America, 1970-1979." Paper presented at the Annual Meeting of the Community Development Society, Blacksburg, Virginia.

Clapp, James A., *Growth Management: Practices and Issues.* 1975. Sacramento: Assembly Committee on Local Government.

Clark, Colin. 1960. *Conditions of Economic Progress.* N.Y.: St. Martin's Press.

Clarke, Gary J. 1975. *Health Programs in the States, A Survey.* New Brunswick: Eagleton Institute of Politics, Rutgers University.

Clemente, Frank. 1977. "Preface to the New Rural America." *The Annals* 429: vii.

Clinard, Marshall. 1966. *Slums and Community Development.* New York: Free Press of Glencoe.

Cohen, Richard A. 1977. "Small Town Revitalization Planning: Case Studies and a Critique." *AIP Journal*, January 1977, pp. 3–12.

——, and Bert E. Swanson. 1976. *The Small Town in America: A Guide for Study and Community Development.* Rensselearville, N.Y.: The Institute on Man and Science.

Conrad, Jon and Barry C. Field. 1976. *Rural Development: Goals, Economic Growth and Community Preferences.* Massachusetts Agricultural Experiment Station Bulletin No. 634. Amherst: University of Mass.

Cornman, John M. and J. Patrick Madden. 1977. *The Essential Process for a Successful Rural Strategy.* Washington, D.C.: National Rural Center.

Cox, Fred M., John L. Erlich, Jack Rothman, and John E. Trapman, eds. 1974. *Community-Action, Planning, Development: A Case Book.* Itasca, Ill.: F. E. Peacock.

——, eds. 1974. *Strategies of Community Organization*, 2nd ed. Itasca, Illinois: F. E. Peacock.

——, eds. 1977. *Tactics and Techniques of Community Practice.* Itasca, Illinois: F. E. Peacock.

Cronin, Joseph M. 1975. "The Interdependence of Higher Education." *Daedalus* 104, no. 1: 108–12.

Crozier, Michel. 1973. *The Stalled Society.* N.Y.: Viking Press.

Davie, Michael. 1972. *In the Future Now, A Report from California.* London: Hamilton.

Davis, Kingsley and Frederick Styles. 1971. *California's Twenty Million.* Population Monograph Series No. 10. Berkeley: University of California.

Davis, Richard N. 1978. "Economic Development Attitudes in Plumas County." Chico: Center for Business and Economic Research, California State University. Mimeographed.

Davis, Robert M. 1976. "The Circuit City Manager: An Approach for Small Cities." Paper delivered at the League of California Cities Annual Conference in San Diego.

De Jong, Gordon F. and Ralph R. Sell. 1977. "Population Redistribution, Migration and Residential Preferences." *Annals* 429: 130–44.

Del Buono, Xavier. n.d. *A Plan for La Familia Expansion and Improvement, 1978-79*. Sacramento: Department of Education, Division of Adult and Community Education.

——. 1978. *Program and Staff Development Activities Related to the Community Education Effort (La Familia) in California Adult Schools*. Sacramento: Department of Education, Division of Adult and Community Education.

Dilman, Don A. and Russell Dobash. 1972. *Preferences for Community Living and Their Implications for Population Redistribution*. Pullman: College of Agriculture, Washington State University.

Dunham, Arthur. 1970. *The New Community Organization*. N.Y.: Crowell.

Dyson, Freeman. 1977. "The Next Industrial Revolution." *The Key Reporter*, Spring, pp. 2ff.

Ecklein, Joan Levin and Armand Lauffer. 1972. *Community Organizers and Social Planners*. N.Y.: John Wiley and Sons.

Elgin, Duane, Tom Thomas, Tom Logothotti, and Sue Cox. 1974. *City Size and the Quality of Life*. Palo Alto: Stanford Research Institute.

Erlich, Paul and Anne H. Erlich. 1974. *The End of Affluence*. N.Y.: Ballantine.

Etzioni, Amitai. 1968. *The Active Society*. N.Y.: Free Press.

Farmer, James A. Jr., Paul H. Sheats and James Deschler. 1972. *Developing Community Service and Continuing Education Programs in California Higher Education Institutions*, A Report Prepared for the California Coordinating Council for Higher Education.

Farmers Institute Papers. 1896. Vol. 40. Berkeley: Bancroft Library, University of California.

Ferkiss, Victor C. 1969. *Technological Man*. N.Y.: Braziller.

Field, Barry C. 1976. "Economic Analysis and Rural Community Development." In *Rural Development: Goals, Economic Growth and Community Preferences*, edited by Jon M. Conrad and Barry Field, pp. 1–87. Amherst, Massachusetts: Agricultural Experiment Station, Research Bulletin Number 634.

Finnigan, Georgia. 1976. "Nontraditional Information Service." *Special Libraries*, February 1976, pp. 102-3.

Fiske, Emmett P. 1977. "Evaluation of Cooperative Extension Efforts at the County Level: The University of California Example." Paper presented at the annual meeting of the Rural Sociological Society, Madison, Wisconsin.

——. 1976. "Waking Up the Farmers, University of California Farmers' Institute Involvement in California Communities 1891–1903." Unpublished paper. Davis: Department of Agricultural History, University of California.

Franklin, Richard. 1966. *Patterns of Community Development*. Washington, D.C.: Public Affairs Press.

Friedland, William. 1974. *Social Sleepwalkers*. Research Monograph no. 13. Davis: Department of Applied Behavioral Sciences, University of California.

——. 1978. "Technology in Agriculture: Labor and the Rate of Accumulation." Paper presented at the 1978 meeting of the American Sociological Association in San Francisco.

——, and Amy Barton. 1975. *Destalking the Wily Tomato*. Research Monograph no. 15. Davis: Department of Applied Behavioral Sciences, University of California.

Fuchs, Victor R. 1968. *The Service Economy*. N.Y.: National Bureau of Economic Research. Distributed by Columbia University Press.

Fuguitt, Glenn V. 1971. "The Places Left Behind: Population Trends and Policy for Rural America." *Rural Sociology* 36: 449–470.

——, and James J. Zuiches. 1973. "Residential Preferences and Population Distribution: Results of a National Survey." Paper presented at meetings of Rural Sociological Society, 1973. Reprinted in *Where Will All the People Go*. Washington, D.C.: 93rd Cong. Committee on Agriculture and Forestry.

Fujimoto, Isao and Philip Symonds. 1971. *Regional Organization in California*. Davis: Department of Applied Behavioral Sciences, University of California.

Galbraith, John Kenneth. 1962. *Economic Development in Perspective*. Cambridge: Harvard University Press.

——. 1967. *The New Industrial State*. Boston: Houghton Mifflin.

Gans, Sheldon P. and Gerald T. Horton. 1975. *Integration of Human Services*. N.Y.: Praeger.

Gibson, Duane L. 1977. "Professional Certification for Community Development Personnel." *Journal of the Community Development Society* 8, no. 2: 30–38.

Gilmore, John S. 1976. "Boom Towns May Hinder Energy Resource Development." *Science* 191: 535–40.

Glazer, Nathan. 1978. "Theory and Practice in the Social Sciences: The Uninvolved Scholar Has Become A Participant." *Chronicle of Higher Education*, July 1978, p. 28.

Goldschmidt, Walter R. 1946. "Small Business and the Community." Report of the Special Committee to Study Problems of American Small Business. Washington, D.C.: U.S. Sen., 79th Cong., 1946.

Grieshop, James. 1978. *Financing Community School Programs in California*. Berkeley: Cooperative Extension, University of California.

Griessman, B. Eugene. 1969. "A Sociologists' Perspective of Vocational Education Needs in Rural America." In *Review and Synthesis of Research on Vocational Education in Rural Areas*, edited by B. Eugene Griessman and Kenneth G. Densley, pp. 3–31. Columbus, Ohio: Eric Clearinghouse.

Gronbjerg, Kirsten. 1977. *Mass Society and the Extension of Welfare: 1960-70*. Chicago: University of Chicago Press.

Grote, Lenard. 1978. "Coastal Conservation and Development: Balancing Local and Statewide Interests." *Public Affairs Report*, vol. 19.

Hancock, M. Donald and G. Sjoberg. 1972. *Politics in the Post-Welfare State*. N.Y.: Columbia University Press.

Hansen, Niles M., *The Future of Nonmetropolitan America*. 1973. Lexington, Mass.: Lexington Books.

——. 1970a. "How Regional Policy Can Benefit from Economic Theory." *Growth and Change*, January 1970, pp. 20–27.

——. 1970b. *Rural Poverty and the Urban Crisis*. Bloomington: Indiana University Press.

——. 1974. "Rural Poverty and Urban Growth: An Economic Critique of Alternative Spatial Growth Patterns." In *The Development of Rural America*, edited by George Brinkman, pp. 125–140. Lawrence: The University Press of Kansas.

Hansen, W. L. and B. Weisbrod. 1969. "The Distribution of Costs and Benefits of Public Education: The Case of California." *Journal of Human Resources* 4, no. 2: 176–191.

Haren, Claude C. 1974. "Location of Industrial Production and Distribution." In *Rural Industrialization, Problems and Prospects*, edited by L. Whiting, pp. 3–26. Ames: University of Iowa Press.

Harris, Seymour. 1972. *A Statistical Portrait of Higher Education*. N.Y.: McGraw Hill.

Harvey, Prentice. 1975. "The Social and Economic Consequences of Industry in Small Communities and Rural Areas: An Annotated Bibliography." Council of Planning Librarians, Exchange Bibliography, 1940.

Hathaway, Dale. 1970. Address before 27th meeting of the National Manpower Advisory Committee in September 1970. Quoted in "Rural Manpower: The Quest for Parity," *County Manpower Report*, September 1972, no. 5.

Heilbroner, Robert. 1974. *An Inquiry into the Human Prospect*. N.Y.: Norton.

Hicks, John D. 1955. *The American Nation, A History of the United States from 1865 to the Present*, 3rd ed. Cambridge: Houghton Mifflin, Riverside Press.

Hilgard, Eugene W., 1903. Report of the Agricultural Experiment Station of the University of California from July 1, 1901 to June 30, 1903 in *Report to the Regents of the University*. Sacramento.

Hogan, Joan. 1978. "New Patterns in California Local Governance." Davis: University of California. Mimeographed.

Housing and Urban Development, Department of, Office of Community Planning and Development. 1976. *Rapid Growth from Energy Projects: Ideas for State and Local Action*. Washington, D.C.: Government Printing Office.

Huie, John M. 1975. "A Challenge to the Community Development Professional." *Journal of the Community Development Society* vol. 6, no. 2: 14–21.

Humboldt County Labor Market Bulletin. August 1978. Sacramento: California Employment Development Department, Employment Data and Research.

Hunt, Thomas Forsythe. 1917. *Report of the College of Agriculture and the Agricultural Experiment Station of the University of California July 1, 1916 to June 30, 1917*. Berkeley: University of California.

Huntington, Samuel P. 1974. "Postindustrial Politics: How Benign Will It Be?" *Comparative Politics* 6, no. 2: 163–91.

Husen, Torsten. 1974. *The Learning Society*. N.Y.: Harper and Row.

Inglehart, Ronald. 1971. "The Silent Revolution in Europe: Intergenerational Change in Post Industrial Societies." *American Political Science Review* 65: 991–1017.

Inkeles, Alex. 1969. "Making Men Modern: On the Causes and Consequences of Individual Change in Six Countries." *American Journal of Sociology* 75: 208–25.

Janowitz, Morris. 1976. *Social Control of the Welfare State*. N.Y.: Elsevier.

Jones, Victor, David Magleby, and Stanely Scott. 1975. *State Local Relations in California*. Working Paper No. 16. Berkeley: Institute of Governmental Studies, University of California.

Just, Richard E., Andrew Schmitz, and David Zilberman. 1978. "The Social Impact of Technological Change in Agriculture" in *Technological Change, Farm Mechanization and Agricultural Employment*, pp. 124–56. Davis: Division of Agricultural Science, University of California.

Kaplan, Bernard A. 1973. "Participatory Planning in Educational Decision Making." Paper delivered at the annual meeting of the International Society of Educational Planners, June 29, 1973.

Karabel, Jerome. 1972. "Community Colleges and Social Stratification." *Harvard Educational Review* 42: 521–62.

Katz, Molly. 1978. "All in the Family." *Change*, May 1978, pp. 38–9.

Kelly, James G. 1977. "Social and Community Interventions." *Annual Review of Psychology* 28: 323–61.

Kerr, Alex and Robert B. Williamson. 1970. "Regional Economics in the U.S." *Growth and Change*, January 1970, pp. 5–19.

Klopp, F. R. 1978. *City of Arcata Wastewater Treatment, Water Reclamation and Ocean Ranching*, Arcata, Cal.: City Council.

Kramer, Ralph M. and Harry Specht, eds. 1975. *Readings in Community Organization Practice*. Englewood Cliffs, N.J.: Prentice Hall.

Kreitlow, Burton W., E. W. Aiton, and Andrea P. Torrence. 1965. *Leadership for Action in Rural Communities*. Danville, Ill.: The Interstate Printers and Publishers.

Kushman, John E. 1977. "The Index of Medical Underservice as a Predictor of Ability to Obtain Physicians' Services." *American Journal of Agricultural Economics* 59: 192–7.

Landis, Benson Y. 1949. *Rural Welfare Services*. N.Y.: Columbia University Press.

LaPorte, Todd. 1974. *Interactions of Technology and Society, Impacts of Improved Airtransport*. Berkeley: Institute of Governmental Studies, University of California.

——, ed. 1975. *Organized Social Complexity*. Princeton: Princeton University Press.

——, and C. J. Abrams. 1975. "Alternative Patterns of Postindustria: The Californian Experience." In *Politics and the Future of Industrial Society*, edited by Leon Lindberg, pp. 19–56. New York: David McKay.

——, with Ted K. Bradshaw. 1977. "Advanced Industrial California: Employment Patterns." *California Data Brief* 11, no. 4. Berkeley: Institute of Governmental Studies.

Larson, Olaf F. and Everett M. Rogers. 1964. "Rural Society in Transition: The American Setting." In *Our Changing Rural Society: Perspectives and Trends*, edited by James H. Copp, pp. 39–70. Ames: Iowa State University Press.

Lasch, Christopher. 1972. "Toward a Theory of Post-Industrial Society." In *Politics in the Post-Welfare State*, edited by M. Donald Hancock and Gideon Sjoberg, pp. 36–50. N.Y.: Columbia University Press.

Lauderdale, Michael L. and James H. Peterson. 1971. *Community Development*. Washington, D.C.: Education, Training, and Research Sciences Corp.

Lauffer, Armand. 1977. *The Practice of Continuing Education in the Human Services*. N.Y.: McGraw-Hill.

Lawrence Berkeley Laboratory. 1978. Distributed Technologies in California's Future, Interim Report, vol. 1. Berkeley: University of California.

Levy, Marion J. 1966. *Modernization and the Structure of Societies*, vols. 1–2. Princeton: University of Princeton Press.

Lichty, Richard W. and Wayne A. Jesswein. 1978. "Assessing University Impacts Using Interindustry Analysis." *Growth and Change*, April 1978, pp. 24–28.

Lubove, Roy. 1965. *The Professional Altruist*. Cambridge: Harvard University Press.

Luytjes, Jan. 1971. "Note on the Impact of Increased Educational Funds in Lagging Areas." *Growth and Change*, January 1971, pp. 38–41.

Lynd, Robert S. and Helen M. Lynd. 1929. *Middletown*. New York: Harcourt, Brace and World.

MacCannell, Dean. 1979. "Macrostructural Accounting." In *Community Development Research: Concepts, Issues and Strategies*, edited by Edward J. Blakeley. N.Y.: Human Science Press.

——. 1976. *The Tourist—A New Theory of the Leisure Class*. N.Y.: Schocken.

——, and James M. Meyers. 1976. *Planning for Tourism*. Community Development Research Series. Davis: Department of Applied Behavioral Sciences, University of California.

McCarthy, Patrick E. 1975. "Higher Education Expansion without Growth." *Daedalus* 104: 78–86.

McGuire, Chester. 1971. "Rural Development Strategies." Working Paper 162. Berkeley: Institute of Urban and Regional Development, University of California.

McWilliams, Cary. 1949. *California, The Great Expectation*. N.Y.: Current Books.

——. 1971. *Factories in the Field*. Santa Barbara: Peregrine.

——. 1977. "Is California Still Exceptional? A View from a Distance." *California Perspectives: Four Leaders Look at the State of the State*, pp. 13–26. Berkeley: Institute of Governmental Studies.

Mamer, John W. 1977. "The California Farm Labor Market: A Challenge to Management and Leadership." Berkeley: Cooperative Extension. Mimeographed.

——, and Varden Fuller. 1978. "Employment on California Farms." *Technological Change, Farm Mechanization and Agricultural Employment*, pp. 1–32. Davis: Division of Agricultural Sciences, University of California.

Marshall, Ray. 1974. *Rural Workers in Rural Labor Markets*. Salt Lake City: Olympus.

Martin, Philip and Candice Hall. 1978. "Labor Displacement and Public Policy." *Technological Change, Farm Mechanization and Agricultural Employment*, pp. 200–43. Davis: Division of Agricultural Sciences, University of California.

Miernyk, William H. 1977. "Rising Energy Prices and Regional Economic Development." *Growth and Change*, July 1977, pp. 1–7.

Miles, Rufus. 1976. *Awakening from the American Dream*. N.Y.: Universe Books.

Miller, David C. 1977. "Methods for Estimating Societal Futures." In *Methodology of Social Impact Analysis*, edited by Kurt Finsterbusch and C. P. Wolb, pp. 202–10. Strandsburg, Penn.: Douden, Hutchinson and Ross.

Milroy, P. R. 1970. "Problems and Advantages of Rural Locations of High Technology Industries." In *Rural Development: Problems and Advantages of Rural Location for Industrial Plants*, pp. 43–48. Agricultural Policy Institute Series No. 49. Raleigh: North Carolina State University.

Morgan, Neil. 1961. *Westward Tilt: The American West Today*. New York: Random House.

Moore, Wilbert E. 1970. *The Professions: Roles and Rules*. N.Y.: Russell Sage Foundation.

——. 1974. "Social Aspects of Economic Development." In *Handbook of Modern Sociology*, edited by Robert Faris, pp. 882–911. Chicago: Rand McNally.

Morrison, Peter A. 1977. "Demographic Trends that Will Shape Future Housing Demand." *Policy Sciences* 8: 203–15.

Munson, Byron E. 1968. "Structural Analysis of the Community." *Rural Sociology* 33: 450–59.

Musser, Wesley N. and Fred C. White. 1977. "The Potential for Rural-Urban Population Balance." *Growth and Change*, October 1977, pp. 9–14.

Mynko, Lizbeth F. 1974. "Directions in Rural Health Services and Research." *exChange* 2: 20–23. Published by California Department of Health.

NPA Agriculture Committee. 1978. "National Health Insurance and Rural People." *Looking Ahead* 1, no. 4: 1–5.

Nadeau, Remi. 1963. *California: The New Society*. N.Y.: David McKay.

National Academy of Sciences. 1971. *The Quality of Rural Living*. Washington, D.C.: National Academy of Sciences.

Newby, Howard. 1979. "Rural Sociology—A Trend Report." Part 1 of a report commissioned by the International Sociological Association to appear in *Current Sociology* in 1979. Paper read at meetings of the Rural Sociological Association, San Francisco, September 1978.

Northeastern California Higher Education Council. 1977. *Annual Report, 1976–77*. Chico: California State University.

Northern California Signature. 1977. 1, no. 1. Arcata: Center for Community Development, Humboldt State University. NASA Remote Sensing Technology Transfer Project, September-October 1977.

O'Toole, James. 1977. *Work, Learning and the American Future,* San Francisco: Jossey-Bass.

Paltridge, James G., Mary Regan, and Dawn Terkla. 1978. *MidCareer Change: Adult Students in MidCareer Transition and Community Support Systems Developed to Meet their Needs.* Washington, D.C.: Office of Education, Community Services and Continuing Education Division.

Parsons, Tom. 1978. "Professional Certification for Practitioners of Community Development." *Journal of the Community Development Society* 9, no. 1: 4–10.

———. 1977. *Some Practical Outcomes of a Center for Community Development.* Arcata: Humboldt State University, Center for Community Development. Mimeographed.

Pennington, Lucinda. 1978. "Better Mousetraps." *PSA California Magazine* 13, no. 9: 83–85.

Peterson, Richard E. and J. B. Lon Hefferlin. 1975. *Postsecondary Alternatives to Meet the Educational Needs of California's Adults.* Sacramento: Assembly Publications Office.

Ploch, Louis A. 1976. *Community Action as Community Development—A Case Study. Research in the Life Sciences* 23, no. 6: 1–15. Orno: University of Maine.

Portes, Alejandro. 1974. "Modernity and Development: A Critique." *Studies in Comparative International Development* 9: 247–79.

President's National Advisory Commission on Rural Poverty. 1967. *The People Left Behind.* Washington, D.C.: Government Printing Office.

Quante, Wolfgang. 1976. *The Exodus of Corporate Headquarters from New York City.* N.Y.: Praeger.

Reul, Myrtle R. 1974. *Territorial Boundaries of Rural Poverty.* East Lansing: Center for Rural Manpower and Public Affairs, and Cooperative Extension Service, Michigan State University.

Roemer, Milton I. 1976. *Rural Health Care.* St. Louis: C. V. Mosby.

Rohrer, Wayne C. and Louis H. Douglas. 1969. *The Agrarian Transition in America.* N.Y.: Bobbs-Merrill.

Rosenberg, Nathan. 1972. *Technology and American Economic Growth.* N.Y.: Harper and Row.

Ross, Murray G. 1955. *Community Organization: Theory and Principles*. N.Y.: Harper.

Rothman, Jack. 1974. *Planning and Organizing Social Change*, N.Y.: Columbia University Press.

Rural America. 1975. *Toward a Platform for Rural America*, Washington, D.C.: Rural America, Inc.

Salner, Marcia. 1977. "Education beyond High School: California's Resources." *California Data Brief* 1, no. 3. Berkeley: Institute of Governmental Studies, University of California.

——. 1975. *Inventory of Existing Postsecondary Alternatives*. Sacramento: Assembly Publications Office.

Sanders, Irwin T. 1964. "Community Development Programs in Sociological Perspective." In *Our Changing Rural Society*, edited by James H. Copp, pp. 307–40. Ames Iowa State University Press.

——. 1970. "The Concept of Community Development." In *Community Development as a Process*, edited by Lee Cary, pp. 9–31. Columbia: University of Missouri Press.

——, and Gordon F. Lewis. 1976. "Rural Community Studies in the United States: A Decade in Review." In *Annual Review of Sociology*, edited by Alex Inkeles, vol. 2, pp. 35–53. Palo Alto: Annual Review, Inc.

Scheffler, Richard H. and John E. Kushman. 1978. "New Health Practitioners and Rural Health Care." *American Journal of Agricultural Economics* 60, no. 4: 691–94.

Schler, Daniel J. 1970. "The Community Development Process." In *Community Development as a Process*, edited by Lee J. Cary, pp. 113–40. Columbia: University of Missouri Press.

Schmitz, Andrew and David Seckler. 1970. "Mechanized Agriculture and Social Welfare: The Case of the Tomato Harvester." *American Journal of Agricultural Economics* 52: 569–77.

Schrag, Peter. 1973. *The End of the American Future*. N.Y.: Simon and Schuster.

——. 1975. A review of *This is California, Please Keep Out*, by Art Seidenbaum. In *New York Times Book Review*, May 11, 1975.

Schumacher, E. F. 1973. *Small Is Beautiful*. N.Y.: Harper and Row.

Schwarts, Seymour I. 1977. *Energy Conserving Lifestyles*. Report to the California Energy Resources Conservation and Development Commission. Davis: University of California.

Scott, Stanley. 1978. "Coastal Planning in California: A Progress Report." *Public Affairs Report* 19, no. 3 and 4.

———. 1975. *Governing California's Coast*. Berkeley: Institute of Governmental Studies, University of California.

Security Pacific Bank. 1975. *California Coastal Zone Economic Study: An Area Profile*. Los Angeles: Publication of Security Pacific Bank.

Sher, Jonathan P., ed. 1977. *Education in Rural America: A Reassessment of Environmental Wisdom*. Boulder: Westview Press.

———, and Stuart A. Rosenfeld. 1977. *Public Education in Sparsely Populated Areas of the United States*. Washington, D.C.: National Institute of Education.

Shover, John. 1976. *First Majority Last Minority: The Transforming of Rural Life in America*. De Kalb: Northern Illinois University Press.

Small Farm Viability Project. 1978. Technology Task Force Final Report. Sacramento: Department of Economic Development.

Smelser, Neil J. 1974. "Growth, Structural Change, and Conflict in California Public Education, 1950–1970." In *Public Higher Education in California*, edited by N. Smelser and Gabriel Almond, pp. 1–141. Berkeley: University of California Press.

Smith, Bardwell L. 1970. "Educational Trends and the Seventies." *AAUP Bulletin*, September 1970, pp. 130–6.

Smith, Henry Nash. 1957. *Virgin Land*, New York: Vintage Books.

Sneed, Joseph D. 1975. "Summary of Proceedings." In Neil Sneed and Steven A. Waldhorn, *Restructuring the Federal System*, pp. 1–32. N.Y.: Crane Russak.

Synder, L. J. 1971. "Health Care in Rural America." *Social Service Outlook* 6, 4: 12–13. N.Y. State Dept. of Social Services.

Sokolow, Alvin D. 1968. *Governmental Response to Urbanization: Three Townships on the Rural-Urban Gradient*. Washington: U.S. Dept. of Agriculture, Economic Research Service.

———. 1977. "California's New Migration to the Towns of the 'Cow Counties'". *California Journal* 8: 348–50.

——. 1978. "The Redistribution of California's Population: New Growth in Nonmetropolitan Areas." *California Data Brief* 2, no. 1.

Sorensen, Donald M. 1976. "Reverse Migration and the Rural Community Development Problem." Discussion paper No. 9. Corvallis, Oregon: Oregon State University, Western Rural Development Center.

Stadtman, Vern A. 1970. *The University of California 1868-1968*. N.Y.: McGraw Hill.

Stanley, Donald. 1978. "Waiting for Walt." *New West*, March 13, 1978, pp. 19-23.

Starr, Kevin. 1973. *Americans and the California Dream, 1850-1915*. N.Y.: Oxford University Press.

Stebbins, Robert, Theodore Papenfuss, and Florence Amamoto. 1978. *Teaching and Research in the California Desert*. Research Report 78-1. Berkeley: Institute of Governmental Studies.

Steinbeck, John. 1939. *Grapes of Wrath*. N.Y.: Bantam.

Sternlieb, George and James W. Hughes. 1975. *Post-Industrial America: Metropolitan Decline and Inter-Regional Job Shifts*. New Brunswick: Center for Urban Policy Research, Rutgers, The State University.

Stinchcombe, Arthur L. 1968. *Constructing Social Theories*. N.Y.: Harcourt Brace and World.

Stott, E. Keith, Jr., Theodore Fetter, and Laura L. Crites. 1977. *Rural Courts: The Effect of Space and Distance on the Administration of Justice*. Denver: National Center for State Courts.

Thomas, Morgan D. 1975. "Growth Pole Theory, Technological Change, and Regional Economic Growth." *Papers of the Fourteenth European Congress of the Regional Science Association* 34: 1-25.

Thompson, James D. 1967. *Organizations in Action*. N.Y.: McGraw Hill.

Thompson, James D. 1974. "Technology, Polity and Societal Development." *Administrative Science Quarterly* 19: 6-21.

Thompson, Wilbur. 1975. "Economic Processes and Employment Problems in Declining Metropolitan Areas." In *Post-Industrial America: Metropolitan Decline and Inter-regional Job Shifts*, edited by George Sternlieb and James Hughes, pp. 187-96. New Brunswick: The Center for Urban Policy Research, Rutgers, The State University.

Toffler, Alvin. 1969. "Value Impact Forecaster: A Profession of the Future." In *Values and the Future*, edited by Kurt Baier, pp. 1–17. N.Y.: Free Press.

Touraine, Alain. 1971. *The Post Industrial Society*. Translated by Leonard F. X. Mayhew. N.Y.: Random House.

Tracy, Phil. 1977. "The Town that Fought the Feds." *New West*, June 6, 1977, pp. 53–55.

Trattner, Walter I. 1974. *From Poor Law to Welfare State*. N.Y.: Free Press.

Trillin, Calvin. 1978. "U.S. Journal: Locke, California: The Last Chinatown." *The New Yorker*, February 20, 1978, pp. 107–13.

Trow, Martin. 1962. "The Democratization of Higher Education in America." *European Journal of Sociology* 3, no. 2: 231–62.

——. 1970. "Reflections on the Transition from Mass to Universal Higher Education." *Daedalus* 99, no. 1: 1–42.

Tucker, C. Jack. 1976. "Changing Patterns of Migration between Metropolitan and Nonmetropolitan Areas in the United States: Recent Evidence." *Demography* 13, no. 4: 435–43.

Turner, Frederic Jackson. 1962. *The Frontier in American History*. N.Y.: Holt, Rinehart and Winston.

Tweeten, Luther. 1974. "Systems Planning for Rural Development." In *The Development of Rural America*, edited by George Brinkman, pp. 77–108. Lawrence: University Press of Kansas.

——, and George L. Brinkman. 1976. *Micropolitan Development*. Ames: Iowa State University Press.

Ulmer, Melville J. 1969. *The Welfare State: USA*. Boston: Houghton Mifflin.

United Nations. 1963. "Social Progress through Community Development." *International Review of Community Development*, No. 11: 141–151.

U.S., Bureau of the Census. 1970. *Census of Population, Detailed Characteristics, 1970*, Washington, D.C.: Government Printing Office.

U.S., Bureau of the Census. 1969. *1969 Census of Agriculture*. Washington, D.C.: Government Printing Office.

U.S., Bureau of the Census. 1974. *1974 Census of Agriculture* vol. 1, part 5. Washington, D.C.: Government Printing Office.

U.S., Department of Housing and Urban Development, Office of Community Planning Development, 701 Comprehensive Planning Program. 1976. *Rapid Growth from Energy Projects: Ideas for State and Local Action*. Washington, D.C.: Government Printing Office.

U.S., Department of Housing and Urban Development. 1978. *Report of the Task Force on Rural and Non-Metropolitan Areas*. Washington, D.C.: Government Printing Office.

U.S., Congress, Senate. 1975. Special Committee on Aging. *Hearing on the Older Americans Act and the Rural Elderly*. Washington, D.C.: Government Printing Office.

U.S., Congress, Senate. 1978. Subcommittee on Agricultural Research and General Legislation of the Committee on Agriculture, Nutrition, and Forestry. *Rural Research Hearings of 1978*. Washington, D.C.: Government Printing Office.

Vidich, Arthur J. and Joseph Bensman. 1958. *Small Town in Mass Society*. Princeton: Princeton University Press.

Waldhorn, Steven A. and Edward J. Blakely. 1976. *Picket Fence Planning: A Study of Local Government Planning*. Sacramento: The Special Subcommittee on Community Development, Calif. Assembly.

Warner, W. Keith. 1974. "Rural Society in a Post-Industrial Age." *Rural Sociology* 39: 306–318.

Warner, W. Lloyd. 1953. *American Life: Dream and Reality*. Chicago: Phoenix Books.

Warren, Roland L. 1963. *The Community in America*. Chicago: Rand McNally.

——. 1975. "External Forces Affecting Local Communities—Bad News and Good News." *Journal of the Community Development Society* 6, no. 2: 5–13.

Watkins, Beverly. 1977. "Certification of Professionals: A Bonanza for Extension Programs." *Chronicle of Higher Education*, April 11, 1977, p. 8.

Webber, Melvin M. 1968-9. "Planning in an Environment of Change, Part 1: Beyond the Industrial Age; Part 2: Permissive Planning." *The Town Planning Review* 39, no. 3: 179–95; 39, no. 4: 277–95.

Weber, Max. 1968. *Economy and Society*. Translated by G. Roth and A. Vidich. N.J.: Bedminster Press.

Widner, Ralph R. 1974. "Regional Coordination of Communities with Industrialization Potential." In *Rural Industrialization: Problems and Potentials*, edited by Larry R. Whiting, pp. 127–35. Ames: Iowa State University Press.

Wilensky, Harold. 1964. "The Professionalization of Everyone." *The American Journal of Sociology* 70, no. 2: 137–57.

——. 1975. *The Welfare State and Equality*. Berkeley: University of California Press.

Wilms, Wellford W. 1976. "A Prescription for Student Aid: Better Information on Post-secondary Education." *Public Affairs Report* 1.

Woodruffe, Kathleen. 1962. *From Charity to Social Work*. London: Routledge and Kegan Paul.

Woods, John A. 1975. "The End of Growth, the Universities' New Challenge." *California Journal*, August 1975, pp. 286–8.

Wrigley, Robert L. Jr. 1973. "Small Cities Can Help to Revitalize Rural Areas." *Annals*, January 1973, pp. 55–64.

Young, Frank and Ruth Young. 1973. *Comparative Studies of Community Growth*. Rural Sociological Society Monograph 2. Morgantown: West Virginia University Press.

Zuiches, James J. 1970. "In-migration and Growth of Nonmetropolitan Urban Places." *Rural Sociology* 35: 410–20.

——, and Edwin H. Carpenter. 1978. "Residential Preferences and Rural Development Policy." *Rural Development Perspectives*, RDP-1. U.S. Department of Agriculture. Washington, D.C.: Government Printing Office.

INDEX

46, 50; urban distributions of,
23–24
population growth, rural: "reverse
migration" and, 4, 23–28, 125;
social changes due to, 2, 23;
statistics on, 7–8
post-industrialism (*see* advanced
industrialism)
poverty, rural, 118–36; changing
conditions of, 118–20; contributing conditions to, 124–25,
142; defined as problem, 120–
21; disadvantaged groups and,
123–24; extent of, 121–23
(*See also* welfare services)
President's National Commission on
Rural Poverty, 66, 120–21
professional services sector, 58
professions: community development as, 29, 31–32, 137–60;
created by technology, 16–17;
in economic development, 36,
38; educational resources for,
83; in rural employment, 40–
45; in service sector, 20, 38,
42, 58; volunteerism vs., 158
Proposition 13 (Jarvis-Ganns Initiative), 21, 73, 74, 75, 88, 96,
107, 117, 127
public administration skills of community developer, 155
public facilities, growth of, 60–61
public policy, 2; community developer and, 147, 155; components (subsets) of, 30; expectations of, 115; interde-
pendence in, 114–17, 133–36
public service sector (*see* government)
publishing industry, 44

qualitative technique, 9
Quante, Wolfgang, 58
quasi-governmental agencies, 63

racial tensions, 3
real estate industry, 57

recertification programs, 80
reciprocal interdependence (Thompson), 111–12
Redwood National Park, 56
Regan, Mary, 85–86
regional planning, 39, 62–63, 101;
government interdependence
and, 106–08; in housing
Demonstration project, 133–
36; new role of community
developers in, 147–48, 158
research: by community developer,
155; government-sponsored,
47, 52; by industries, 90;
libraries, 91; social anticipation, 10–11; university-
sponsored, 22, 50, 51, 88–90
resource allocation, 31
retirement communities, 25, 54, 125
"reverse migration," 4, 23–28, 125
Rogers, Everett, 2
Rosenberg, Nathan, 15–16
Rosenfeld, Stuart A., 66
"rural," Census definition of, 7
rural advanced industrialism: in
California, as prototype, 6–11;
concept development of, 5, 13;
future-study methodologies on,
9–11; as new frontier, 1, 3, 23,
121; receptivity to change of,
144–46; social anticipation research in, 10–11; themes in,
summarized, 3–5 (*See also* advanced industrialism)
Rural America, Inc., 2, 5, 66, 160
Rural America Act (1972), 26
Rural Development Act, 105
Rural Economic Institute, 51
Rural Health Federation, 131
Rural Outreach Program, 85
rural society, emerging problems in,
2–3
Rural Sociological Society, 1

Sacramento Regional Area Planning
Commission (SRAPC), 108
"safety valve" theory, 140

ABOUT THE AUTHORS

TED K. BRADSHAW's current scholarly interests include analyses of California's development as an advanced industrial society, social change in rural communities, organizational interdependence, and life styles. He has written articles and papers on the state's economic development, educational system, governmental agencies, changing energy institutions, and a variety of emerging policy issues.

Mr. Bradshaw is currently research sociologist on the staff of the Institute of Governmental Studies, University of California, Berkeley, where he edits *California Data Brief*, published by the Institute.

EDWARD J. BLAKELY is an active consultant for several international agencies and nations on problems of economic and social development. He is a member of the Employment Commission and the Private Industry Council for the city of Oakland, California.

Blakely is the author of several books, articles, and monographs on community development in the United States and the Third World, including *Toward a Theory of Training People for the War on Poverty* (New York: Vantage Press, 1972). He was also editor of *Community Development Research* (New York: Human Sciences Press, 1979) and is now Assistant Vice-President, Academic Personnel Systemwide, University of California, Berkeley.